SPIDER-MAN
ONE MORE DAY

SPIDER-MAN: ONE MORE DAY. Contains material originally published in magazine form as AMAZING SPIDER-MAN #544-545, SENSATIONAL SPIDER-MAN #41, FRIENDLY NEIGHBORHOOD SPIDER-MAN #24 and MARVEL SPOTLIGHT: SPIDER-MAN – ONE MORE DAY/BRAND NEW DAY. First printing 2008. ISBN# 978-0-7851-2633-1. Published by MARVEL PUBLISHING, INC., a subsidiary of MARVEL ENTERTAINMENT, INC. OFFICE OF PUBLICATION: 417 5th Avenue, New York, NY 10016. Copyright © 2007 and 2008 Marvel Characters, Inc. All rights reserved. $24.99 per copy in the U.S. and $40.00 in Canada (GST #R127032852); Canadian Agreement #40668537. All characters featured in this issue and the distinctive names and likenesses thereof, and all related indicia are trademarks of Marvel Characters, Inc. No similarity between any of the names, characters, persons, and/or institutions in this magazine with those of any living or dead person or institution is intended, and any such similarity which may exist is purely coincidental. **Printed in the U.S.A.** ALAN FINE, CEO Marvel Toys & Publishing Divisions and CMO Marvel Entertainment, Inc.; DAVID GABRIEL, SVP of Publishing Sales & Circulation; DAVID BOGART, SVP of Business Affairs & Talent Management; MICHAEL PASCIULLO, VP of Merchandising & Communications; JIM O'KEEFE, VP of Operations & Logistics; DAN CARR, Executive Director of Publishing Technology; JUSTIN F. GABRIE, Director of Editorial Operations; SUSAN CRESPI, Production Manager; STAN LEE, Chairman Emeritus. For information regarding advertising in Marvel Comics or on Marvel.com, please contact Mitch Dane, Advertising

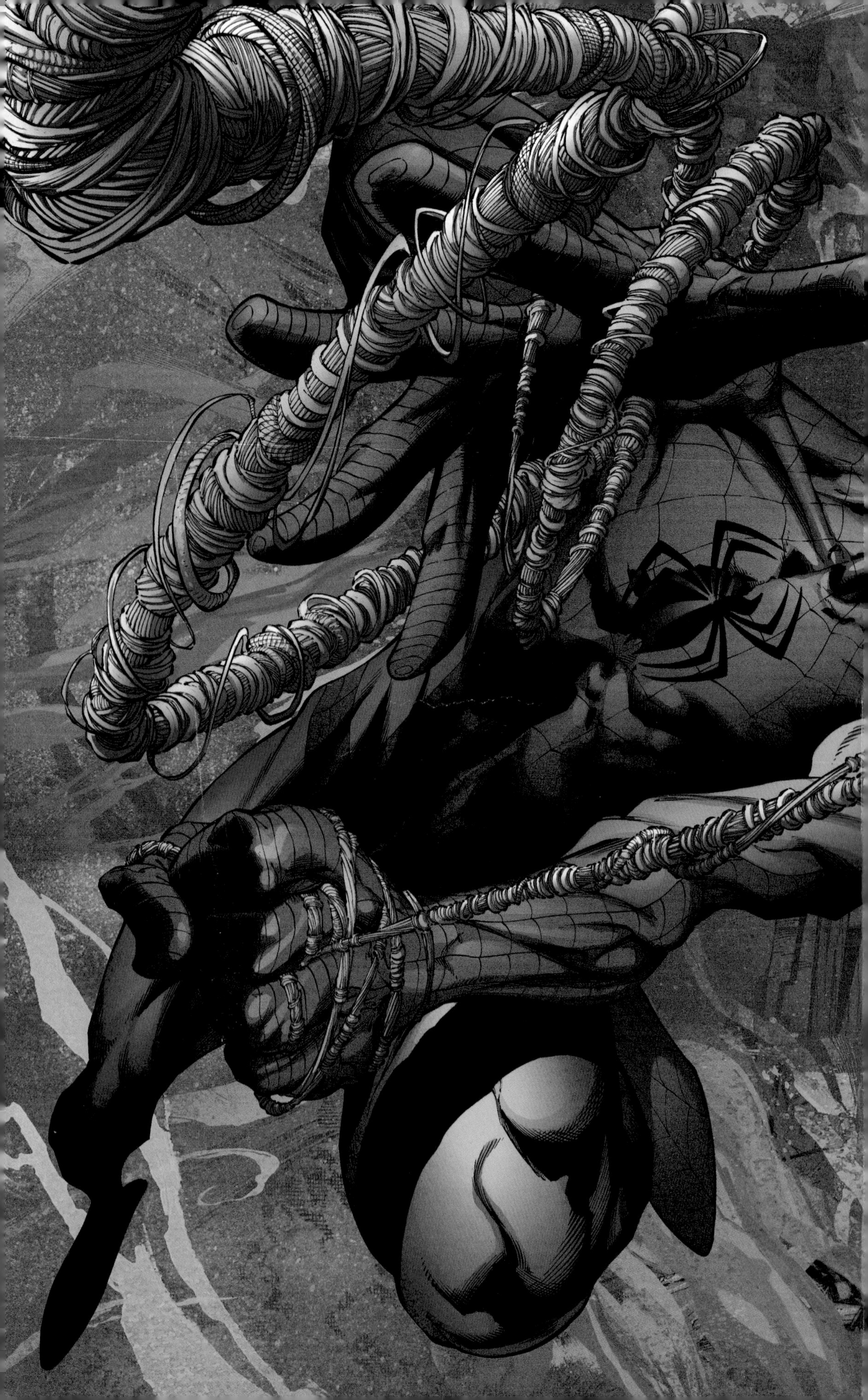

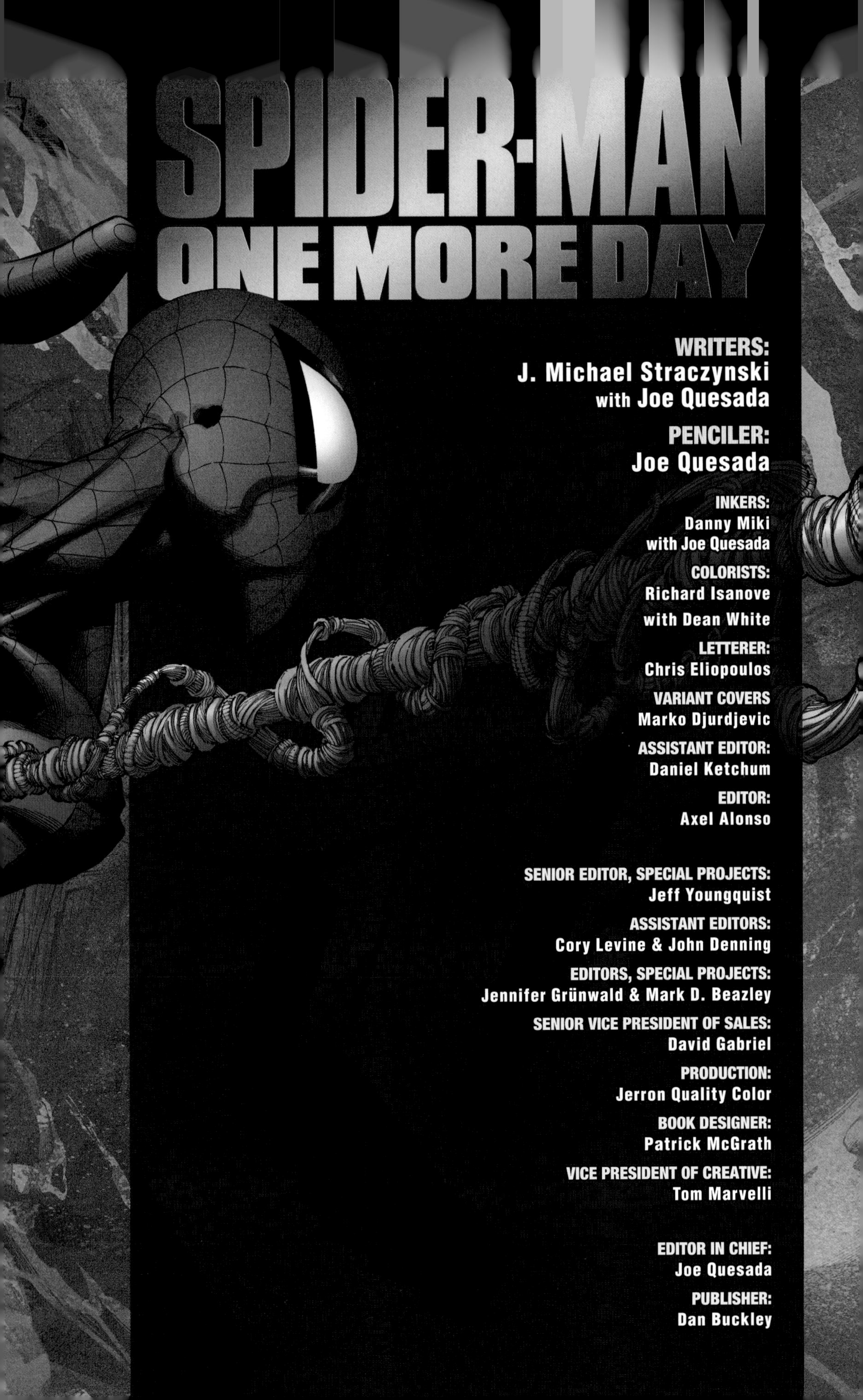

SPIDER-MAN
ONE MORE DAY

WRITERS:
J. Michael Straczynski
with Joe Quesada

PENCILER:
Joe Quesada

INKERS:
Danny Miki
with Joe Quesada

COLORISTS:
Richard Isanove
with Dean White

LETTERER:
Chris Eliopoulos

VARIANT COVERS
Marko Djurdjevic

ASSISTANT EDITOR:
Daniel Ketchum

EDITOR:
Axel Alonso

SENIOR EDITOR, SPECIAL PROJECTS:
Jeff Youngquist

ASSISTANT EDITORS:
Cory Levine & John Denning

EDITORS, SPECIAL PROJECTS:
Jennifer Grünwald & Mark D. Beazley

SENIOR VICE PRESIDENT OF SALES:
David Gabriel

PRODUCTION:
Jerron Quality Color

BOOK DESIGNER:
Patrick McGrath

VICE PRESIDENT OF CREATIVE:
Tom Marvelli

EDITOR IN CHIEF:
Joe Quesada

PUBLISHER:
Dan Buckley

PREVIOUSLY...

When high-school student Peter Parker was bitten by a radioactive spider, he gained the proportional strength, agility and abilities of the arachnid. A selfish decision cost him the life of his beloved Uncle Ben, inspiring Peter's vow to always use his great powers responsibly, to choose action over inaction when someone is in need.

After years of super-heroic deeds as the Amazing Spider-Man, Peter descended into some of the worst days of his life. It began when he publicly unmasked at the request of his mentor Tony Stark, a.k.a. Iron Man, as a sign of support for the Superhuman Registration Act. It was a difficult decision, but his Aunt May and wife Mary Jane supported his choice. Soon, disagreements with the Act's supporters led to another tough choice: to denounce registration and join Captain America's underground forces. After a massive battle between super heroes, Captain America was arrested and assassinated. A fugitive from the law, Spider-Man fled with his family to a seedy motel, their finances evaporating, while his enemies conspired against him and his vulnerable family.

While incarcerated, Wilson Fisk, the Kingpin of Crime, dispatched a sniper to kill Peter and his family. Though Peter protected Mary Jane from the sniper's bullet, Aunt May was shot instead. Hospitalized under an alias, May Parker lay comatose, while Spider-Man sought justice — dressed in his cloth black costume, reflecting his grim demeanor. To make matters worse, the original Venom, cancer victim Eddie Brock, attempted to kill May during his hospital stay. Infiltrating Rykers Island prison, Spider-Man beat the Kingpin to within an inch of his life.

Still, May's life was slipping away. Peter tried giving May a transfusion of his own blood, but nothing improved. The police grew suspicious while investigating May's case. In desperation, Peter recklessly struck an officer, stole an ambulance and transferred May to another hospital. Painting himself into a corner, it was likely just a matter of time before May would die and he would have to face the law.

In a séance via Madame Web, May had told Peter to let her go. But in Peter's mind, his life as Spider-Man and his decision to unmask led to her shooting. Could he live with himself if he had not tried any means necessary to save her life? He knew fantastic and powerful people — could they help? Could he withstand the blood of another loved one on his hands? The clock was ticking. What would he do for

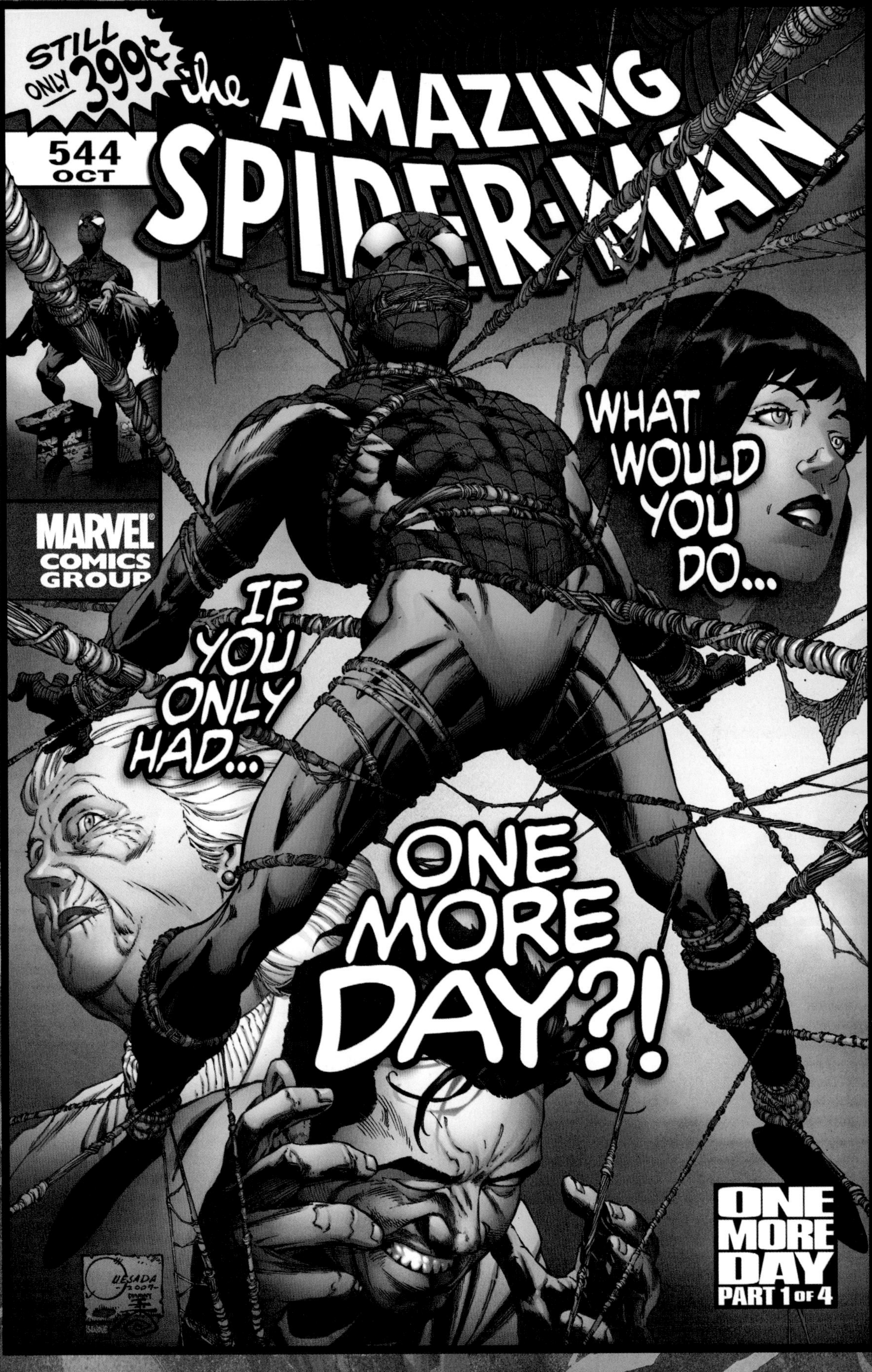
STILL ONLY 399¢
the AMAZING SPIDER-MAN
544 OCT
MARVEL COMICS GROUP
WHAT WOULD YOU DO...
IF YOU ONLY HAD...
ONE MORE DAY?!
ONE MORE DAY PART 1 OF 4

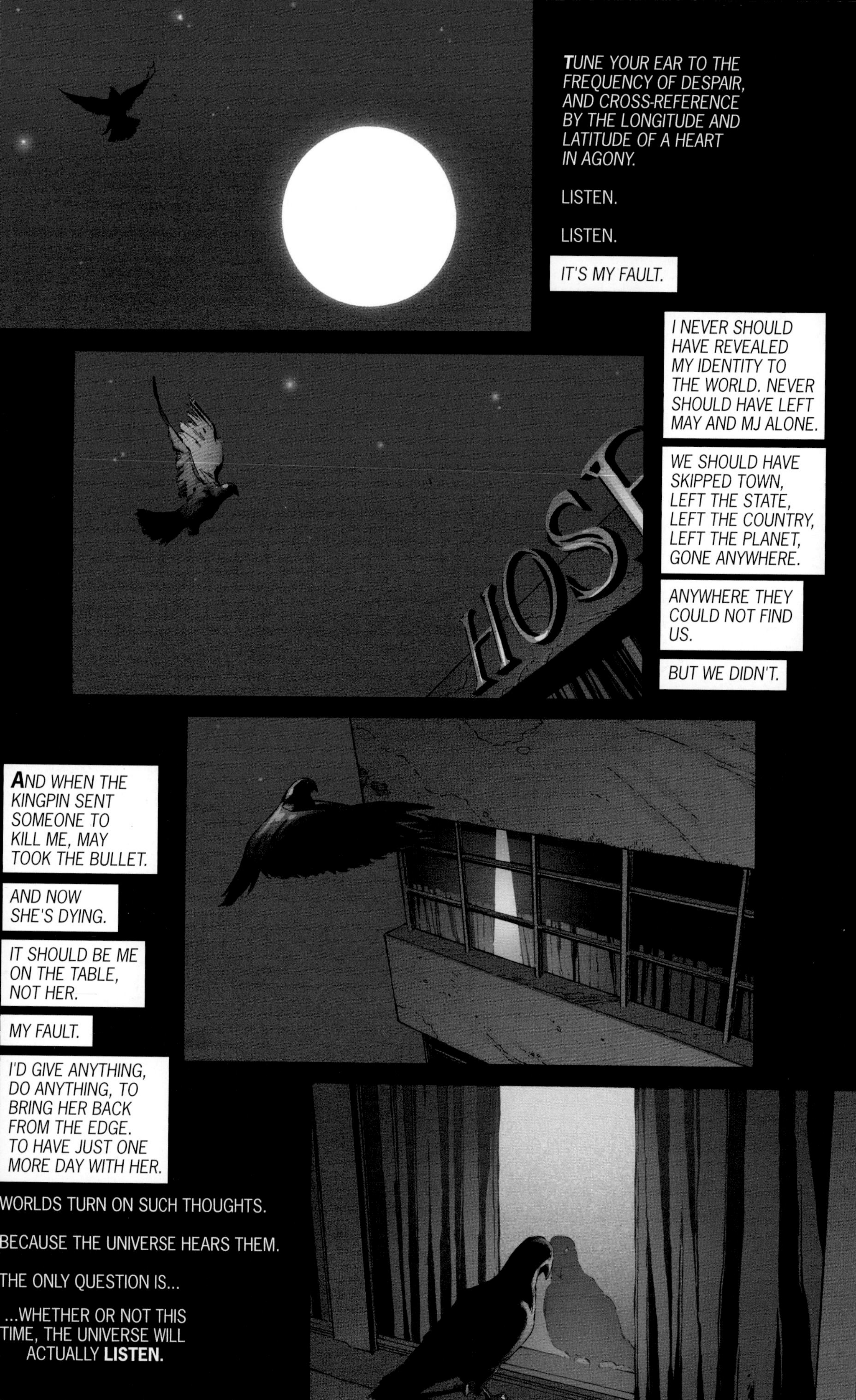
TUNE YOUR EAR TO THE FREQUENCY OF DESPAIR, AND CROSS-REFERENCE BY THE LONGITUDE AND LATITUDE OF A HEART IN AGONY.
LISTEN.
LISTEN.
IT'S MY FAULT.
I NEVER SHOULD HAVE REVEALED MY IDENTITY TO THE WORLD. NEVER SHOULD HAVE LEFT MAY AND MJ ALONE.
WE SHOULD HAVE SKIPPED TOWN, LEFT THE STATE, LEFT THE COUNTRY, LEFT THE PLANET, GONE ANYWHERE.
ANYWHERE THEY COULD NOT FIND US.
BUT WE DIDN'T.
HOSP
AND WHEN THE KINGPIN SENT SOMEONE TO KILL ME, MAY TOOK THE BULLET.
AND NOW SHE'S DYING.
IT SHOULD BE ME ON THE TABLE, NOT HER.
MY FAULT.
I'D GIVE ANYTHING, DO ANYTHING, TO BRING HER BACK FROM THE EDGE. TO HAVE JUST ONE MORE DAY WITH HER.
WORLDS TURN ON SUCH THOUGHTS.
BECAUSE THE UNIVERSE HEARS THEM.
THE ONLY QUESTION IS...
...WHETHER OR NOT THIS TIME, THE UNIVERSE WILL ACTUALLY LISTEN.

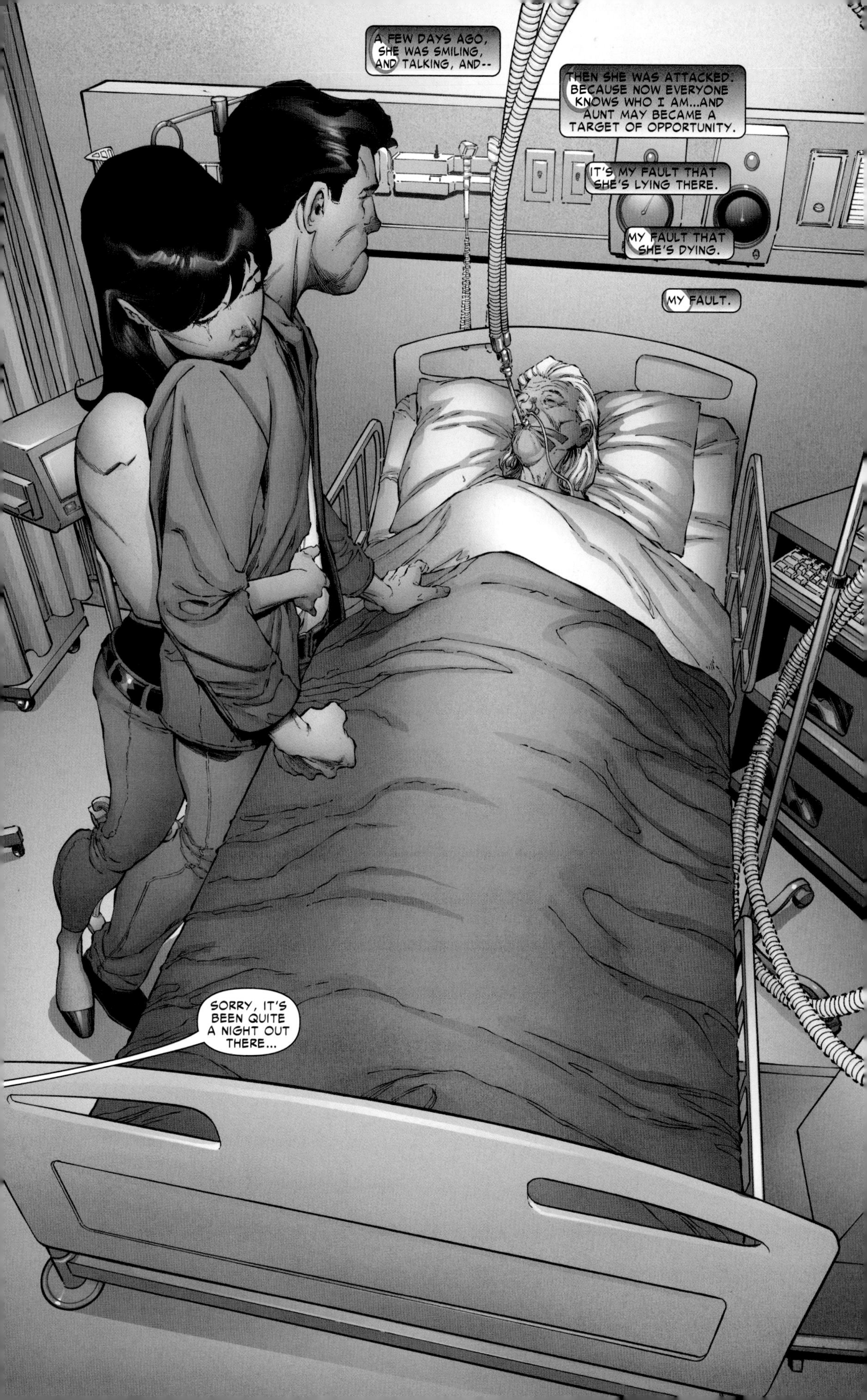
A FEW DAYS AGO, SHE WAS SMILING, AND TALKING, AND--
THEN SHE WAS ATTACKED. BECAUSE NOW EVERYONE KNOWS WHO I AM...AND AUNT MAY BECAME A TARGET OF OPPORTUNITY.
IT'S MY FAULT THAT SHE'S LYING THERE.
MY FAULT THAT SHE'S DYING.
MY FAULT.
SORRY, IT'S BEEN QUITE A NIGHT OUT THERE...

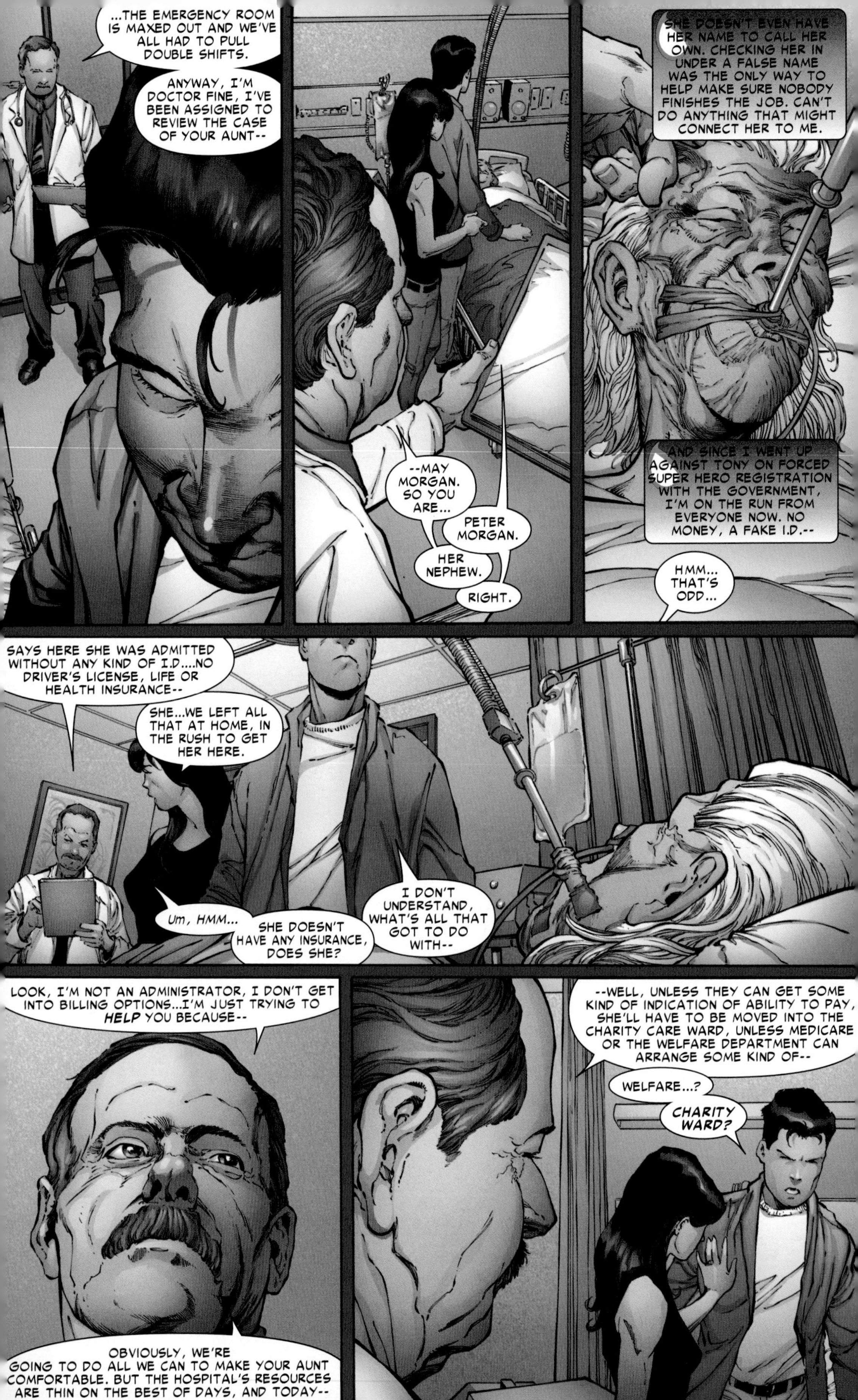
...THE EMERGENCY ROOM IS MAXED OUT AND WE'VE ALL HAD TO PULL DOUBLE SHIFTS.
ANYWAY, I'M DOCTOR FINE, I'VE BEEN ASSIGNED TO REVIEW THE CASE OF YOUR AUNT--
--MAY MORGAN. SO YOU ARE...
PETER MORGAN.
HER NEPHEW.
RIGHT.
SHE DOESN'T EVEN HAVE HER NAME TO CALL HER OWN. CHECKING HER IN UNDER A FALSE NAME WAS THE ONLY WAY TO HELP MAKE SURE NOBODY FINISHES THE JOB. CAN'T DO ANYTHING THAT MIGHT CONNECT HER TO ME.
AND SINCE I WENT UP AGAINST TONY ON FORCED SUPER HERO REGISTRATION WITH THE GOVERNMENT, I'M ON THE RUN FROM EVERYONE NOW. NO MONEY, A FAKE I.D.--
HMM... THAT'S ODD...
SAYS HERE SHE WAS ADMITTED WITHOUT ANY KIND OF I.D....NO DRIVER'S LICENSE, LIFE OR HEALTH INSURANCE--
SHE...WE LEFT ALL THAT AT HOME, IN THE RUSH TO GET HER HERE.
Um, HMM...
SHE DOESN'T HAVE ANY INSURANCE, DOES SHE?
I DON'T UNDERSTAND, WHAT'S ALL THAT GOT TO DO WITH--
LOOK, I'M NOT AN ADMINISTRATOR, I DON'T GET INTO BILLING OPTIONS...I'M JUST TRYING TO HELP YOU BECAUSE--
OBVIOUSLY, WE'RE GOING TO DO ALL WE CAN TO MAKE YOUR AUNT COMFORTABLE. BUT THE HOSPITAL'S RESOURCES ARE THIN ON THE BEST OF DAYS, AND TODAY--
--WELL, UNLESS THEY CAN GET SOME KIND OF INDICATION OF ABILITY TO PAY, SHE'LL HAVE TO BE MOVED INTO THE CHARITY CARE WARD, UNLESS MEDICARE OR THE WELFARE DEPARTMENT CAN ARRANGE SOME KIND OF--
WELFARE...?
CHARITY WARD?

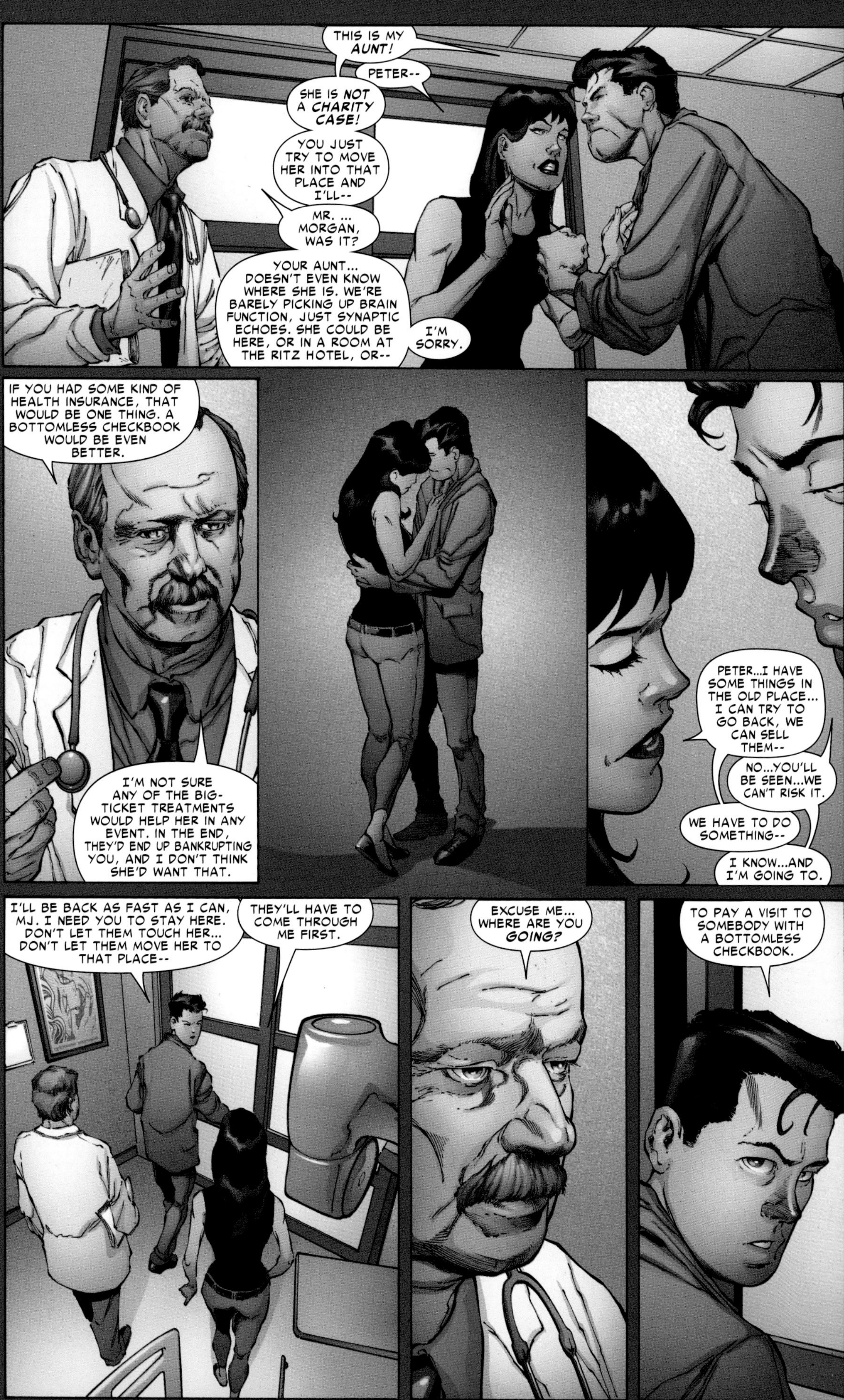
THIS IS MY AUNT!
PETER--
SHE IS NOT A CHARITY CASE!
YOU JUST TRY TO MOVE HER INTO THAT PLACE AND I'LL--
MR. ... MORGAN, WAS IT?
YOUR AUNT... DOESN'T EVEN KNOW WHERE SHE IS. WE'RE BARELY PICKING UP BRAIN FUNCTION, JUST SYNAPTIC ECHOES. SHE COULD BE HERE, OR IN A ROOM AT THE RITZ HOTEL, OR--
I'M SORRY.
IF YOU HAD SOME KIND OF HEALTH INSURANCE, THAT WOULD BE ONE THING. A BOTTOMLESS CHECKBOOK WOULD BE EVEN BETTER.
I'M NOT SURE ANY OF THE BIG-TICKET TREATMENTS WOULD HELP HER IN ANY EVENT. IN THE END, THEY'D END UP BANKRUPTING YOU, AND I DON'T THINK SHE'D WANT THAT.
PETER...I HAVE SOME THINGS IN THE OLD PLACE... I CAN TRY TO GO BACK, WE CAN SELL THEM--
NO...YOU'LL BE SEEN...WE CAN'T RISK IT.
WE HAVE TO DO SOMETHING--
I KNOW...AND I'M GOING TO.
I'LL BE BACK AS FAST AS I CAN, MJ. I NEED YOU TO STAY HERE. DON'T LET THEM TOUCH HER... DON'T LET THEM MOVE HER TO THAT PLACE--
THEY'LL HAVE TO COME THROUGH ME FIRST.
EXCUSE ME... WHERE ARE YOU GOING?
TO PAY A VISIT TO SOMEBODY WITH A BOTTOMLESS CHECKBOOK.

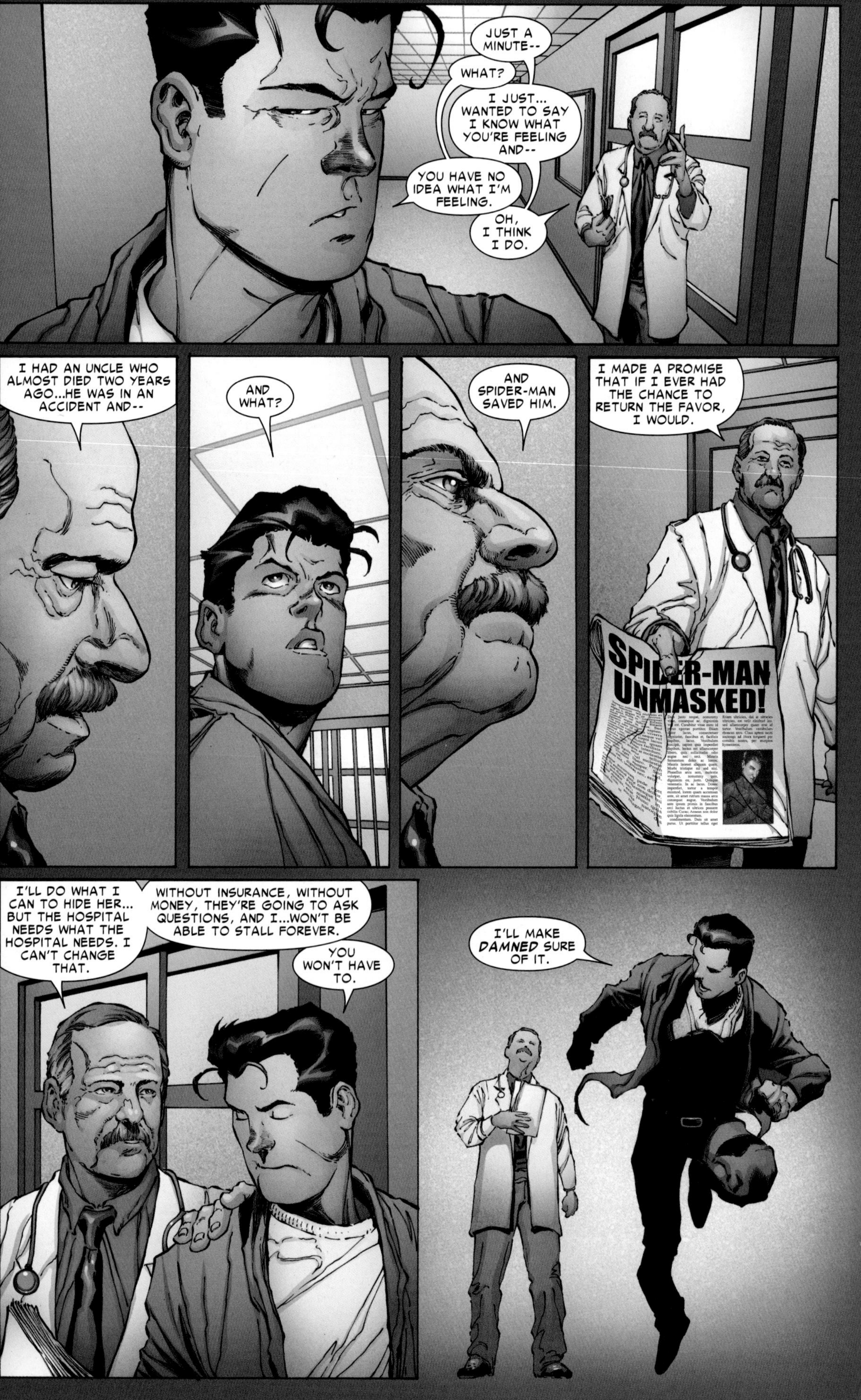
JUST A MINUTE--
WHAT?
I JUST... WANTED TO SAY I KNOW WHAT YOU'RE FEELING AND--
YOU HAVE NO IDEA WHAT I'M FEELING.
OH, I THINK I DO.
I HAD AN UNCLE WHO ALMOST DIED TWO YEARS AGO...HE WAS IN AN ACCIDENT AND--
AND WHAT?
AND SPIDER-MAN SAVED HIM.
I MADE A PROMISE THAT IF I EVER HAD THE CHANCE TO RETURN THE FAVOR, I WOULD.
SPIDER-MAN UNMASKED!
I'LL DO WHAT I CAN TO HIDE HER... BUT THE HOSPITAL NEEDS WHAT THE HOSPITAL NEEDS. I CAN'T CHANGE THAT.
WITHOUT INSURANCE, WITHOUT MONEY, THEY'RE GOING TO ASK QUESTIONS, AND I...WON'T BE ABLE TO STALL FOREVER.
YOU WON'T HAVE TO.
I'LL MAKE DAMNED SURE OF IT.

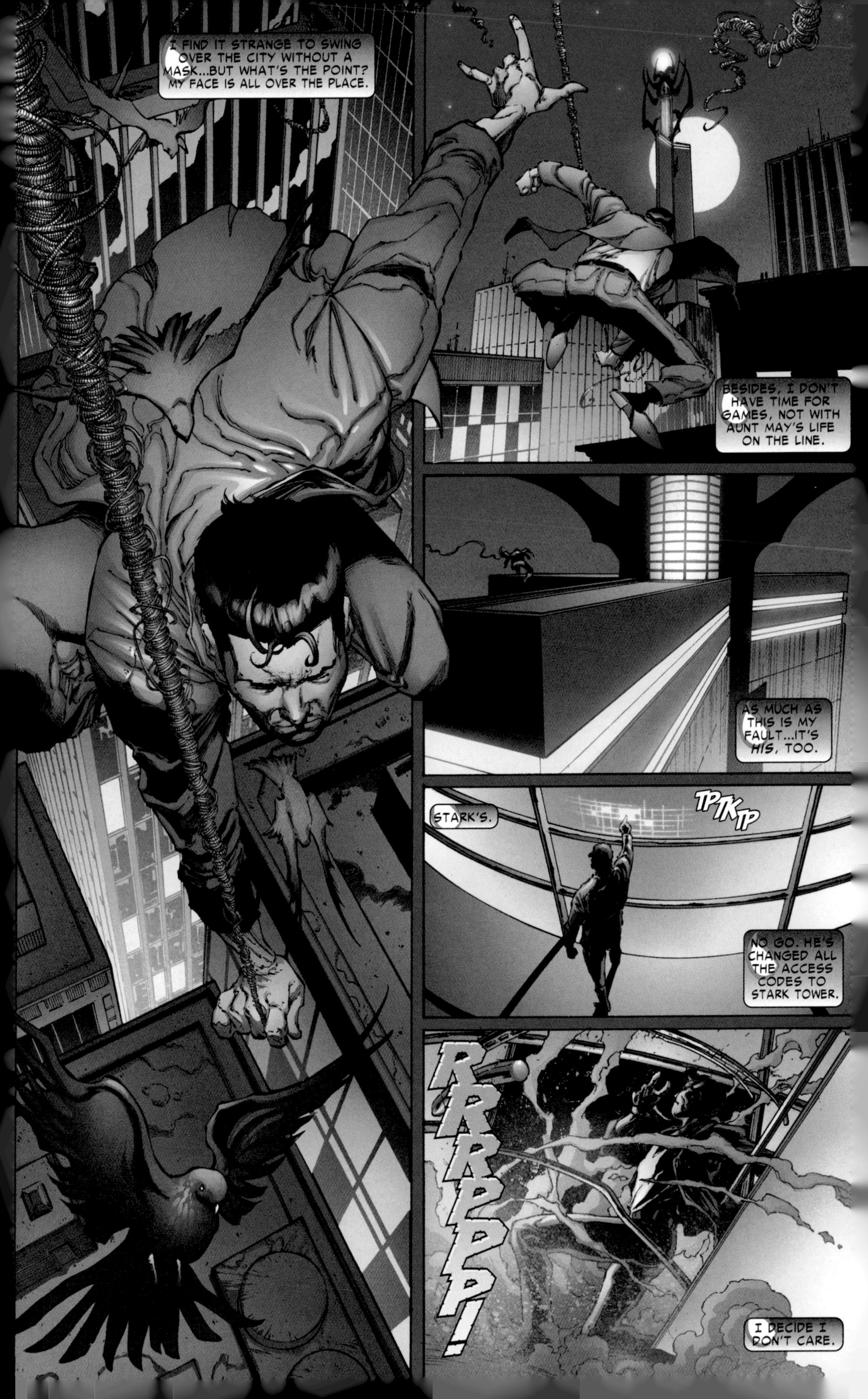
I FIND IT STRANGE TO SWING OVER THE CITY WITHOUT A MASK...BUT WHAT'S THE POINT? MY FACE IS ALL OVER THE PLACE.
BESIDES, I DON'T HAVE TIME FOR GAMES, NOT WITH AUNT MAY'S LIFE ON THE LINE.
AS MUCH AS THIS IS MY FAULT...IT'S *HIS*, TOO.
STARK'S.
TPTKTP
NO GO. HE'S CHANGED ALL THE ACCESS CODES TO STARK TOWER.
RRRPPP!
I DECIDE I DON'T CARE.

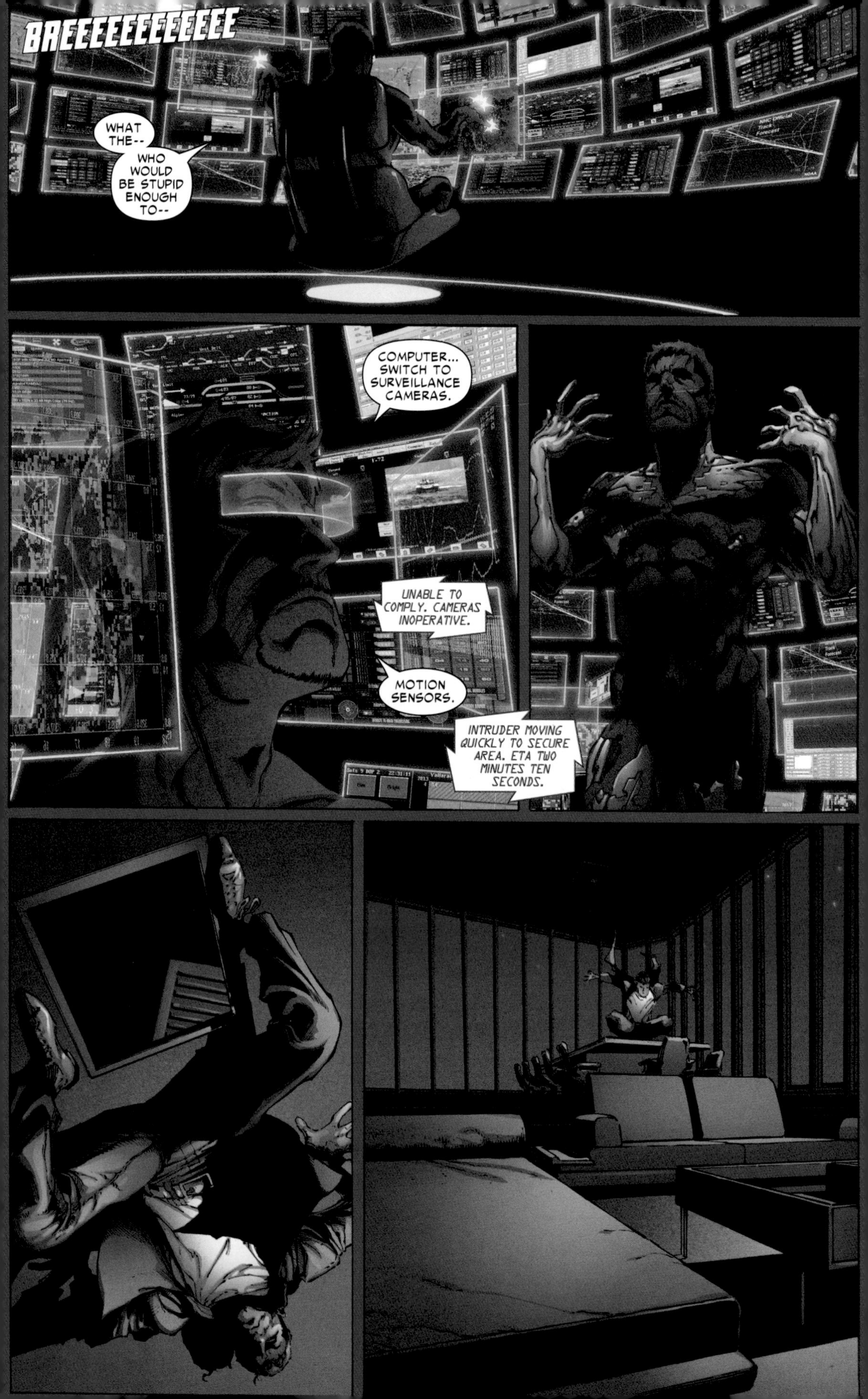
BREEEEEEEEEEEE
WHAT THE-- WHO WOULD BE STUPID ENOUGH TO--
COMPUTER... SWITCH TO SURVEILLANCE CAMERAS.
UNABLE TO COMPLY. CAMERAS INOPERATIVE.
MOTION SENSORS.
INTRUDER MOVING QUICKLY TO SECURE AREA. ETA TWO MINUTES TEN SECONDS.

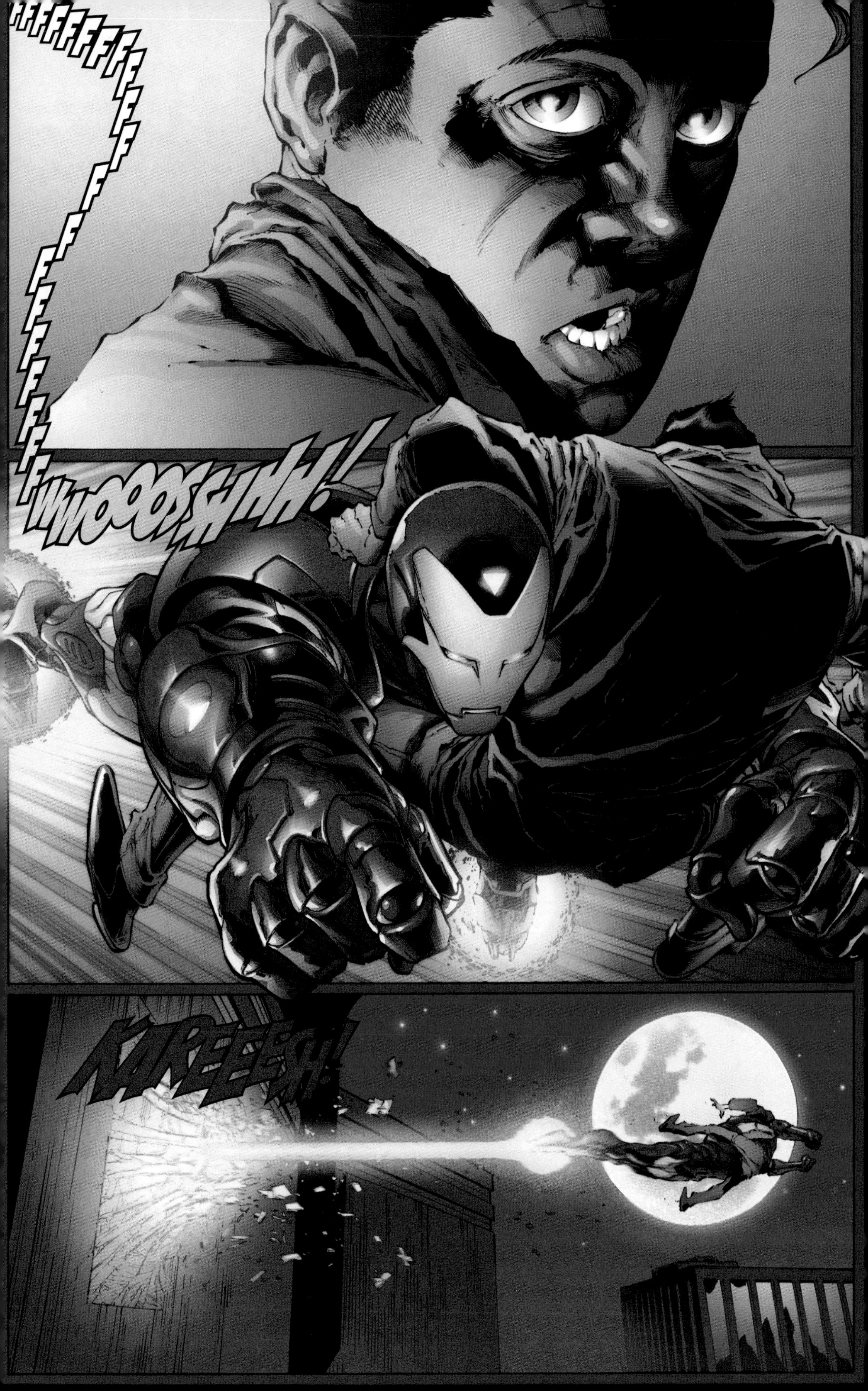
FFFFFFFFFFFFFFFFFFFFFFFFFWWOOOSHHH!
KAREEESH!

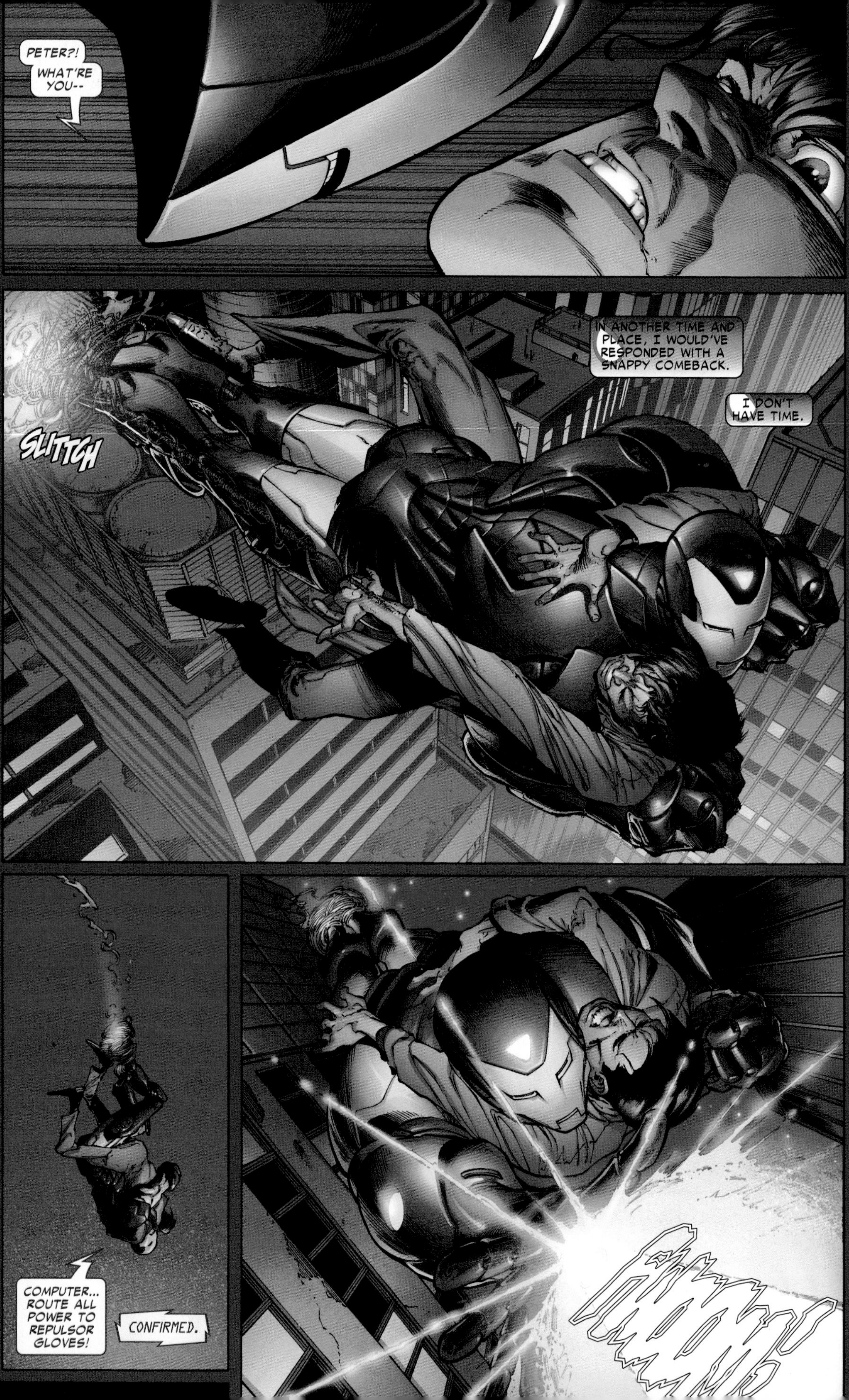
PETER?! WHAT'RE YOU--
IN ANOTHER TIME AND PLACE, I WOULD'VE RESPONDED WITH A SNAPPY COMEBACK.
I DON'T HAVE TIME.
SLITTCH
COMPUTER... ROUTE ALL POWER TO REPULSOR GLOVES!
CONFIRMED.

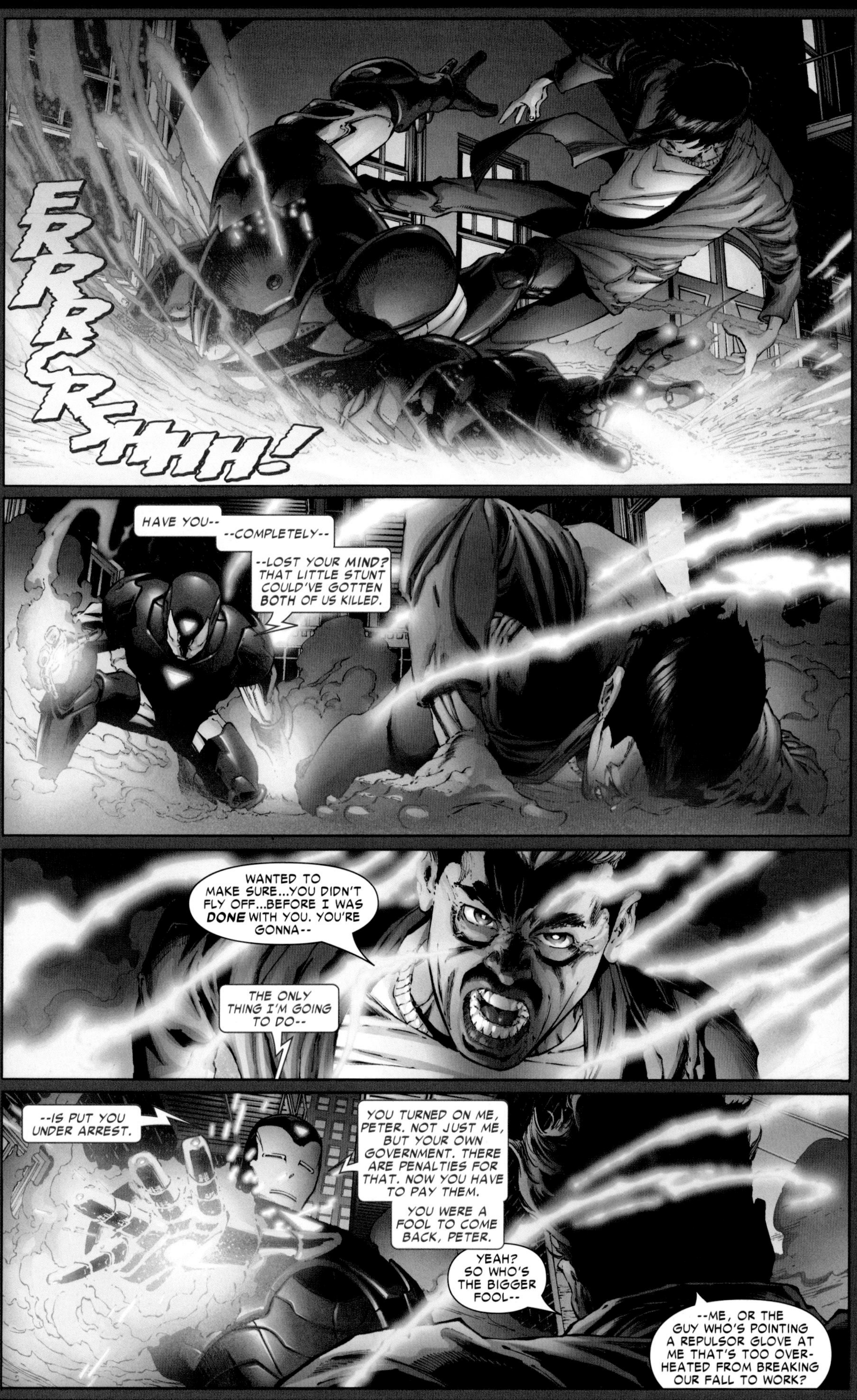
ERRRGRHHH!
HAVE YOU--
--COMPLETELY--
--LOST YOUR MIND? THAT LITTLE STUNT COULD'VE GOTTEN BOTH OF US KILLED.
WANTED TO MAKE SURE...YOU DIDN'T FLY OFF...BEFORE I WAS DONE WITH YOU. YOU'RE GONNA--
THE ONLY THING I'M GOING TO DO--
--IS PUT YOU UNDER ARREST.
YOU TURNED ON ME, PETER. NOT JUST ME, BUT YOUR OWN GOVERNMENT. THERE ARE PENALTIES FOR THAT. NOW YOU HAVE TO PAY THEM.
YOU WERE A FOOL TO COME BACK, PETER.
YEAH? SO WHO'S THE BIGGER FOOL--
--ME, OR THE GUY WHO'S POINTING A REPULSOR GLOVE AT ME THAT'S TOO OVER-HEATED FROM BREAKING OUR FALL TO WORK?

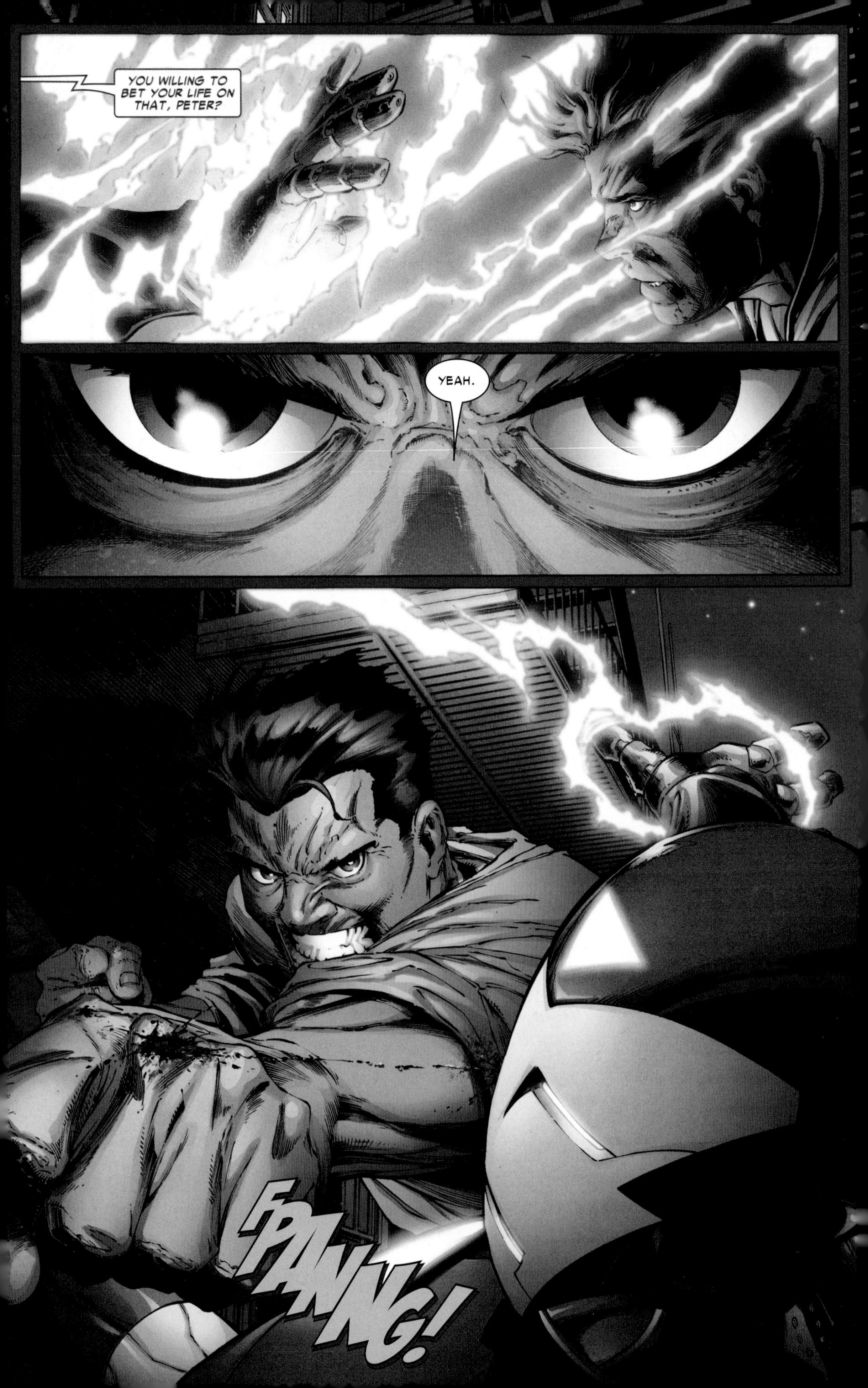
YOU WILLING TO BET YOUR LIFE ON THAT, PETER?
YEAH.
FPANNG!

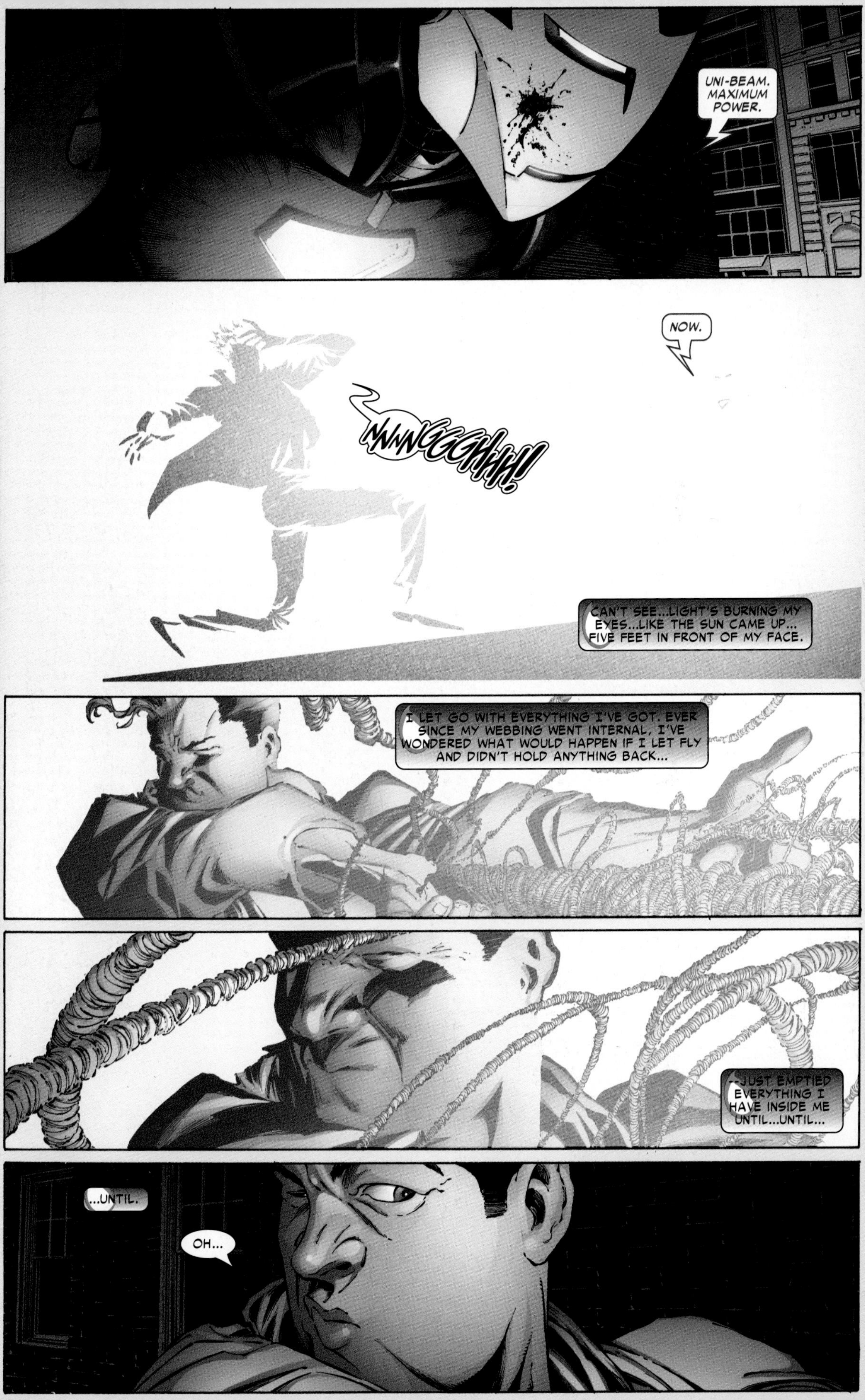
UNI-BEAM. MAXIMUM POWER.
NOW.
NNNNGGGHHH!
CAN'T SEE...LIGHT'S BURNING MY EYES...LIKE THE SUN CAME UP... FIVE FEET IN FRONT OF MY FACE.
I LET GO WITH EVERYTHING I'VE GOT. EVER SINCE MY WEBBING WENT INTERNAL, I'VE WONDERED WHAT WOULD HAPPEN IF I LET FLY AND DIDN'T HOLD ANYTHING BACK...
--JUST EMPTIED EVERYTHING I HAVE INSIDE ME UNTIL...UNTIL...
...UNTIL.
OH...

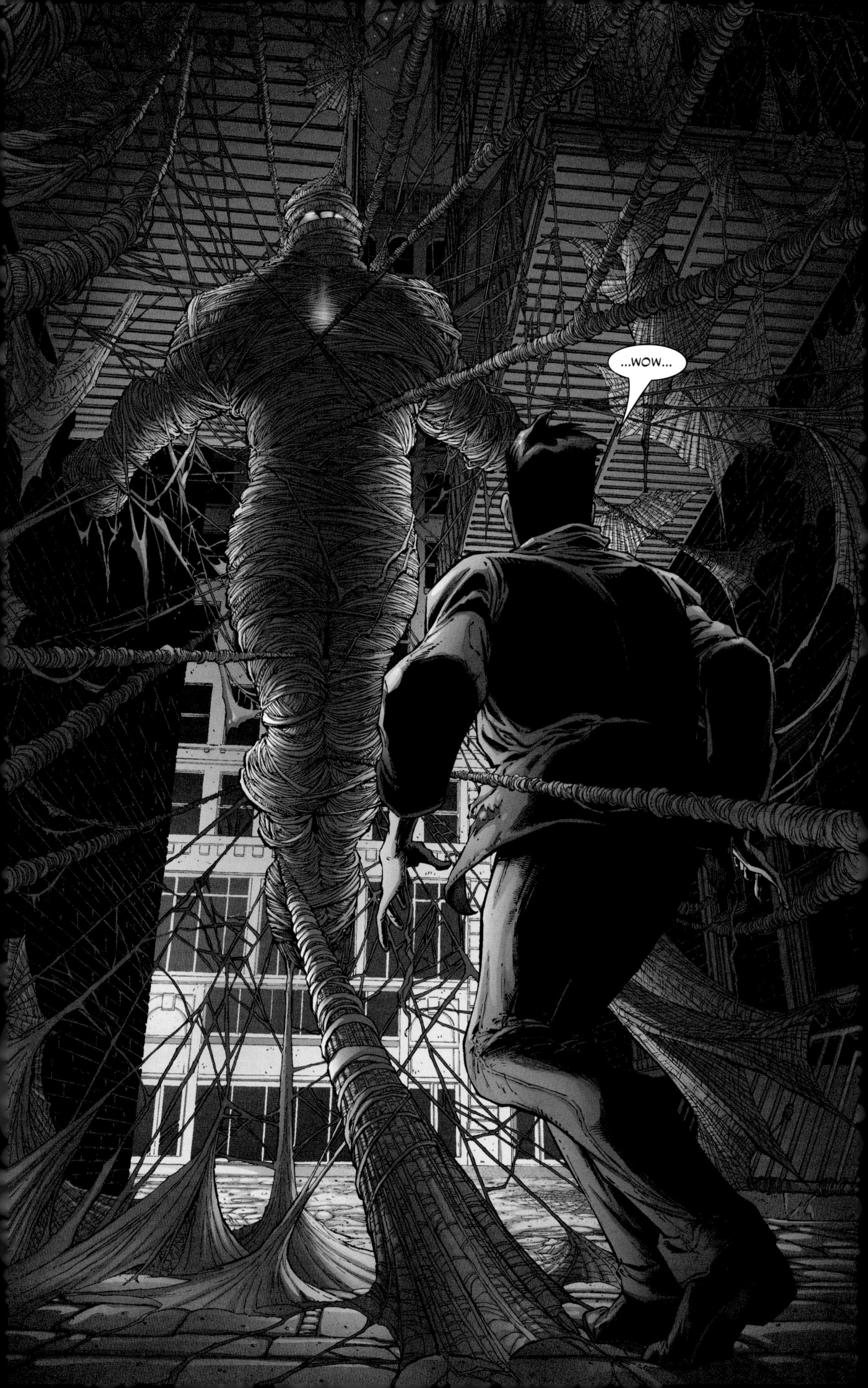
...WOW...

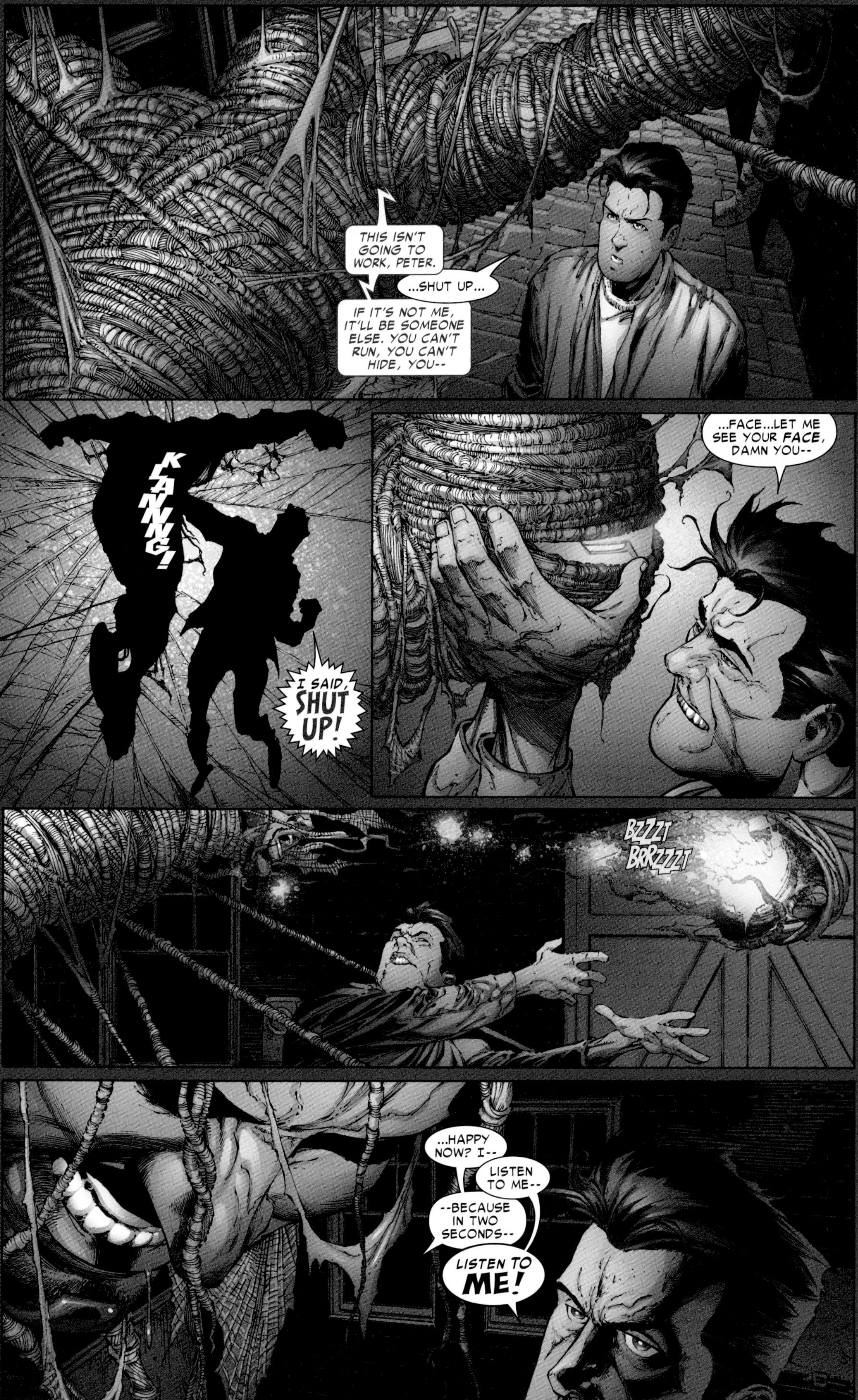
THIS ISN'T GOING TO WORK, PETER.
...SHUT UP...
IF IT'S NOT ME, IT'LL BE SOMEONE ELSE. YOU CAN'T RUN, YOU CAN'T HIDE, YOU--
KLANNNG!
I SAID, SHUT UP!
...FACE...LET ME SEE YOUR FACE, DAMN YOU--
BZZZZT
BRRZZZZT
...HAPPY NOW? I--
LISTEN TO ME--
--BECAUSE IN TWO SECONDS--
LISTEN TO ME!

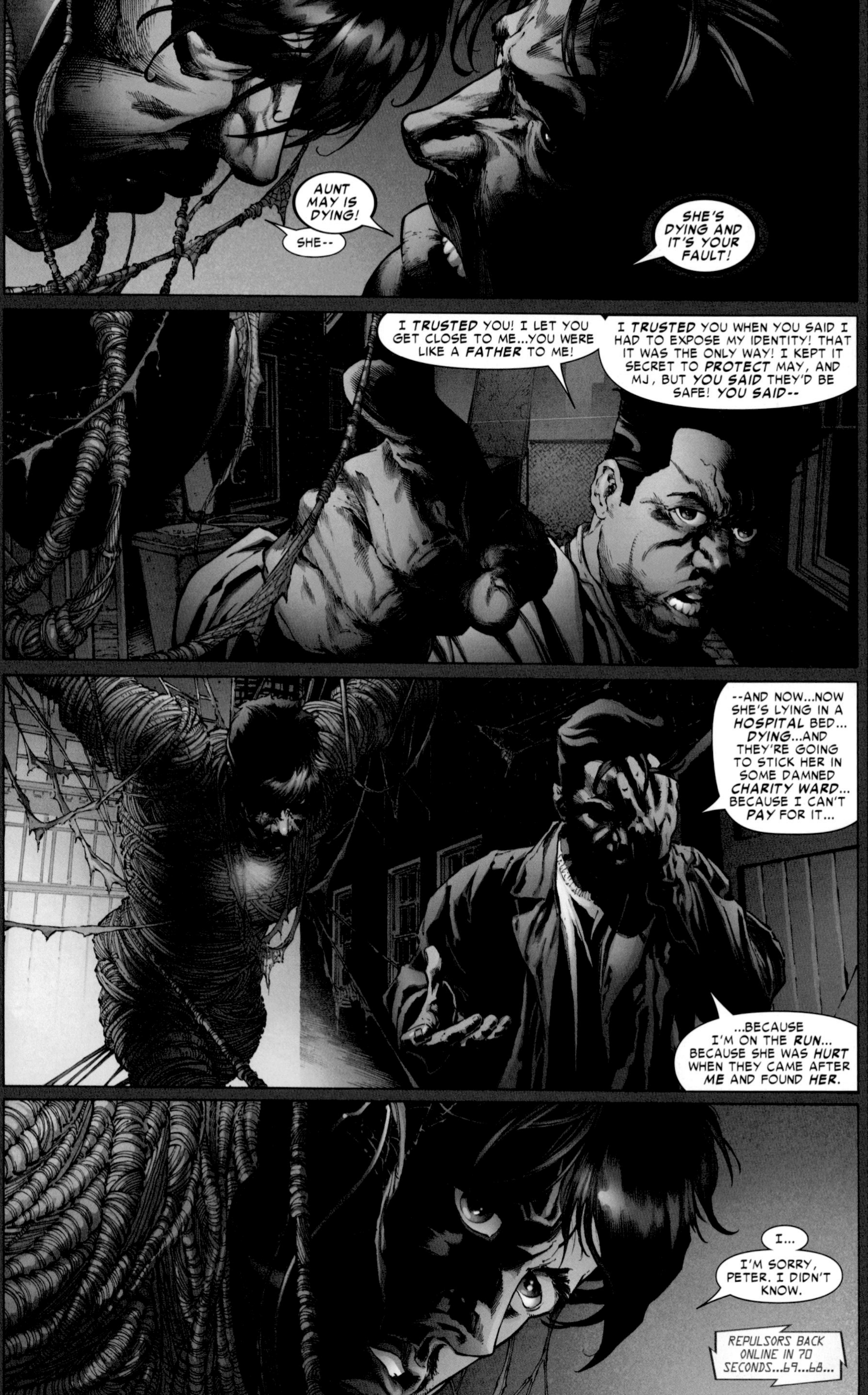
AUNT MAY IS DYING!
SHE--
SHE'S DYING AND IT'S YOUR FAULT!
I TRUSTED YOU! I LET YOU GET CLOSE TO ME...YOU WERE LIKE A FATHER TO ME!
I TRUSTED YOU WHEN YOU SAID I HAD TO EXPOSE MY IDENTITY! THAT IT WAS THE ONLY WAY! I KEPT IT SECRET TO PROTECT MAY, AND MJ, BUT YOU SAID THEY'D BE SAFE! YOU SAID--
--AND NOW...NOW SHE'S LYING IN A HOSPITAL BED... DYING...AND THEY'RE GOING TO STICK HER IN SOME DAMNED CHARITY WARD... BECAUSE I CAN'T PAY FOR IT...
...BECAUSE I'M ON THE RUN... BECAUSE SHE WAS HURT WHEN THEY CAME AFTER ME AND FOUND HER.
I...
I'M SORRY, PETER. I DIDN'T KNOW.
REPULSORS BACK ONLINE IN 70 SECONDS...69...68...

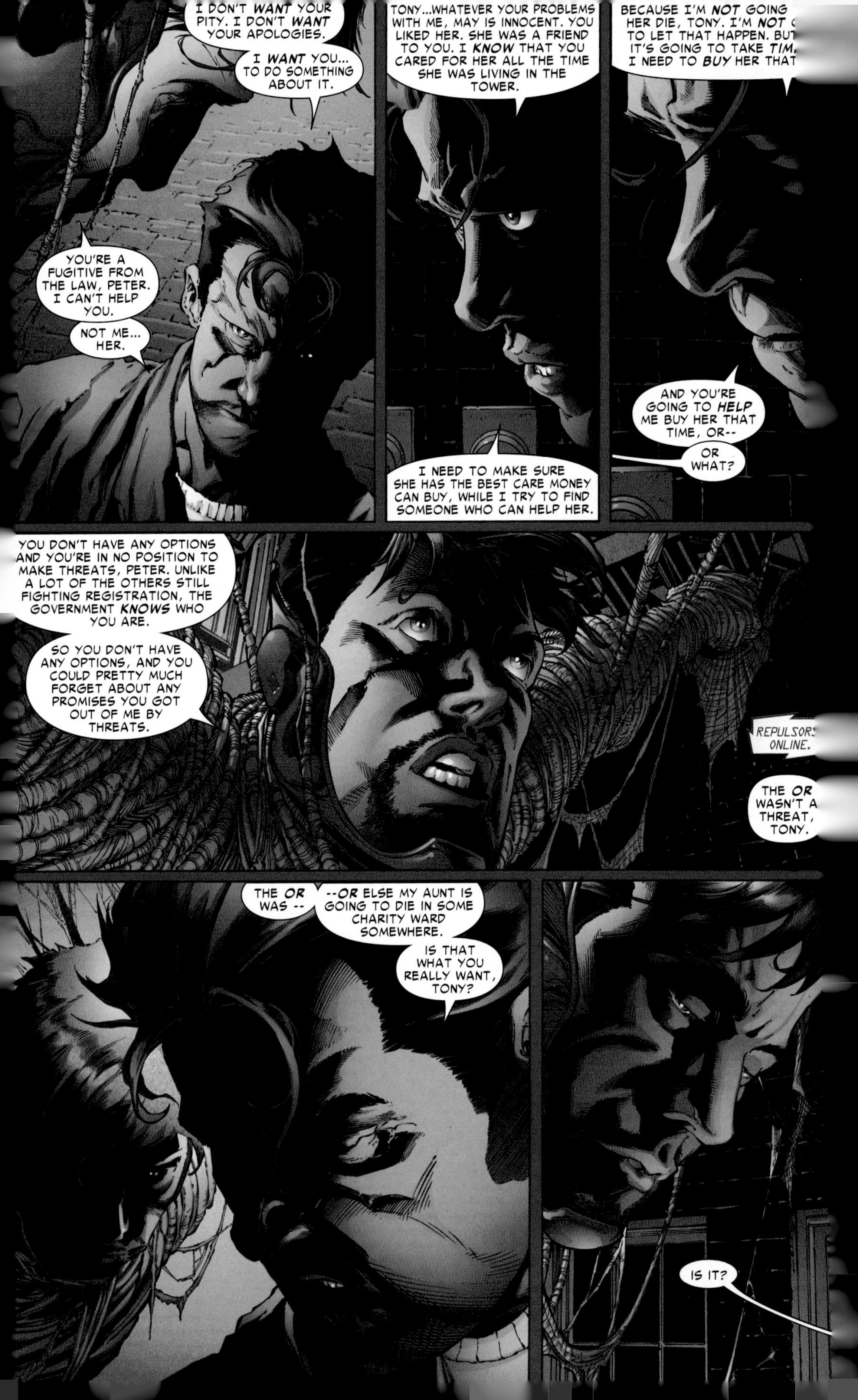
I DON'T WANT YOUR PITY. I DON'T WANT YOUR APOLOGIES.
I WANT YOU... TO DO SOMETHING ABOUT IT.
YOU'RE A FUGITIVE FROM THE LAW, PETER. I CAN'T HELP YOU.
NOT ME... HER.
TONY...WHATEVER YOUR PROBLEMS WITH ME, MAY IS INNOCENT. YOU LIKED HER. SHE WAS A FRIEND TO YOU. I KNOW THAT YOU CARED FOR HER ALL THE TIME SHE WAS LIVING IN THE TOWER.
I NEED TO MAKE SURE SHE HAS THE BEST CARE MONEY CAN BUY, WHILE I TRY TO FIND SOMEONE WHO CAN HELP HER.
BECAUSE I'M NOT GOING HER DIE, TONY. I'M NOT TO LET THAT HAPPEN. BUT IT'S GOING TO TAKE TIM I NEED TO BUY HER THAT
AND YOU'RE GOING TO HELP ME BUY HER THAT TIME, OR--
OR WHAT?
YOU DON'T HAVE ANY OPTIONS AND YOU'RE IN NO POSITION TO MAKE THREATS, PETER. UNLIKE A LOT OF THE OTHERS STILL FIGHTING REGISTRATION, THE GOVERNMENT KNOWS WHO YOU ARE.
SO YOU DON'T HAVE ANY OPTIONS, AND YOU COULD PRETTY MUCH FORGET ABOUT ANY PROMISES YOU GOT OUT OF ME BY THREATS.
REPULSORS ONLINE.
THE OR WASN'T A THREAT, TONY.
THE OR WAS --
--OR ELSE MY AUNT IS GOING TO DIE IN SOME CHARITY WARD SOMEWHERE.
IS THAT WHAT YOU REALLY WANT, TONY?
IS IT?

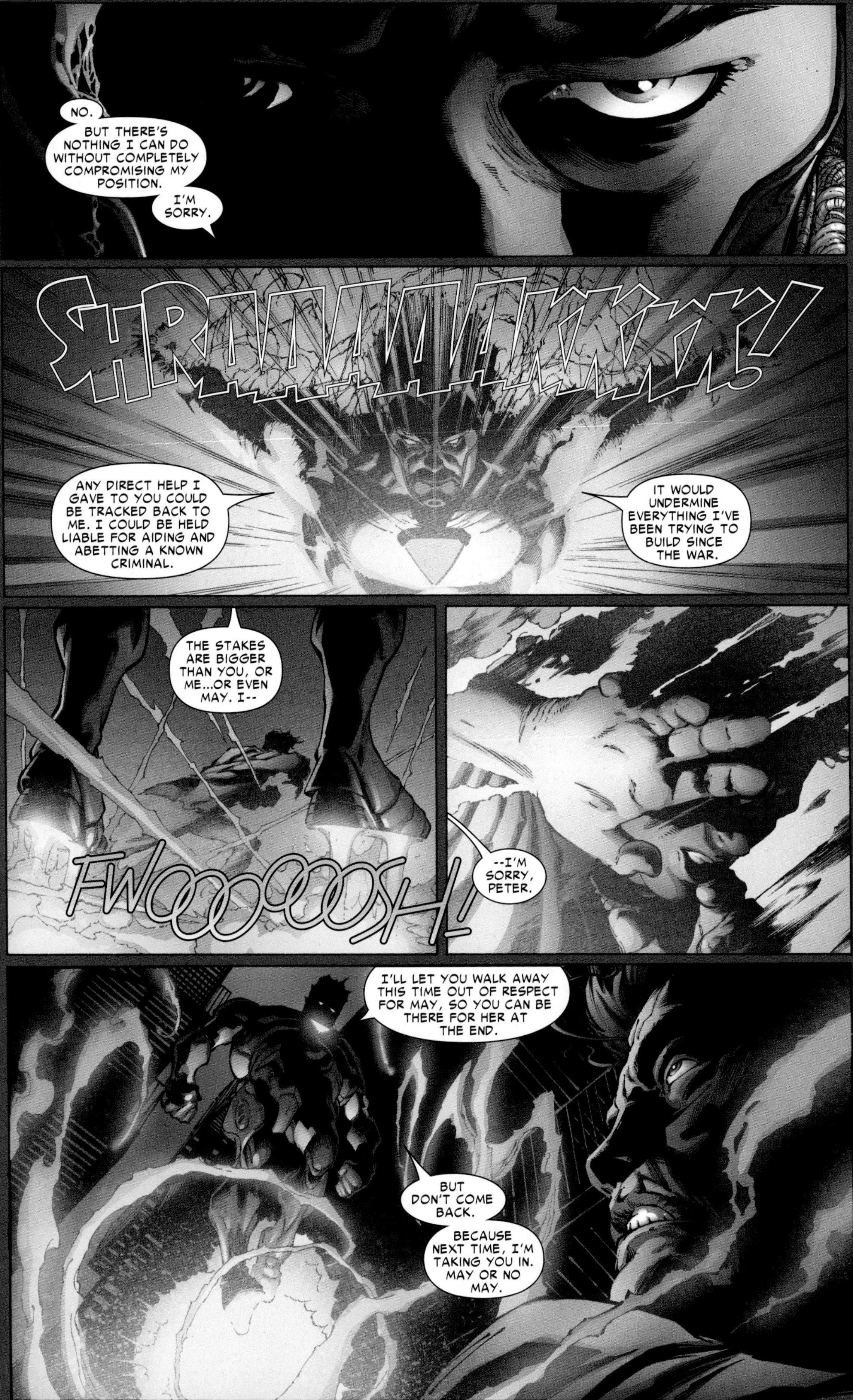
NO.
BUT THERE'S NOTHING I CAN DO WITHOUT COMPLETELY COMPROMISING MY POSITION.
I'M SORRY.
SHRAAAAAKKKK!
ANY DIRECT HELP I GAVE TO YOU COULD BE TRACKED BACK TO ME. I COULD BE HELD LIABLE FOR AIDING AND ABETTING A KNOWN CRIMINAL.
IT WOULD UNDERMINE EVERYTHING I'VE BEEN TRYING TO BUILD SINCE THE WAR.
THE STAKES ARE BIGGER THAN YOU, OR ME...OR EVEN MAY. I--
FWOOOOOOSH!
--I'M SORRY, PETER.
I'LL LET YOU WALK AWAY THIS TIME OUT OF RESPECT FOR MAY, SO YOU CAN BE THERE FOR HER AT THE END.
BUT DON'T COME BACK.
BECAUSE NEXT TIME, I'M TAKING YOU IN. MAY OR NO MAY.

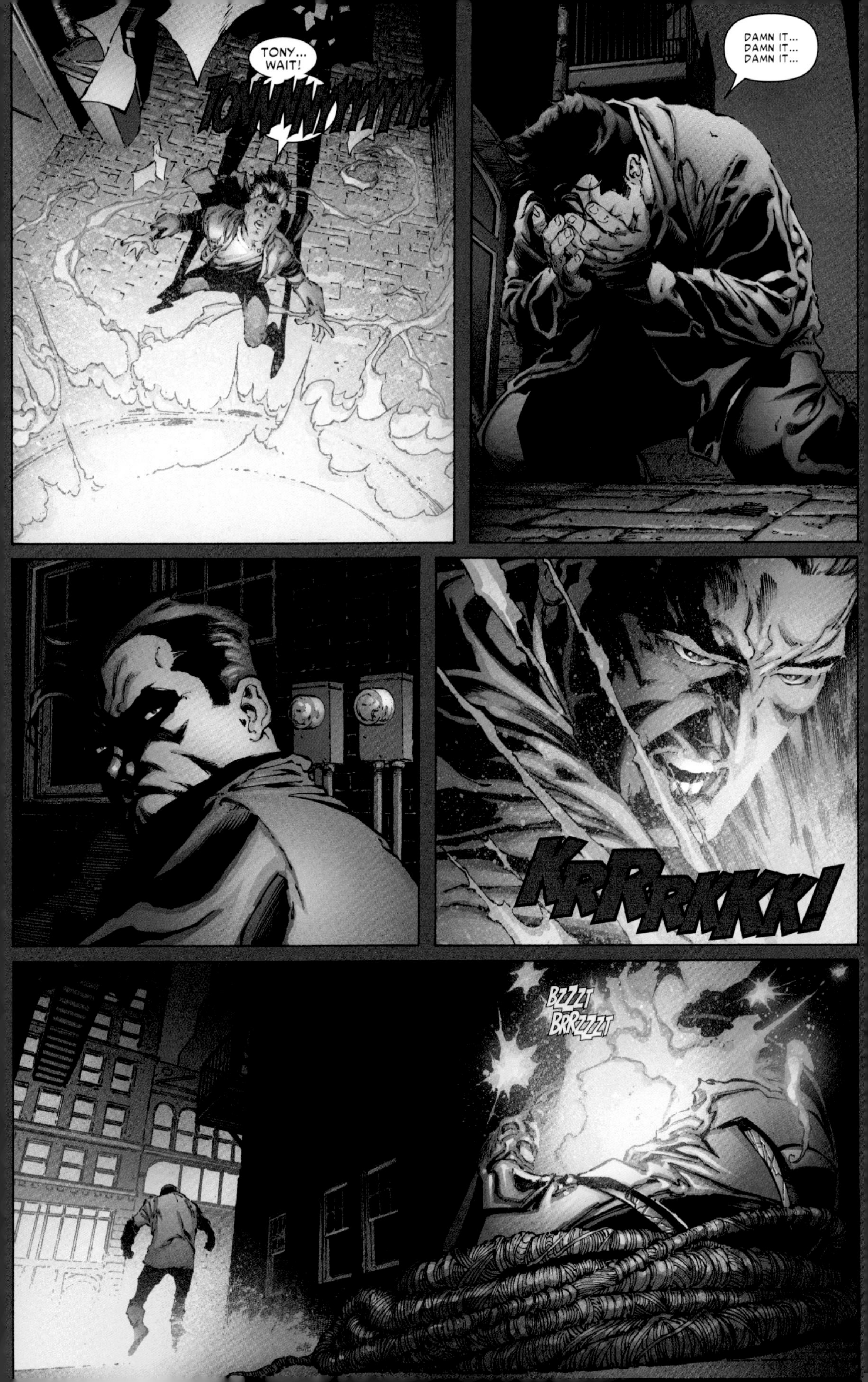
TONY... WAIT!
TONNNNYYYYYY!
DAMN IT... DAMN IT... DAMN IT...
KRRRKKK!
BZZZT
BRRZZZZT

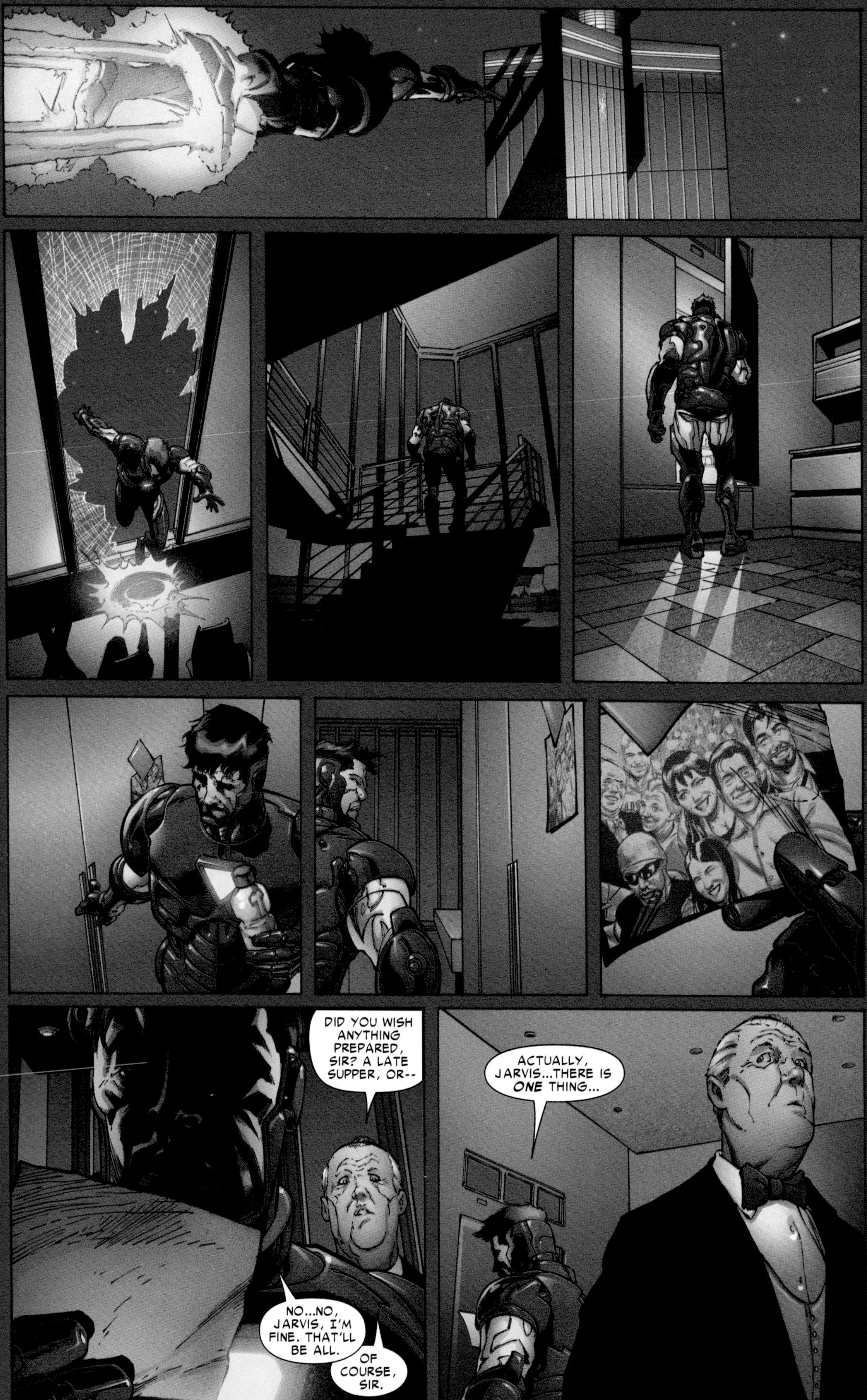
DID YOU WISH ANYTHING PREPARED, SIR? A LATE SUPPER, OR--
NO...NO, JARVIS, I'M FINE. THAT'LL BE ALL.
OF COURSE, SIR.
ACTUALLY, JARVIS...THERE IS ONE THING...

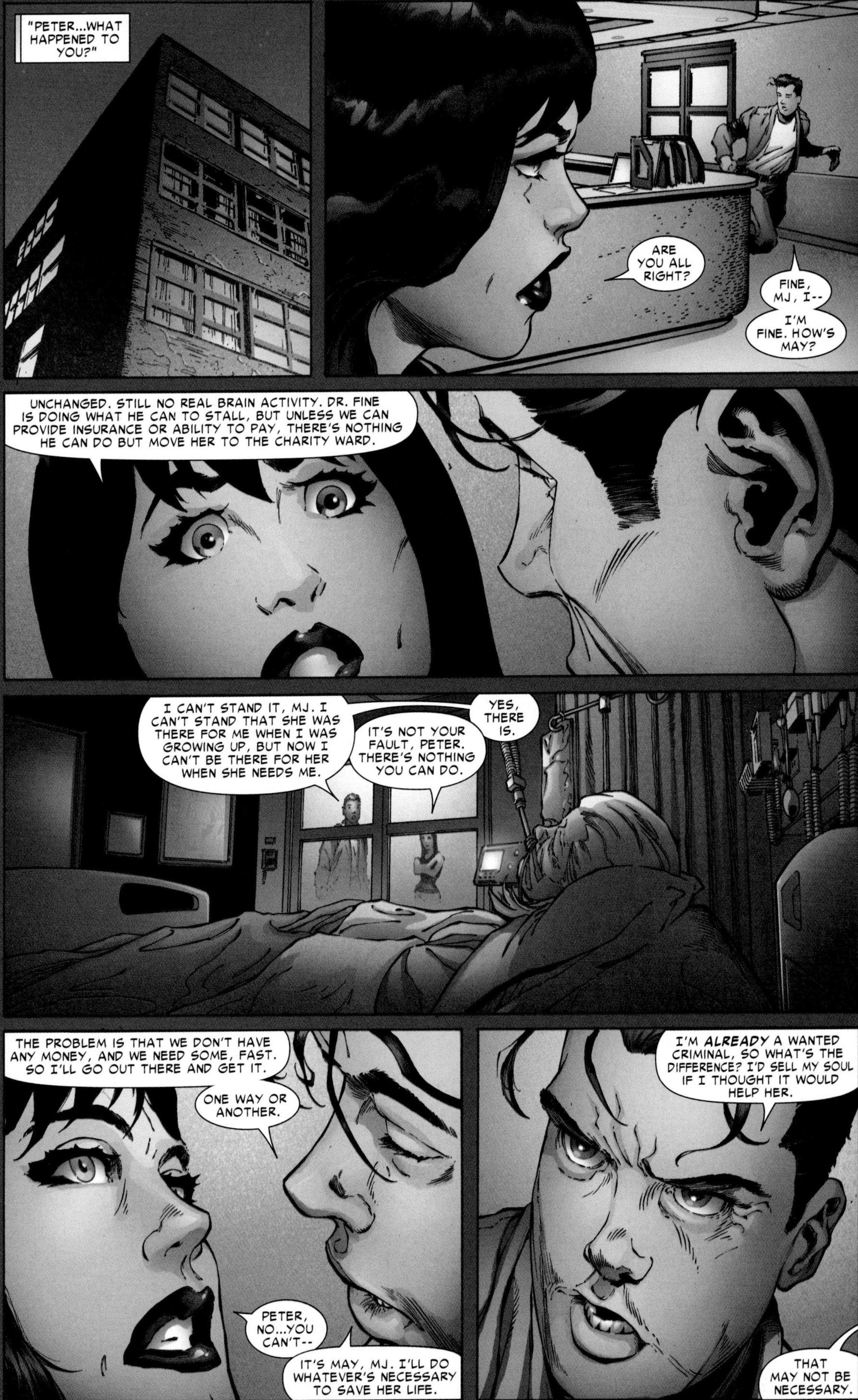
"PETER...WHAT HAPPENED TO YOU?"
ARE YOU ALL RIGHT?
FINE, MJ, I--
I'M FINE. HOW'S MAY?
UNCHANGED. STILL NO REAL BRAIN ACTIVITY. DR. FINE IS DOING WHAT HE CAN TO STALL, BUT UNLESS WE CAN PROVIDE INSURANCE OR ABILITY TO PAY, THERE'S NOTHING HE CAN DO BUT MOVE HER TO THE CHARITY WARD.
I CAN'T STAND IT, MJ. I CAN'T STAND THAT SHE WAS THERE FOR ME WHEN I WAS GROWING UP, BUT NOW I CAN'T BE THERE FOR HER WHEN SHE NEEDS ME.
IT'S NOT YOUR FAULT, PETER. THERE'S NOTHING YOU CAN DO.
YES, THERE IS.
THE PROBLEM IS THAT WE DON'T HAVE ANY MONEY, AND WE NEED SOME, FAST. SO I'LL GO OUT THERE AND GET IT.
ONE WAY OR ANOTHER.
PETER, NO...YOU CAN'T--
IT'S MAY, MJ. I'LL DO WHATEVER'S NECESSARY TO SAVE HER LIFE.
I'M ALREADY A WANTED CRIMINAL, SO WHAT'S THE DIFFERENCE? I'D SELL MY SOUL IF I THOUGHT IT WOULD HELP HER.
THAT MAY NOT BE NECESSARY.

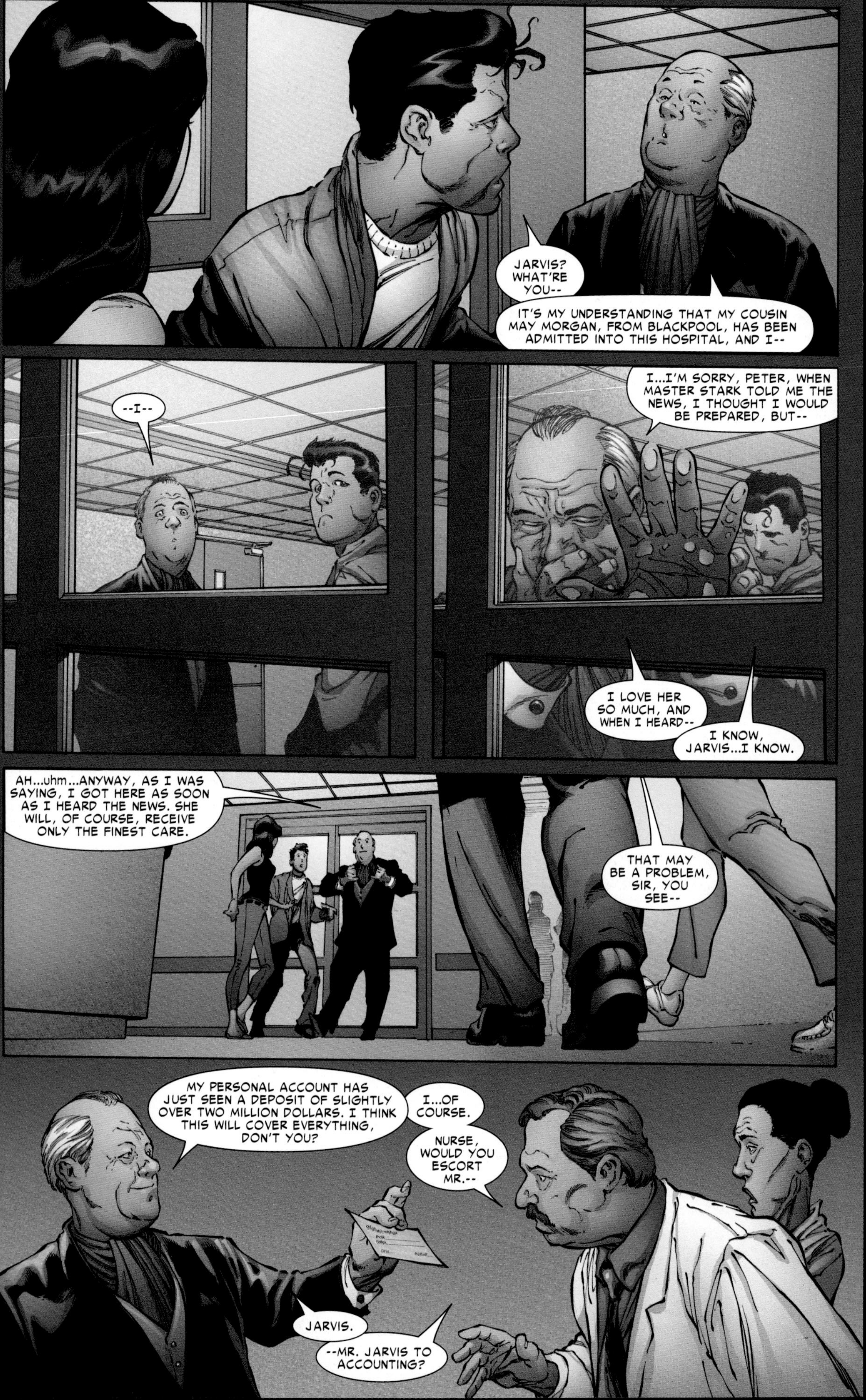
JARVIS? WHAT'RE YOU--
IT'S MY UNDERSTANDING THAT MY COUSIN MAY MORGAN, FROM BLACKPOOL, HAS BEEN ADMITTED INTO THIS HOSPITAL, AND I--
--I--
I...I'M SORRY, PETER, WHEN MASTER STARK TOLD ME THE NEWS, I THOUGHT I WOULD BE PREPARED, BUT--
I LOVE HER SO MUCH, AND WHEN I HEARD--
I KNOW, JARVIS...I KNOW.
AH...uhm...ANYWAY, AS I WAS SAYING, I GOT HERE AS SOON AS I HEARD THE NEWS. SHE WILL, OF COURSE, RECEIVE ONLY THE FINEST CARE.
THAT MAY BE A PROBLEM, SIR, YOU SEE--
MY PERSONAL ACCOUNT HAS JUST SEEN A DEPOSIT OF SLIGHTLY OVER TWO MILLION DOLLARS. I THINK THIS WILL COVER EVERYTHING, DON'T YOU?
I...OF COURSE.
NURSE, WOULD YOU ESCORT MR.--
JARVIS.
--MR. JARVIS TO ACCOUNTING?

OF COURSE. RIGHT THIS WAY, SIR.

I'M NOT SURE HOW YOU PULLED THIS OFF, SON, BUT...WELL DONE.

THANKS... THOUGH I SUSPECT--

"--I WON'T BE ABLE TO GO BACK A SECOND TIME... FOR ANYTHING."

NOT NECESSARY. WE CAN MAKE HER LAST DAYS AS COMFORTABLE AS--

THEY'RE NOT HER LAST DAYS. WE'VE GOT HER STABILIZED, NOW I CAN--

SON... LISTEN TO ME.

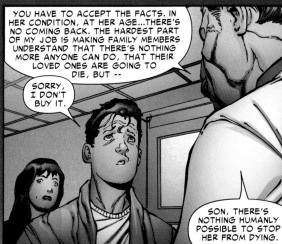

YOU HAVE TO ACCEPT THE FACTS. IN HER CONDITION, AT HER AGE...THERE'S NO COMING BACK. THE HARDEST PART OF MY JOB IS MAKING FAMILY MEMBERS UNDERSTAND THAT THERE'S NOTHING MORE ANYONE CAN DO, THAT THEIR LOVED ONES ARE GOING TO DIE, BUT --

SORRY, I DON'T BUY IT.

SON, THERE'S NOTHING HUMANLY POSSIBLE TO STOP HER FROM DYING.

MAYBE NOT IN THE WORLD YOU LIVE IN, DOC...BUT IN THE CROWD I HANG OUT WITH...I'LL FIND SOMEBODY.

COUNT ON IT.

C'MON, MJ.

I SEE THE LOOK ON HIS FACE AS WE LEAVE THE BUILDING. HE DOESN'T BELIEVE IT.

DOESN'T MATTER. IT'S NOT GOING TO STOP ME.

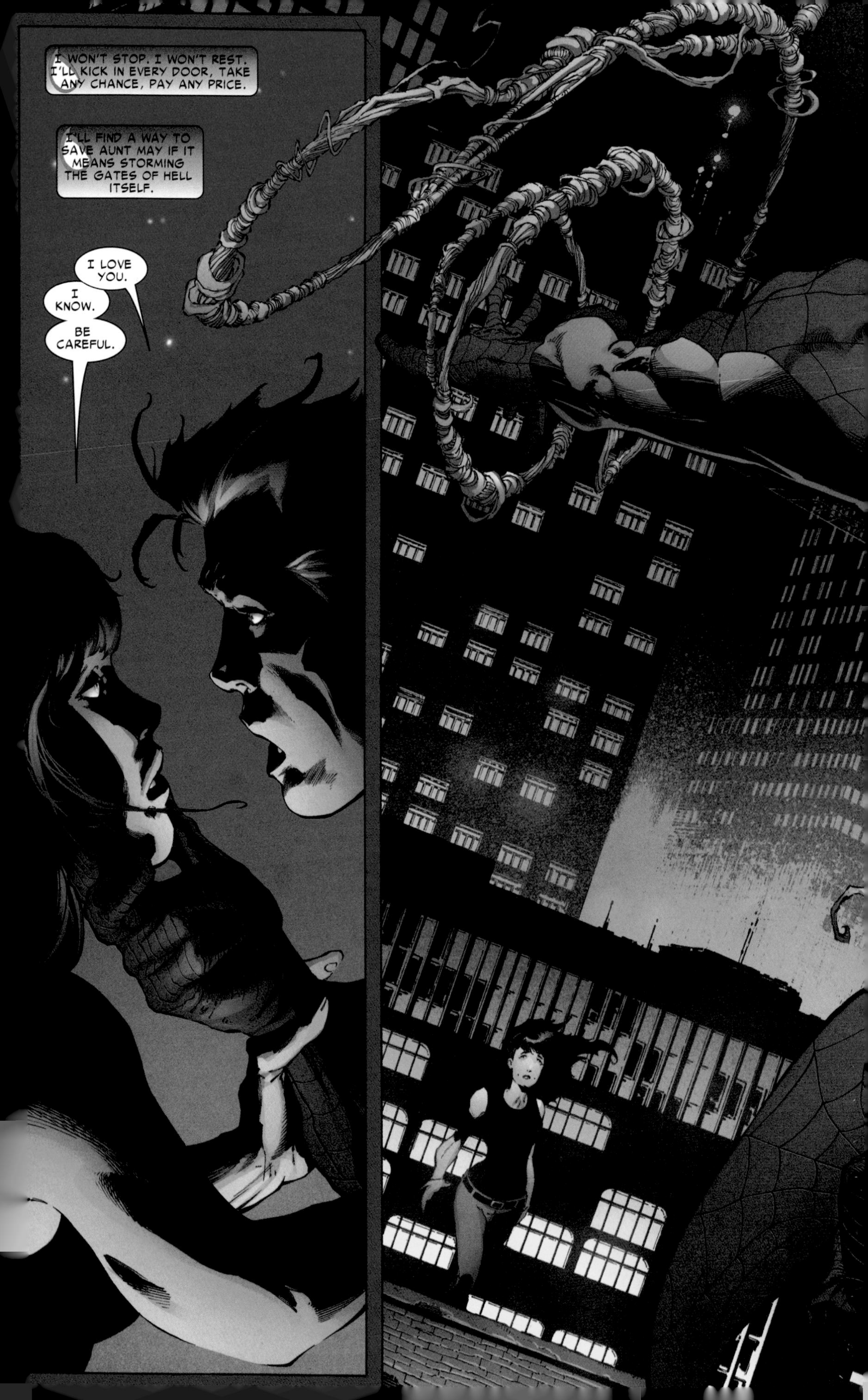
I WON'T STOP. I WON'T REST. I'LL KICK IN EVERY DOOR, TAKE ANY CHANCE, PAY ANY PRICE.
I'LL FIND A WAY TO SAVE AUNT MAY IF IT MEANS STORMING THE GATES OF HELL ITSELF.
I LOVE YOU.
I KNOW.
BE CAREFUL.

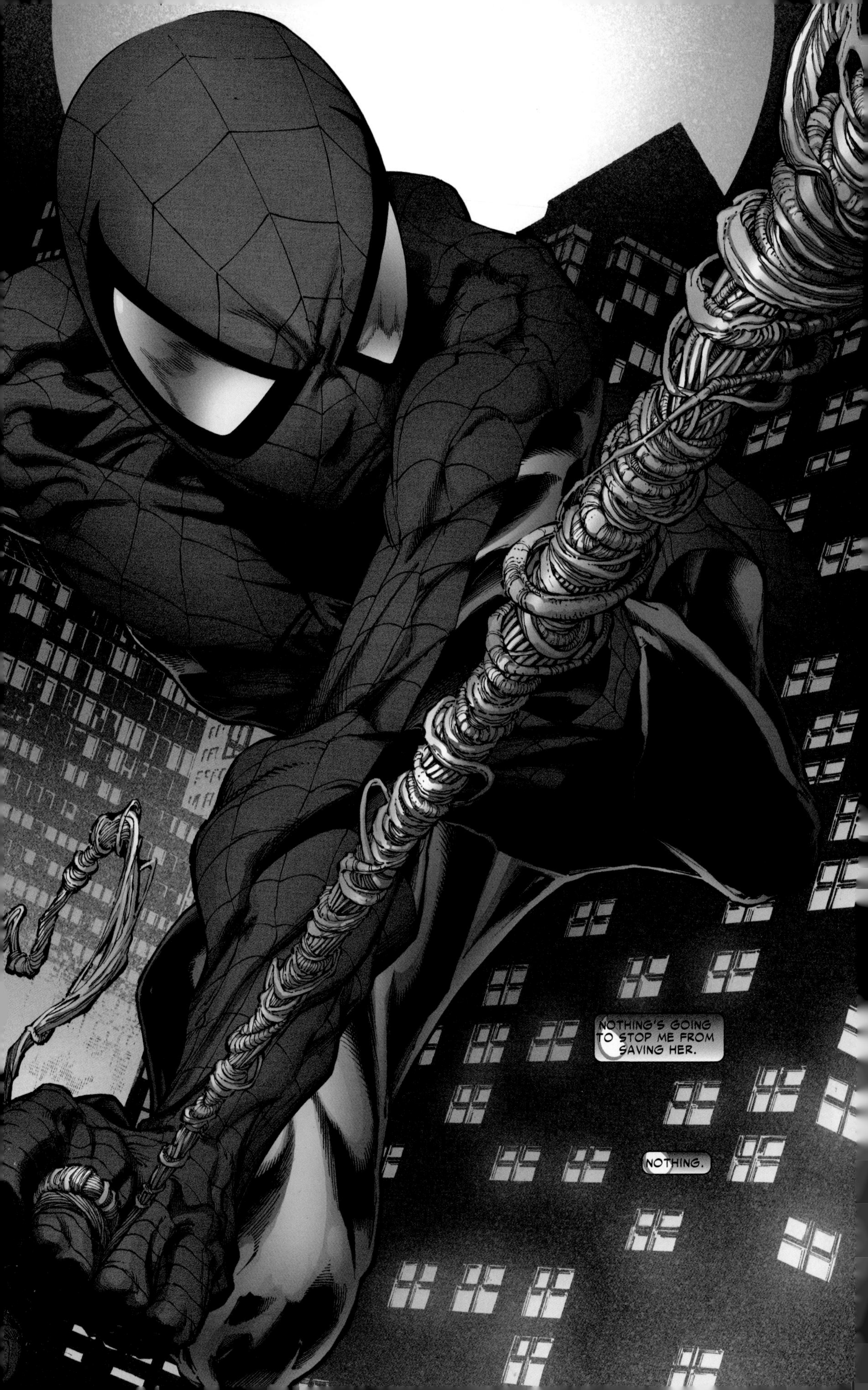
NOTHING'S GOING TO STOP ME FROM SAVING HER.
NOTHING.

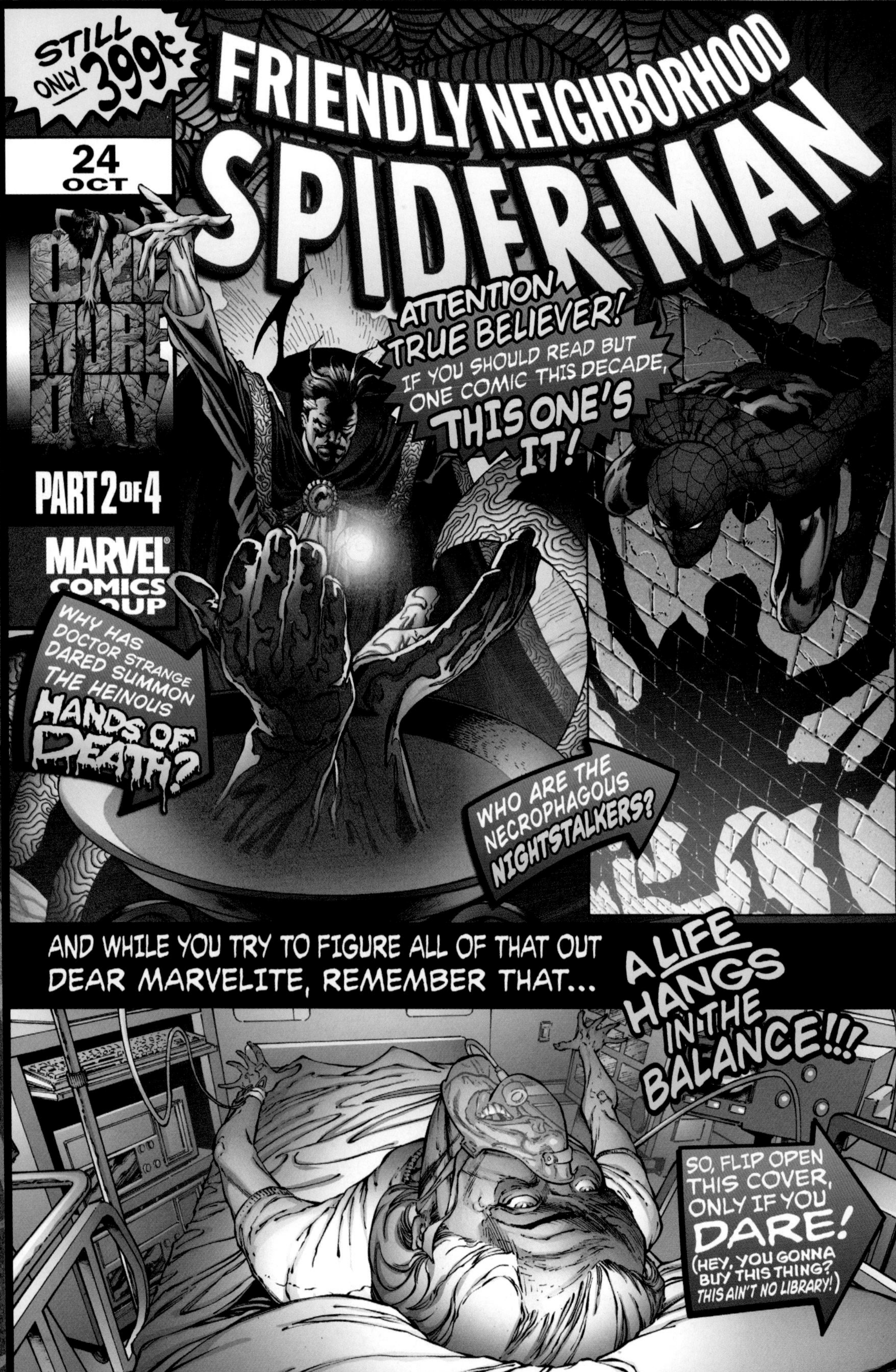

STILL ONLY 399¢
24 OCT
FRIENDLY NEIGHBORHOOD SPIDER-MAN
ONE MORE DAY
PART 2 OF 4
MARVEL COMICS GROUP
ATTENTION TRUE BELIEVER! IF YOU SHOULD READ BUT ONE COMIC THIS DECADE, THIS ONE'S IT!
WHY HAS DOCTOR STRANGE DARED SUMMON THE HEINOUS HANDS OF DEATH?
WHO ARE THE NECROPHAGOUS NIGHTSTALKERS?
AND WHILE YOU TRY TO FIGURE ALL OF THAT OUT DEAR MARVELITE, REMEMBER THAT...
A LIFE HANGS IN THE BALANCE!!!
SO, FLIP OPEN THIS COVER, ONLY IF YOU DARE!
(HEY, YOU GONNA BUY THIS THING? THIS AIN'T NO LIBRARY!)

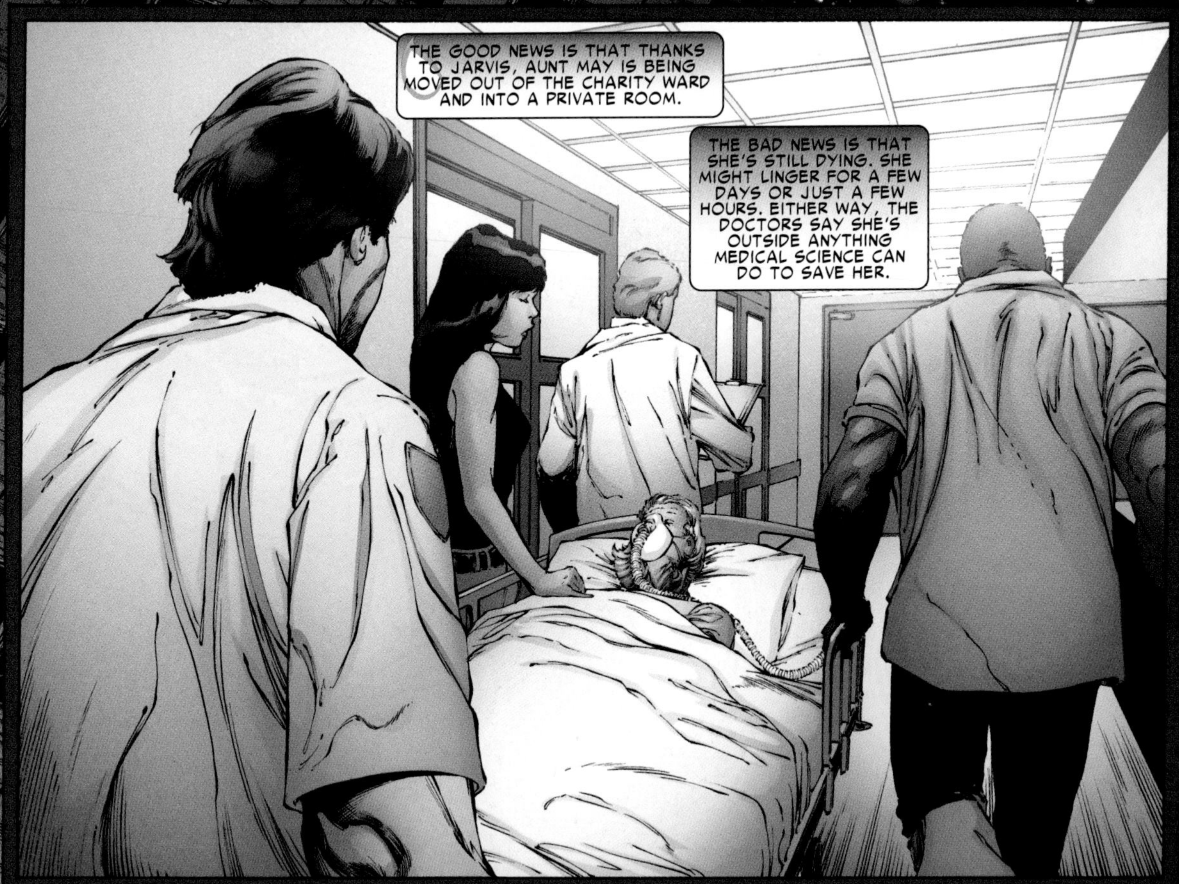
THE GOOD NEWS IS THAT THANKS TO JARVIS, AUNT MAY IS BEING MOVED OUT OF THE CHARITY WARD AND INTO A PRIVATE ROOM.
THE BAD NEWS IS THAT SHE'S STILL DYING. SHE MIGHT LINGER FOR A FEW DAYS OR JUST A FEW HOURS. EITHER WAY, THE DOCTORS SAY SHE'S OUTSIDE ANYTHING MEDICAL SCIENCE CAN DO TO SAVE HER.

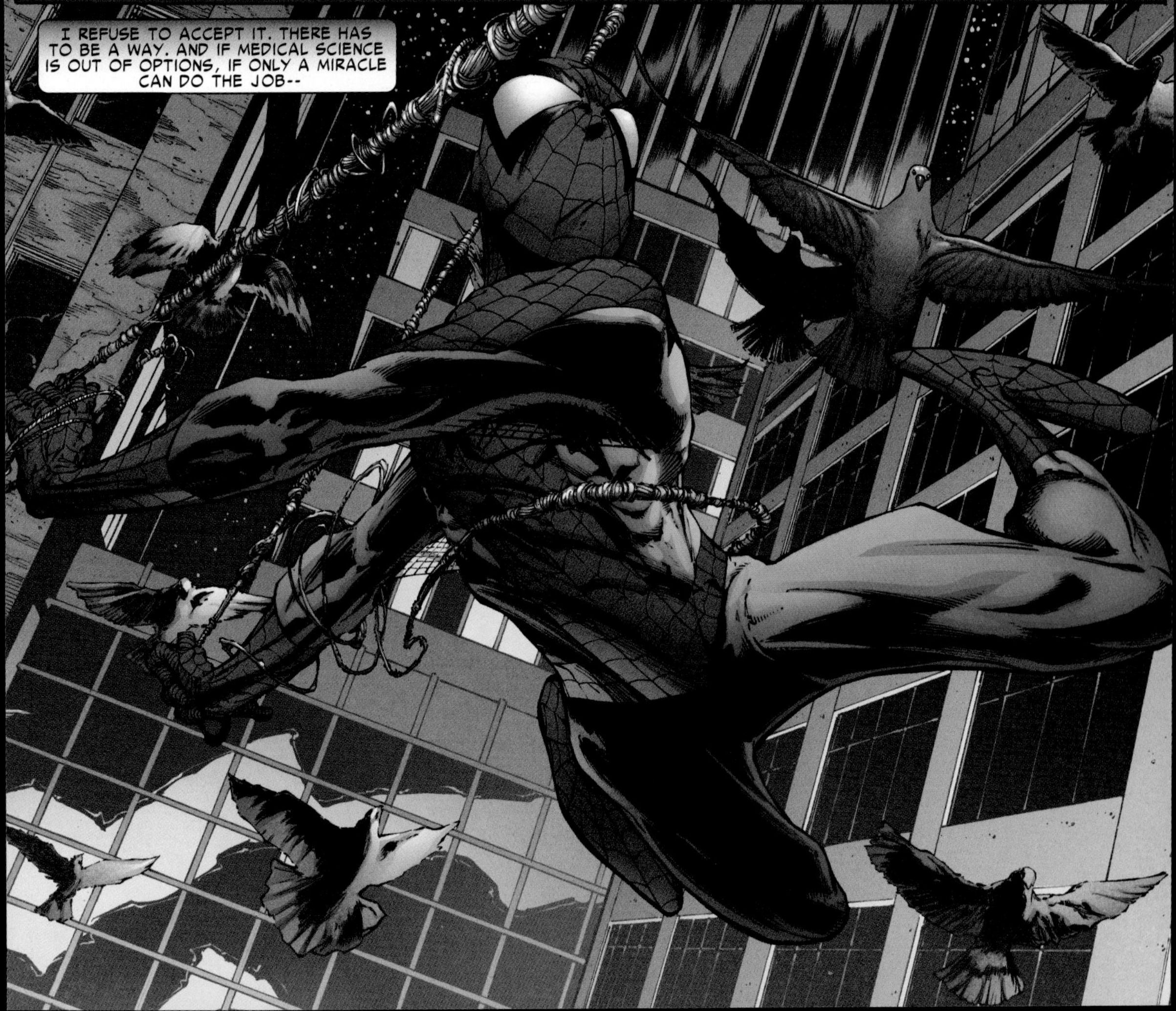
I REFUSE TO ACCEPT IT. THERE HAS TO BE A WAY. AND IF MEDICAL SCIENCE IS OUT OF OPTIONS, IF ONLY A MIRACLE CAN DO THE JOB--

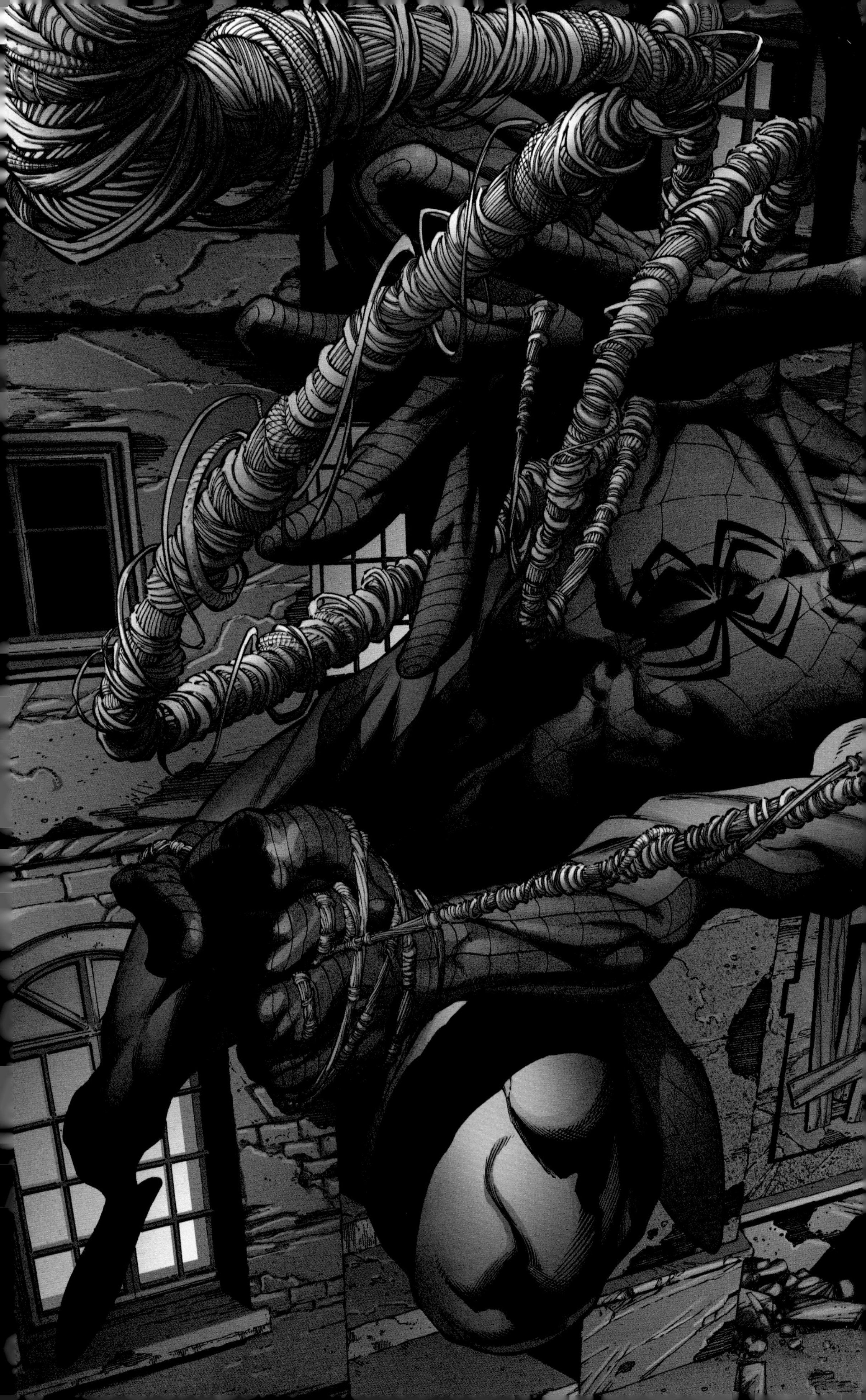

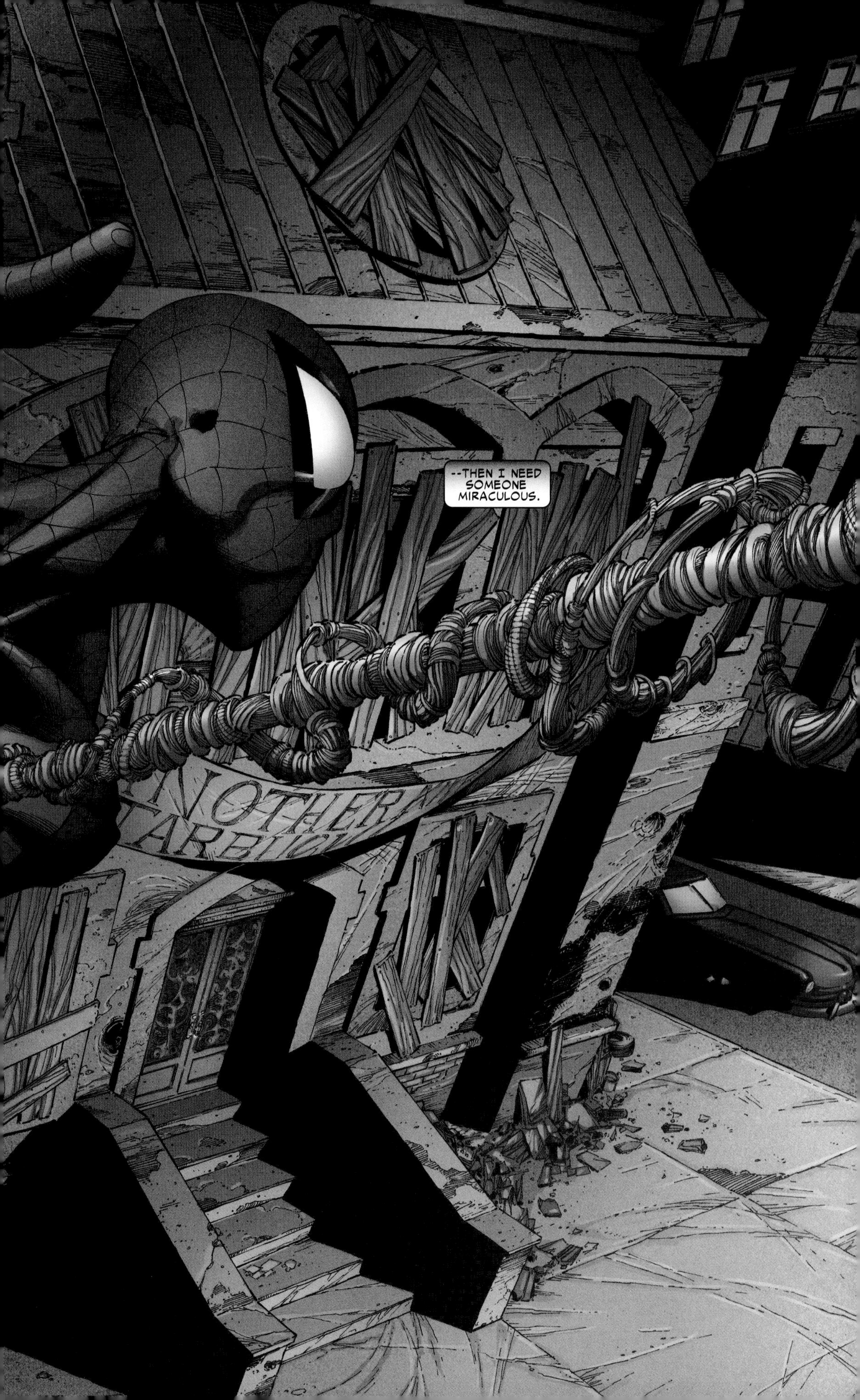
--THEN I NEED SOMEONE MIRACULOUS.

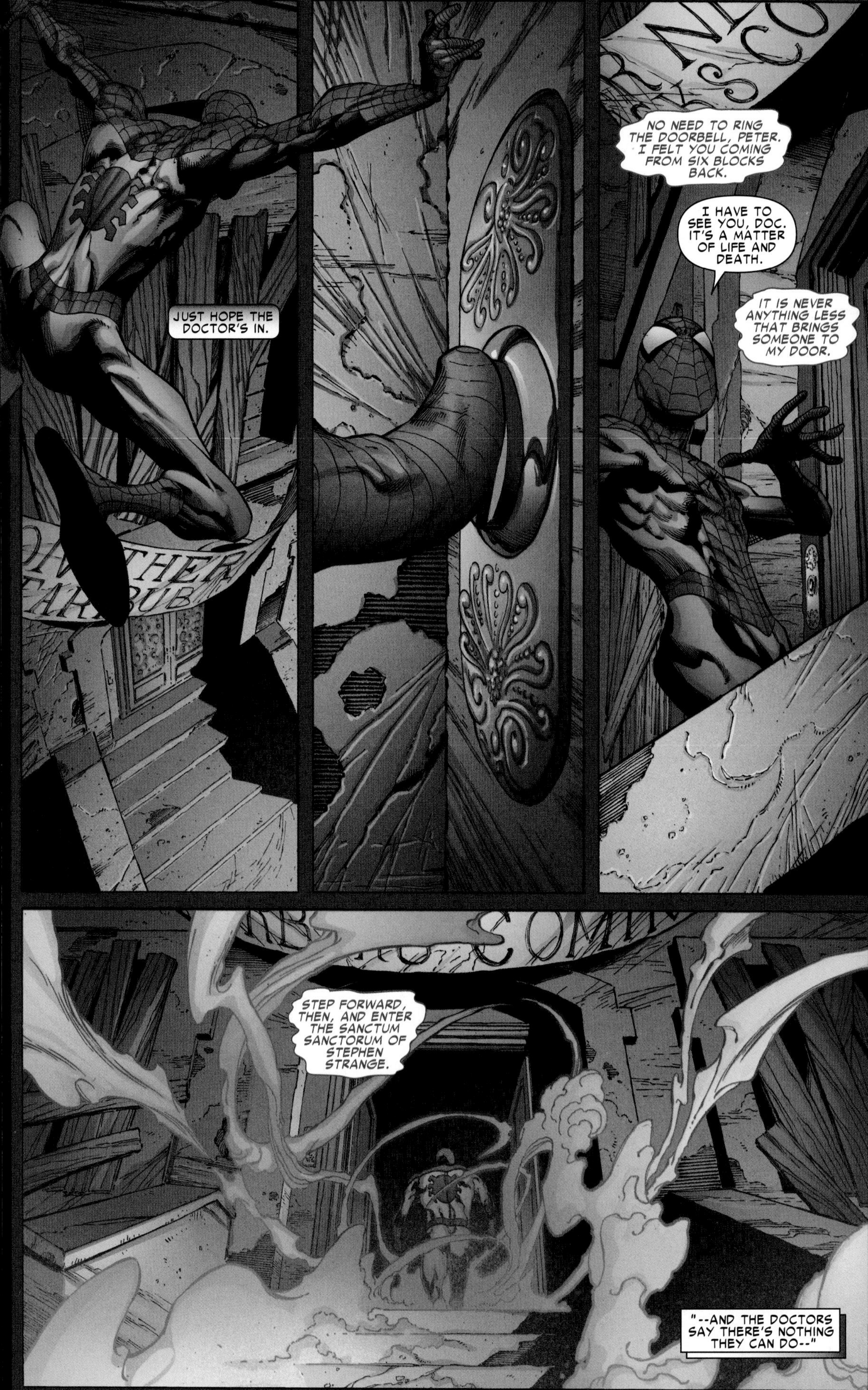

JUST HOPE THE DOCTOR'S IN.
NO NEED TO RING THE DOORBELL, PETER. I FELT YOU COMING FROM SIX BLOCKS BACK.
I HAVE TO SEE YOU, DOC. IT'S A MATTER OF LIFE AND DEATH.
IT IS NEVER ANYTHING LESS THAT BRINGS SOMEONE TO MY DOOR.
STEP FORWARD, THEN, AND ENTER THE SANCTUM SANCTORUM OF STEPHEN STRANGE.
"--AND THE DOCTORS SAY THERE'S NOTHING THEY CAN DO--"

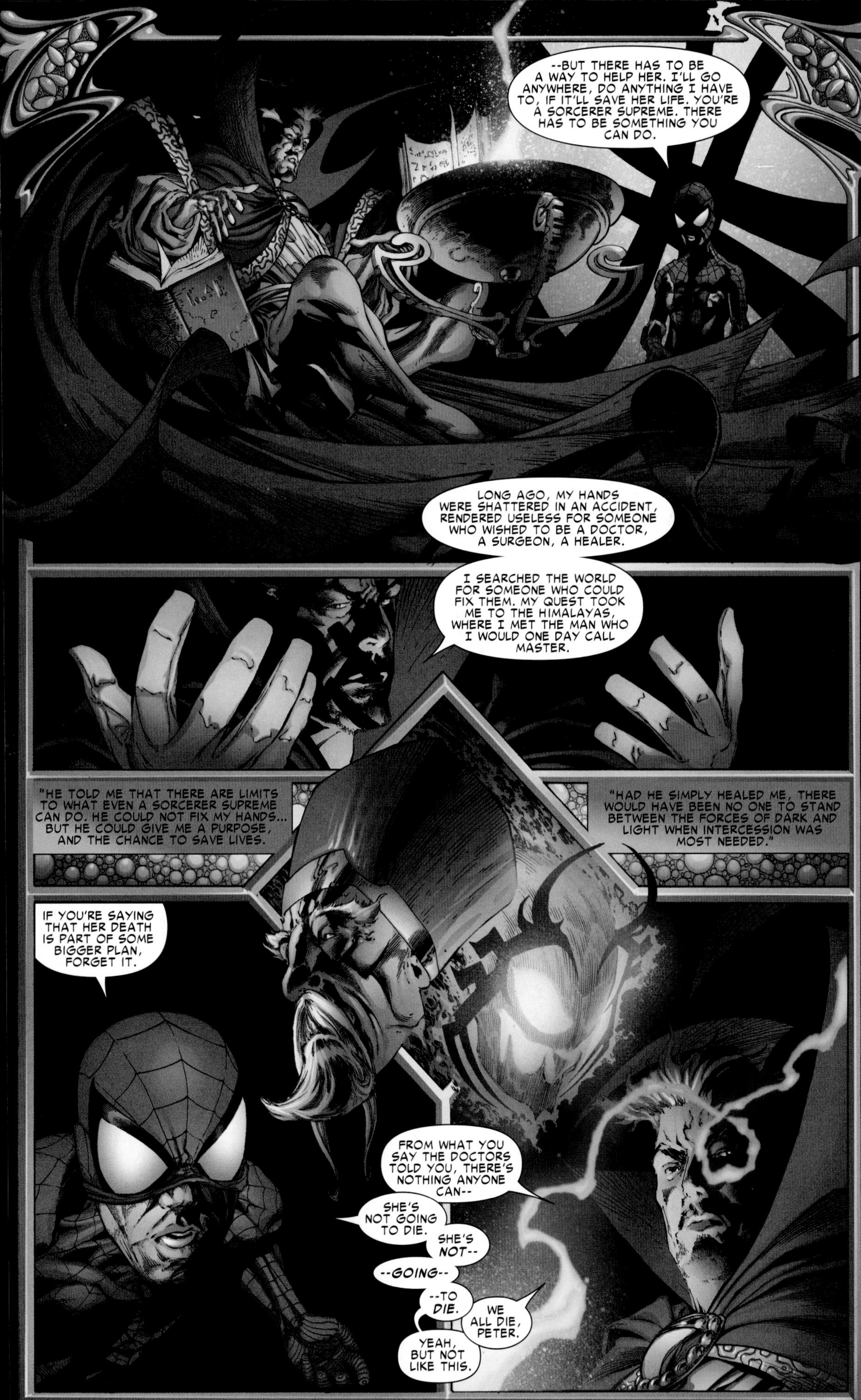
--BUT THERE HAS TO BE A WAY TO HELP HER. I'LL GO ANYWHERE, DO ANYTHING I HAVE TO, IF IT'LL SAVE HER LIFE. YOU'RE A SORCERER SUPREME. THERE HAS TO BE SOMETHING YOU CAN DO.
LONG AGO, MY HANDS WERE SHATTERED IN AN ACCIDENT, RENDERED USELESS FOR SOMEONE WHO WISHED TO BE A DOCTOR, A SURGEON, A HEALER.
I SEARCHED THE WORLD FOR SOMEONE WHO COULD FIX THEM. MY QUEST TOOK ME TO THE HIMALAYAS, WHERE I MET THE MAN WHO I WOULD ONE DAY CALL MASTER.
"HE TOLD ME THAT THERE ARE LIMITS TO WHAT EVEN A SORCERER SUPREME CAN DO. HE COULD NOT FIX MY HANDS... BUT HE COULD GIVE ME A PURPOSE, AND THE CHANCE TO SAVE LIVES.
"HAD HE SIMPLY HEALED ME, THERE WOULD HAVE BEEN NO ONE TO STAND BETWEEN THE FORCES OF DARK AND LIGHT WHEN INTERCESSION WAS MOST NEEDED."
IF YOU'RE SAYING THAT HER DEATH IS PART OF SOME BIGGER PLAN, FORGET IT.
FROM WHAT YOU SAY THE DOCTORS TOLD YOU, THERE'S NOTHING ANYONE CAN--
SHE'S NOT GOING TO DIE.
SHE'S *NOT*--
--*GOING*--
--TO *DIE*.
WE ALL DIE, PETER.
YEAH, BUT NOT LIKE THIS.

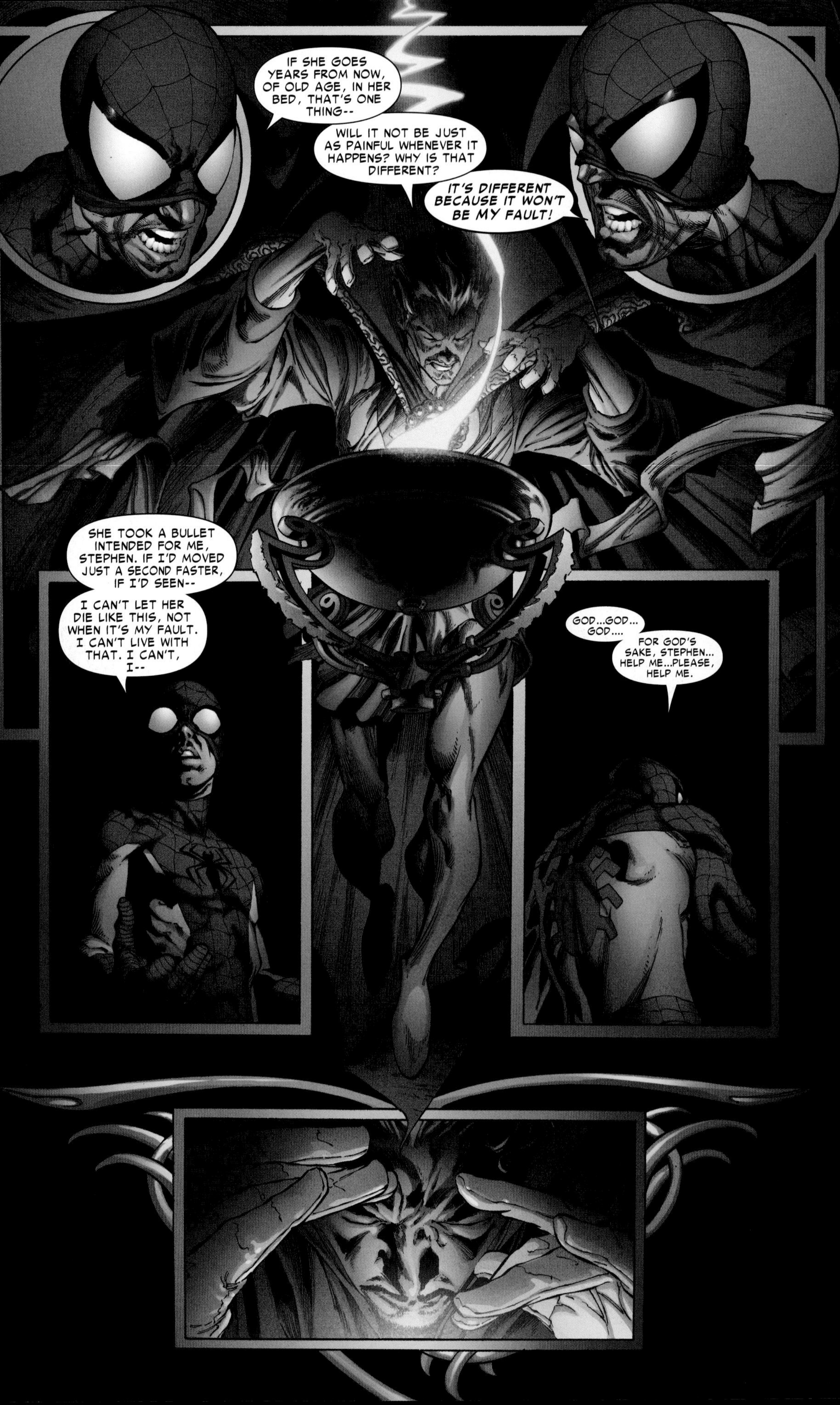
IF SHE GOES YEARS FROM NOW, OF OLD AGE, IN HER BED, THAT'S ONE THING--
WILL IT NOT BE JUST AS PAINFUL WHENEVER IT HAPPENS? WHY IS THAT DIFFERENT?
IT'S DIFFERENT BECAUSE IT WON'T BE MY FAULT!
SHE TOOK A BULLET INTENDED FOR ME, STEPHEN. IF I'D MOVED JUST A SECOND FASTER, IF I'D SEEN--
I CAN'T LET HER DIE LIKE THIS, NOT WHEN IT'S MY FAULT. I CAN'T LIVE WITH THAT. I CAN'T, I--
GOD...GOD... GOD....
FOR GOD'S SAKE, STEPHEN... HELP ME...PLEASE, HELP ME.

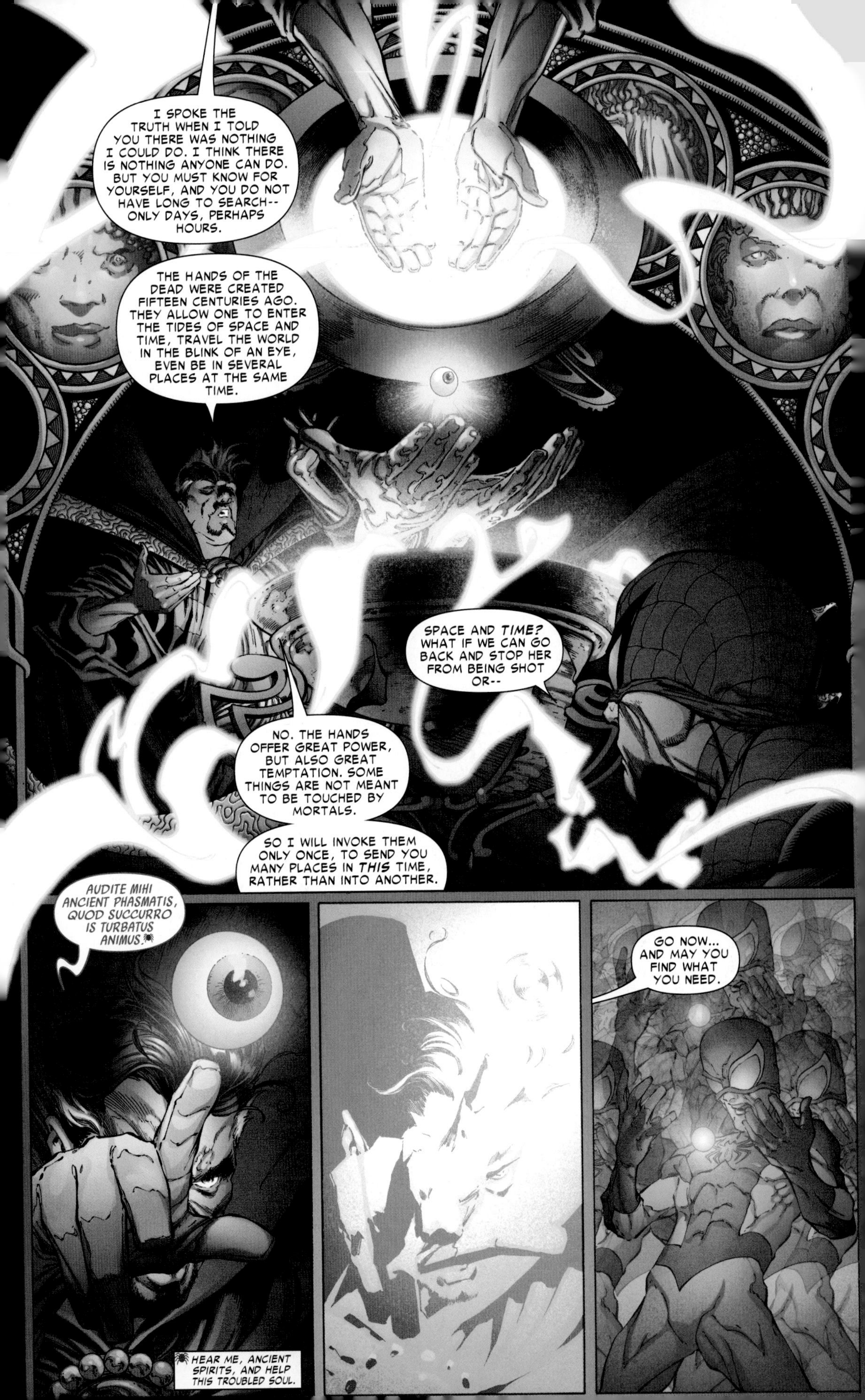
I SPOKE THE TRUTH WHEN I TOLD YOU THERE WAS NOTHING I COULD DO. I THINK THERE IS NOTHING ANYONE CAN DO. BUT YOU MUST KNOW FOR YOURSELF, AND YOU DO NOT HAVE LONG TO SEARCH-- ONLY DAYS, PERHAPS HOURS.
THE HANDS OF THE DEAD WERE CREATED FIFTEEN CENTURIES AGO. THEY ALLOW ONE TO ENTER THE TIDES OF SPACE AND TIME, TRAVEL THE WORLD IN THE BLINK OF AN EYE, EVEN BE IN SEVERAL PLACES AT THE SAME TIME.
SPACE AND *TIME?* WHAT IF WE CAN GO BACK AND STOP HER FROM BEING SHOT OR--
NO. THE HANDS OFFER GREAT POWER, BUT ALSO GREAT TEMPTATION. SOME THINGS ARE NOT MEANT TO BE TOUCHED BY MORTALS.
SO I WILL INVOKE THEM ONLY ONCE, TO SEND YOU MANY PLACES IN *THIS* TIME, RATHER THAN INTO ANOTHER.
AUDITE MIHI ANCIENT PHASMATIS, QUOD SUCCURRO IS TURBATUS ANIMUS.
HEAR ME, ANCIENT SPIRITS, AND HELP THIS TROUBLED SOUL.
GO NOW... AND MAY YOU FIND WHAT YOU NEED.

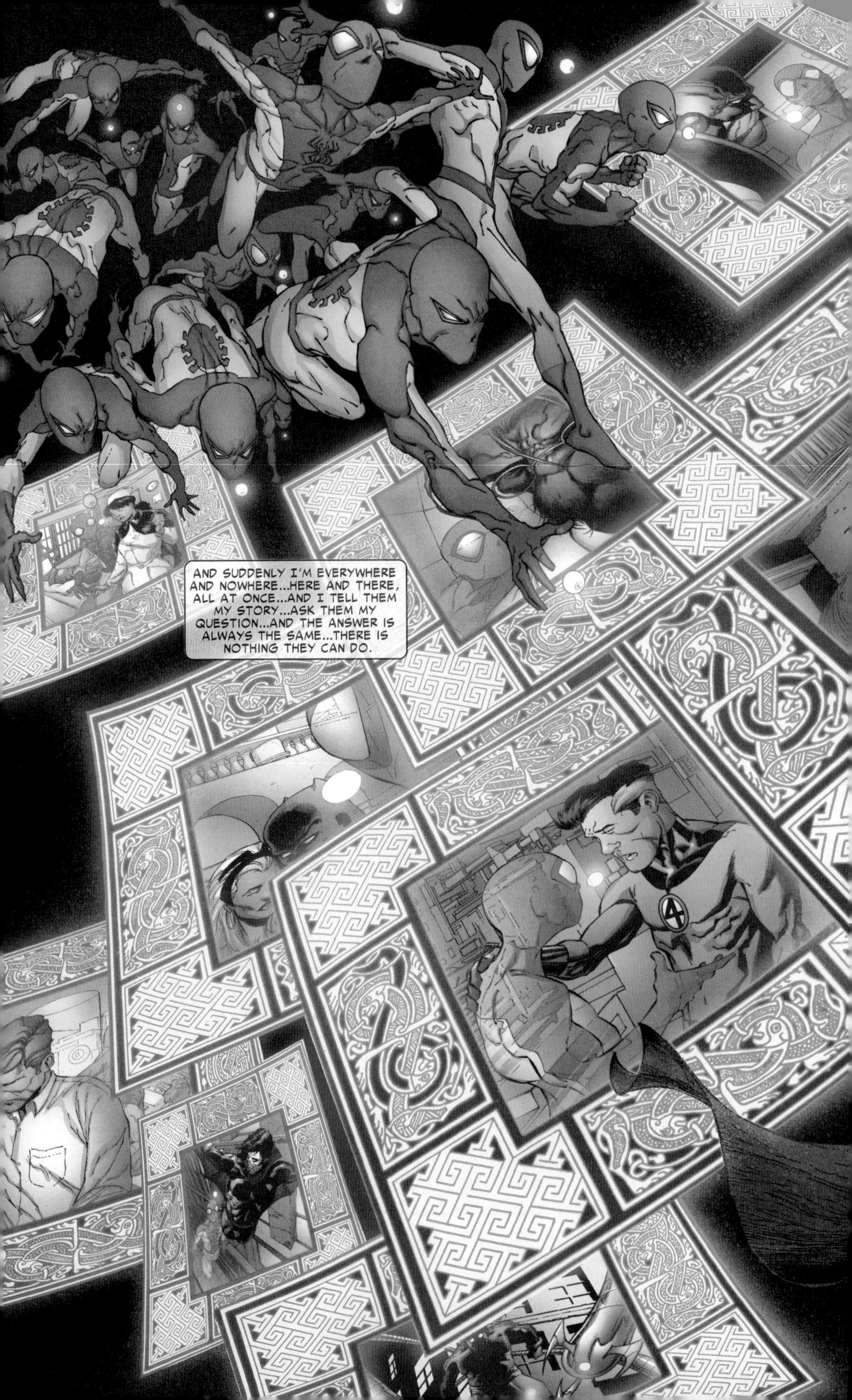
AND SUDDENLY I'M EVERYWHERE AND NOWHERE...HERE AND THERE, ALL AT ONCE...AND I TELL THEM MY STORY...ASK THEM MY QUESTION...AND THE ANSWER IS ALWAYS THE SAME...THERE IS NOTHING THEY CAN DO.

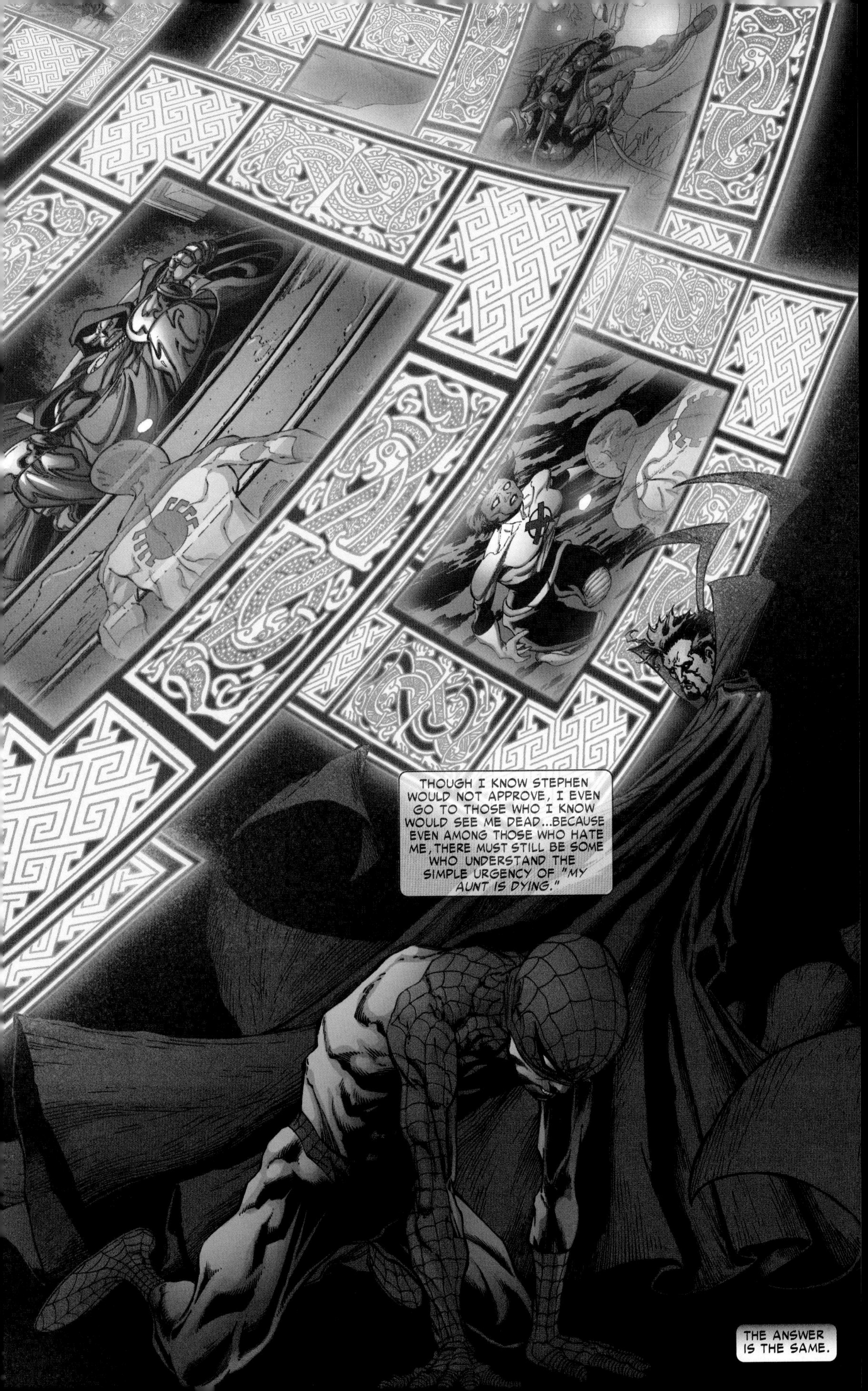
THOUGH I KNOW STEPHEN WOULD NOT APPROVE, I EVEN GO TO THOSE WHO I KNOW WOULD SEE ME DEAD...BECAUSE EVEN AMONG THOSE WHO HATE ME, THERE MUST STILL BE SOME WHO UNDERSTAND THE SIMPLE URGENCY OF "MY AUNT IS DYING."
THE ANSWER IS THE SAME.

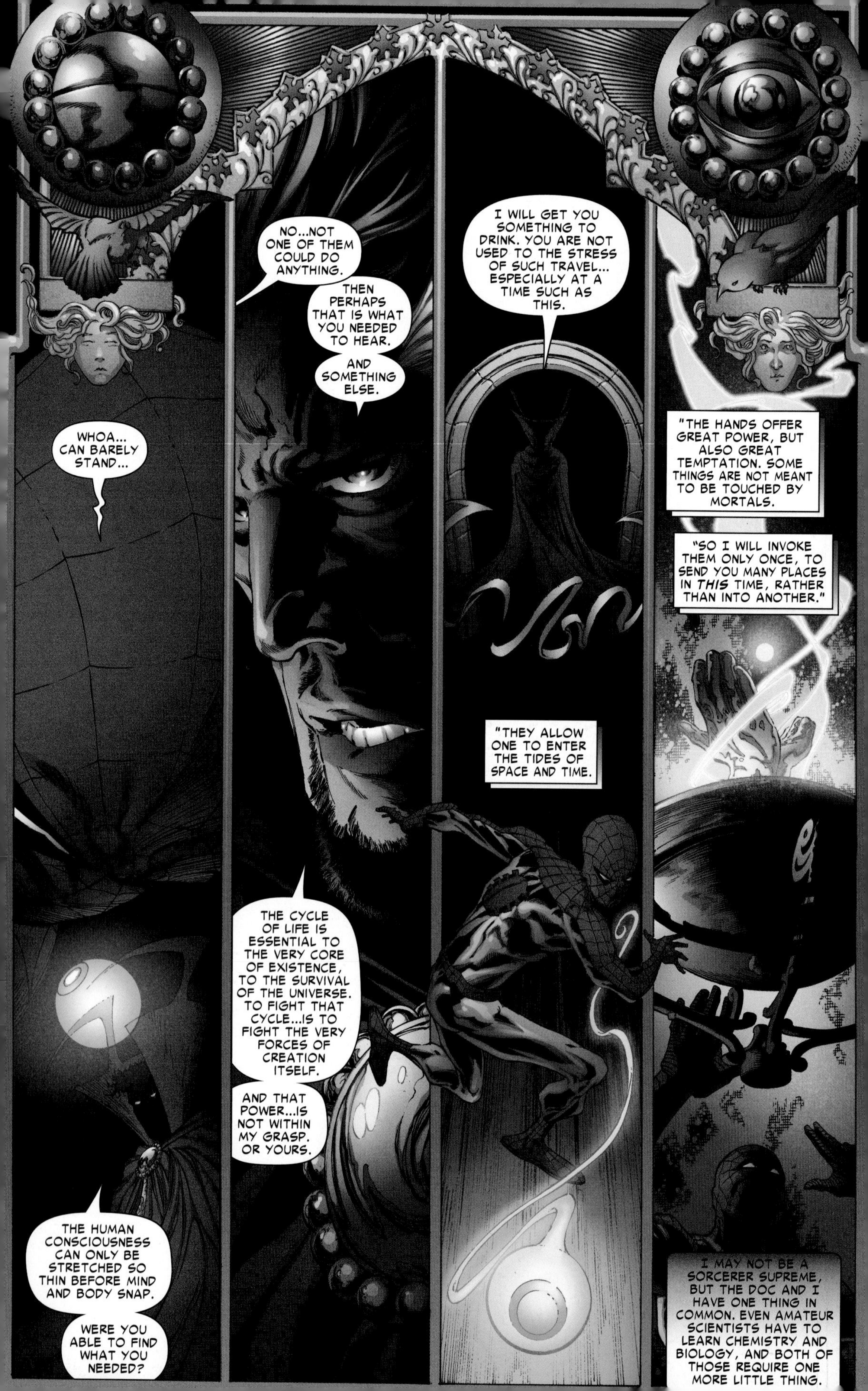
WHOA... CAN BARELY STAND...
NO...NOT ONE OF THEM COULD DO ANYTHING.
THEN PERHAPS THAT IS WHAT YOU NEEDED TO HEAR.
AND SOMETHING ELSE.
I WILL GET YOU SOMETHING TO DRINK. YOU ARE NOT USED TO THE STRESS OF SUCH TRAVEL... ESPECIALLY AT A TIME SUCH AS THIS.
"THE HANDS OFFER GREAT POWER, BUT ALSO GREAT TEMPTATION. SOME THINGS ARE NOT MEANT TO BE TOUCHED BY MORTALS.
"SO I WILL INVOKE THEM ONLY ONCE, TO SEND YOU MANY PLACES IN *THIS* TIME, RATHER THAN INTO ANOTHER."
"THEY ALLOW ONE TO ENTER THE TIDES OF SPACE AND TIME.
THE CYCLE OF LIFE IS ESSENTIAL TO THE VERY CORE OF EXISTENCE, TO THE SURVIVAL OF THE UNIVERSE. TO FIGHT THAT CYCLE...IS TO FIGHT THE VERY FORCES OF CREATION ITSELF.
AND THAT POWER...IS NOT WITHIN MY GRASP. OR YOURS.
THE HUMAN CONSCIOUSNESS CAN ONLY BE STRETCHED SO THIN BEFORE MIND AND BODY SNAP.
WERE YOU ABLE TO FIND WHAT YOU NEEDED?
I MAY NOT BE A SORCERER SUPREME, BUT THE DOC AND I HAVE ONE THING IN COMMON. EVEN AMATEUR SCIENTISTS HAVE TO LEARN CHEMISTRY AND BIOLOGY, AND BOTH OF THOSE REQUIRE ONE MORE LITTLE THING.

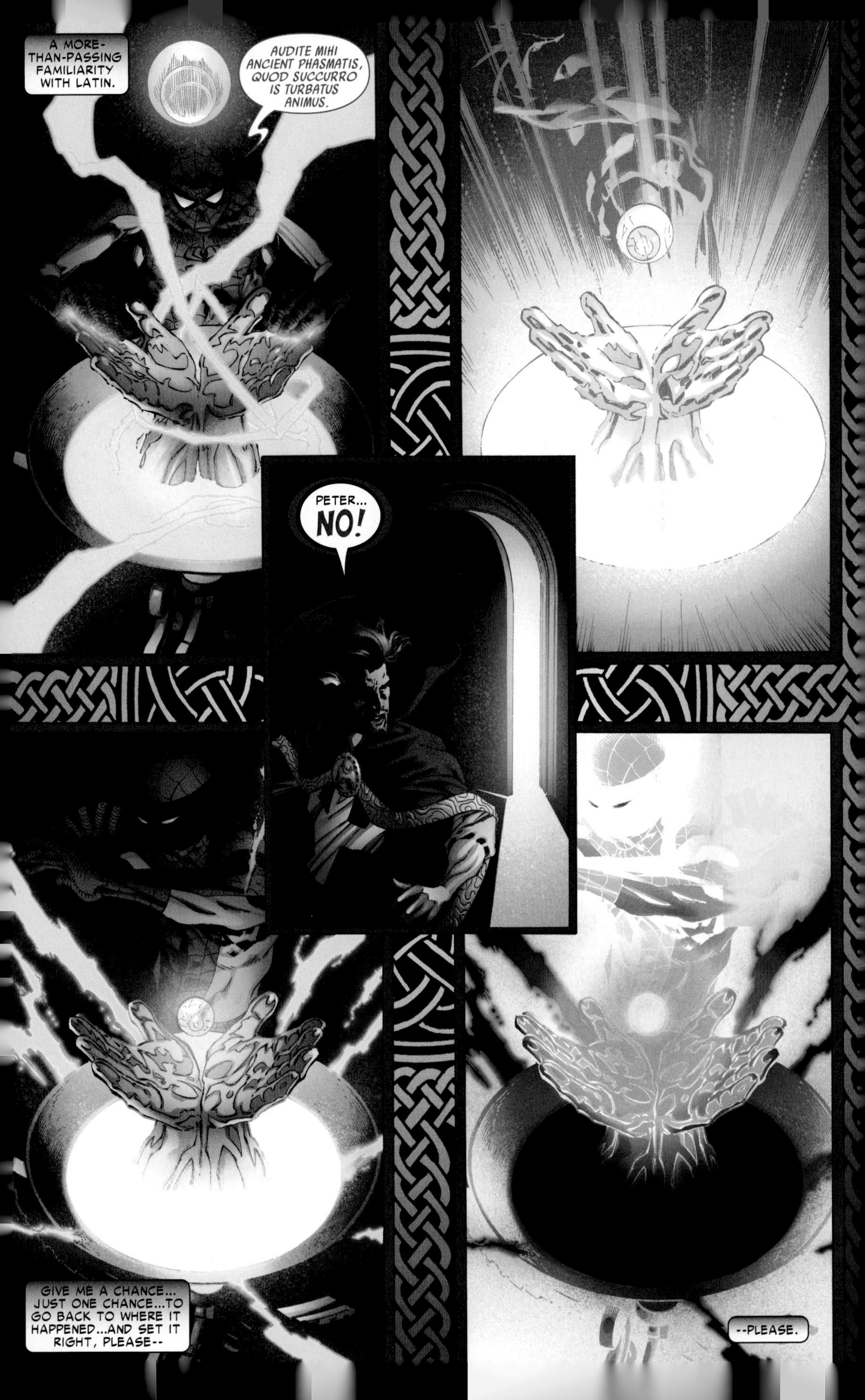
A MORE-THAN-PASSING FAMILIARITY WITH LATIN.
AUDITE MIHI ANCIENT PHASMATIS, QUOD SUCCURRO IS TURBATUS ANIMUS.
PETER... NO!
GIVE ME A CHANCE... JUST ONE CHANCE...TO GO BACK TO WHERE IT HAPPENED...AND SET IT RIGHT, PLEASE--
--PLEASE.

WHERE AM I?
WHEN AM I?
WHAT--
--AM I?
WAIT--
THERE HE IS. THAT'S HIM. THE ONE WHO SHOT MAY.
THERE THEY ARE... MAY AND MJ, RIGHT IN THE LINE OF FIRE. I SHOULD BE SHOWING UP ANY SECOND.
ONLY HAVE ONE CHANCE. HAVE TO TAKE HIM OUT FAST, BEFORE--
WHAT THE--
--CAN'T TOUCH HIM, HE CAN'T EVEN FEEL ME.

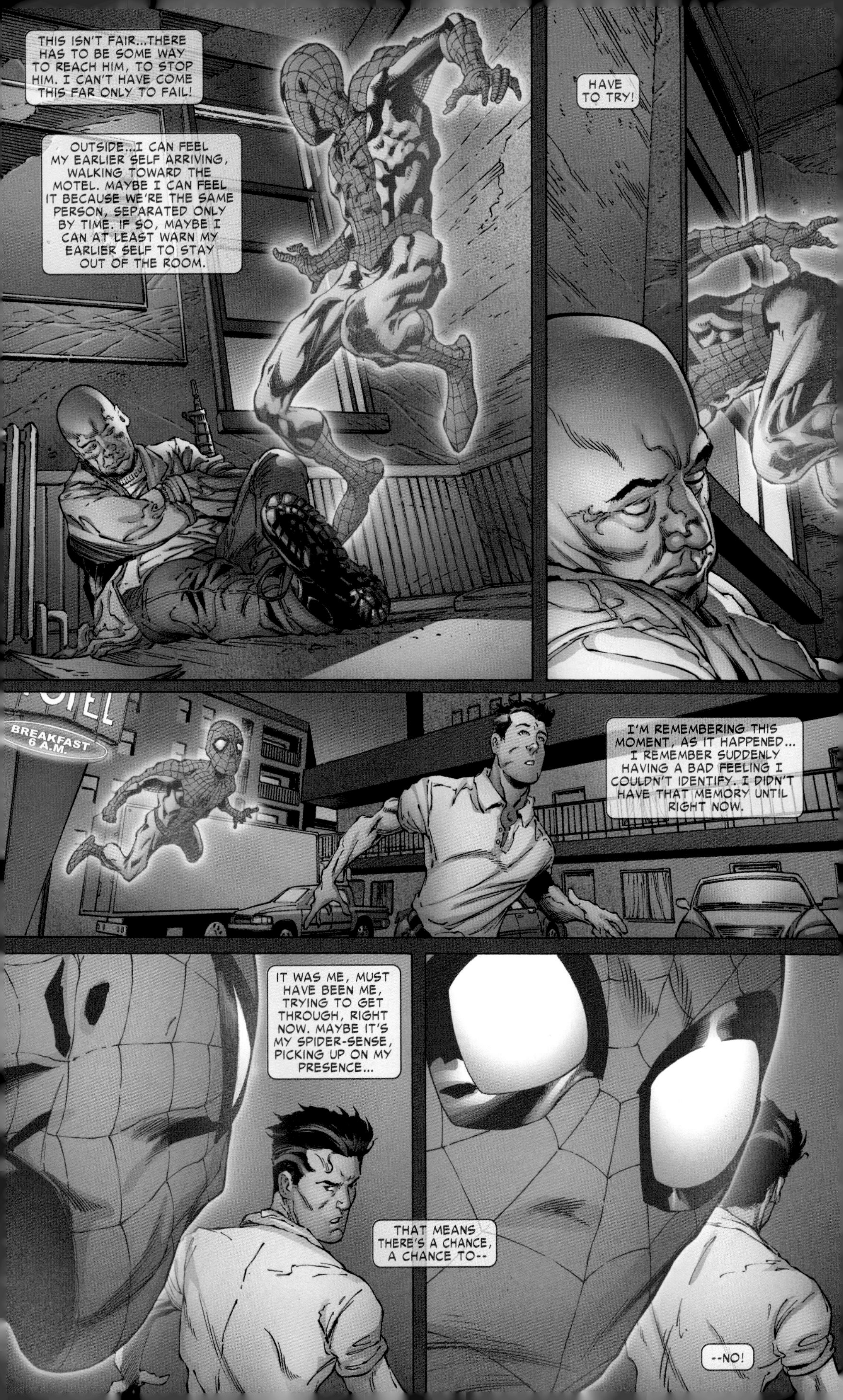
THIS ISN'T FAIR...THERE HAS TO BE SOME WAY TO REACH HIM, TO STOP HIM. I CAN'T HAVE COME THIS FAR ONLY TO FAIL!
OUTSIDE...I CAN FEEL MY EARLIER SELF ARRIVING, WALKING TOWARD THE MOTEL. MAYBE I CAN FEEL IT BECAUSE WE'RE THE SAME PERSON, SEPARATED ONLY BY TIME. IF SO, MAYBE I CAN AT LEAST WARN MY EARLIER SELF TO STAY OUT OF THE ROOM.
HAVE TO TRY!
BREAKFAST 6 A.M.
I'M REMEMBERING THIS MOMENT, AS IT HAPPENED... I REMEMBER SUDDENLY HAVING A BAD FEELING I COULDN'T IDENTIFY. I DIDN'T HAVE THAT MEMORY UNTIL RIGHT NOW.
IT WAS ME, MUST HAVE BEEN ME, TRYING TO GET THROUGH, RIGHT NOW. MAYBE IT'S MY SPIDER-SENSE, PICKING UP ON MY PRESENCE...
THAT MEANS THERE'S A CHANCE, A CHANCE TO--
--NO!

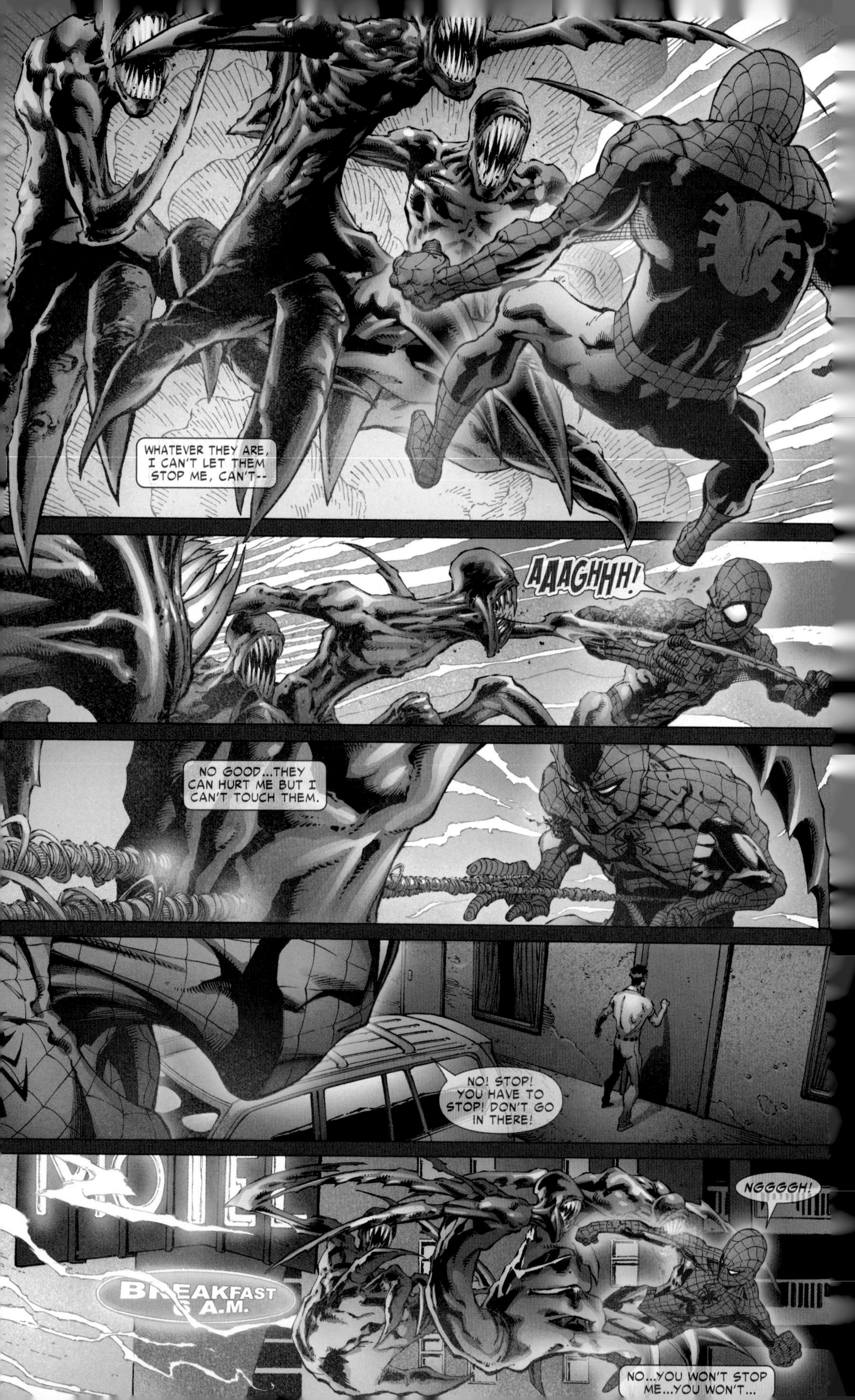

WHATEVER THEY ARE, I CAN'T LET THEM STOP ME, CAN'T--
AAAGHHH!
NO GOOD...THEY CAN HURT ME BUT I CAN'T TOUCH THEM.
NO! STOP! YOU HAVE TO STOP! DON'T GO IN THERE!
BREAKFAST 6 A.M.
NGGGGH!
NO...YOU WON'T STOP ME...YOU WON'T...

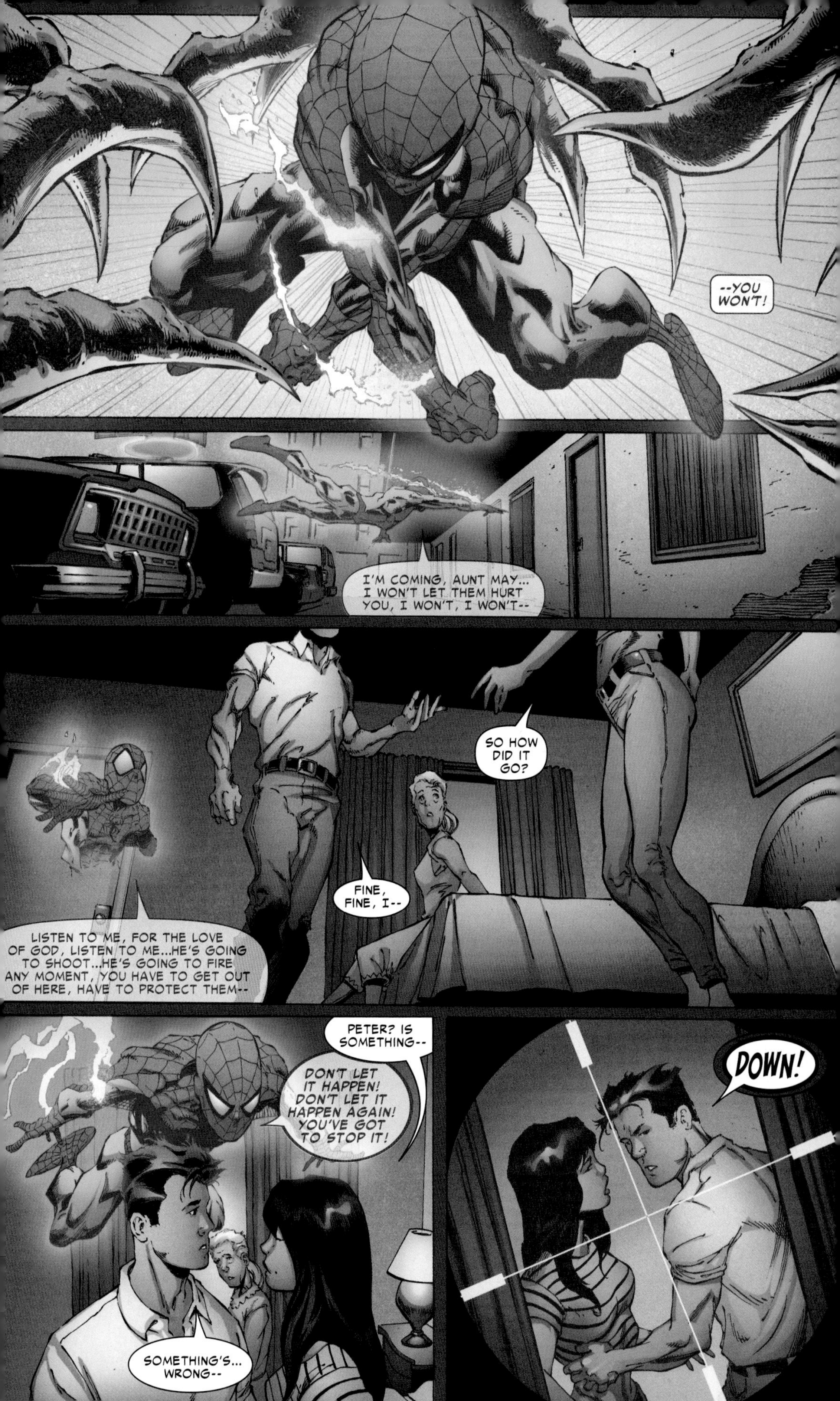
--YOU WON'T!
I'M COMING, AUNT MAY... I WON'T LET THEM HURT YOU, I WON'T, I WON'T--
SO HOW DID IT GO?
FINE, FINE, I--
LISTEN TO ME, FOR THE LOVE OF GOD, LISTEN TO ME...HE'S GOING TO SHOOT...HE'S GOING TO FIRE ANY MOMENT, YOU HAVE TO GET OUT OF HERE, HAVE TO PROTECT THEM--
PETER? IS SOMETHING--
DON'T LET IT HAPPEN! DON'T LET IT HAPPEN AGAIN! YOU'VE GOT TO STOP IT!
SOMETHING'S... WRONG--
DOWN!

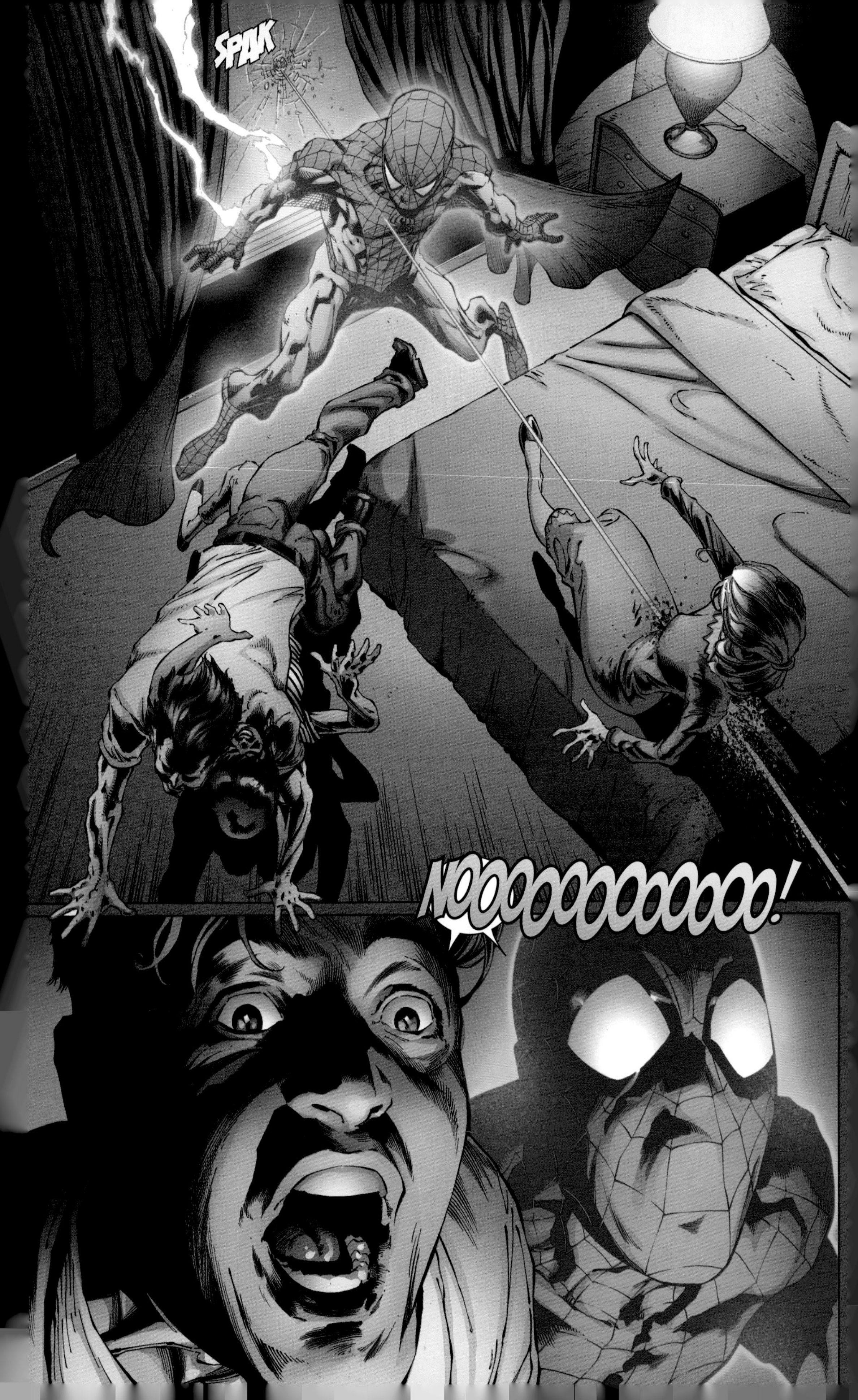
SPAK
NOOOOOOOOOOOOO!

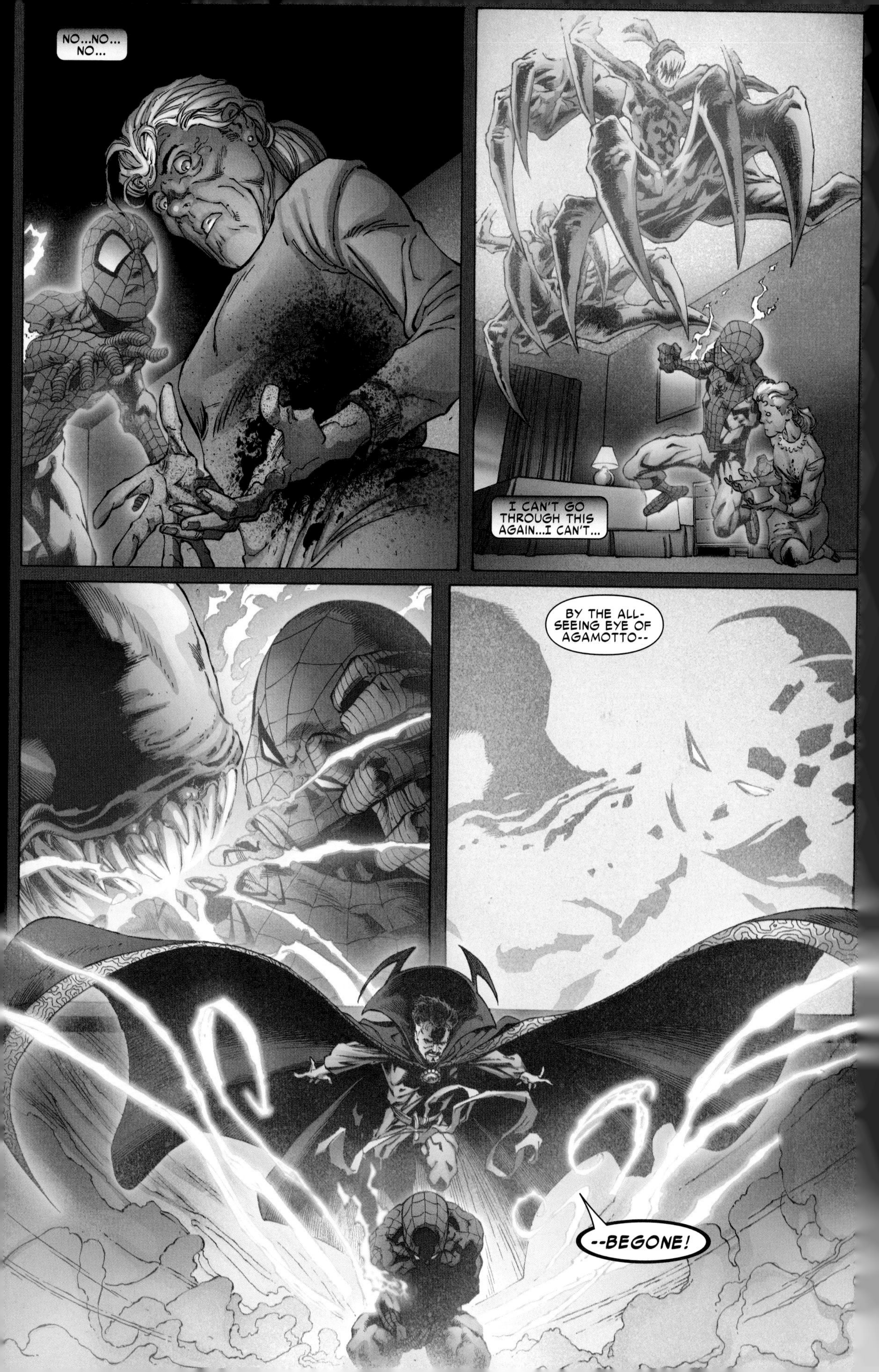
NO...NO... NO...
I CAN'T GO THROUGH THIS AGAIN...I CAN'T...
BY THE ALL-SEEING EYE OF AGAMOTTO--
--BEGONE!

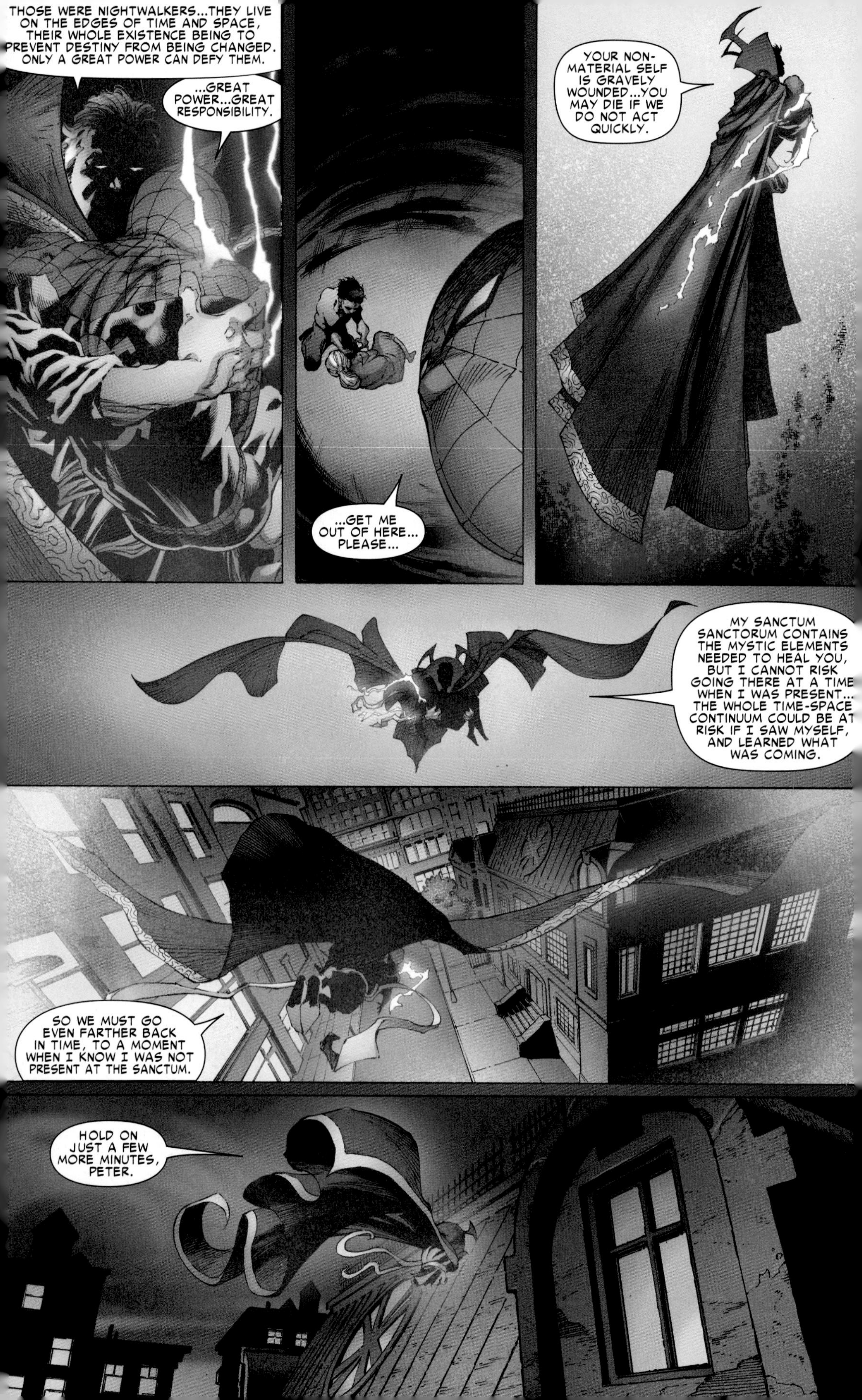
THOSE WERE NIGHTWALKERS...THEY LIVE ON THE EDGES OF TIME AND SPACE, THEIR WHOLE EXISTENCE BEING TO PREVENT DESTINY FROM BEING CHANGED. ONLY A GREAT POWER CAN DEFY THEM.
...GREAT POWER...GREAT RESPONSIBILITY.
...GET ME OUT OF HERE... PLEASE...
YOUR NON-MATERIAL SELF IS GRAVELY WOUNDED...YOU MAY DIE IF WE DO NOT ACT QUICKLY.
MY SANCTUM SANCTORUM CONTAINS THE MYSTIC ELEMENTS NEEDED TO HEAL YOU, BUT I CANNOT RISK GOING THERE AT A TIME WHEN I WAS PRESENT... THE WHOLE TIME-SPACE CONTINUUM COULD BE AT RISK IF I SAW MYSELF, AND LEARNED WHAT WAS COMING.
SO WE MUST GO EVEN FARTHER BACK IN TIME, TO A MOMENT WHEN I KNOW I WAS NOT PRESENT AT THE SANCTUM.
HOLD ON JUST A FEW MORE MINUTES, PETER.

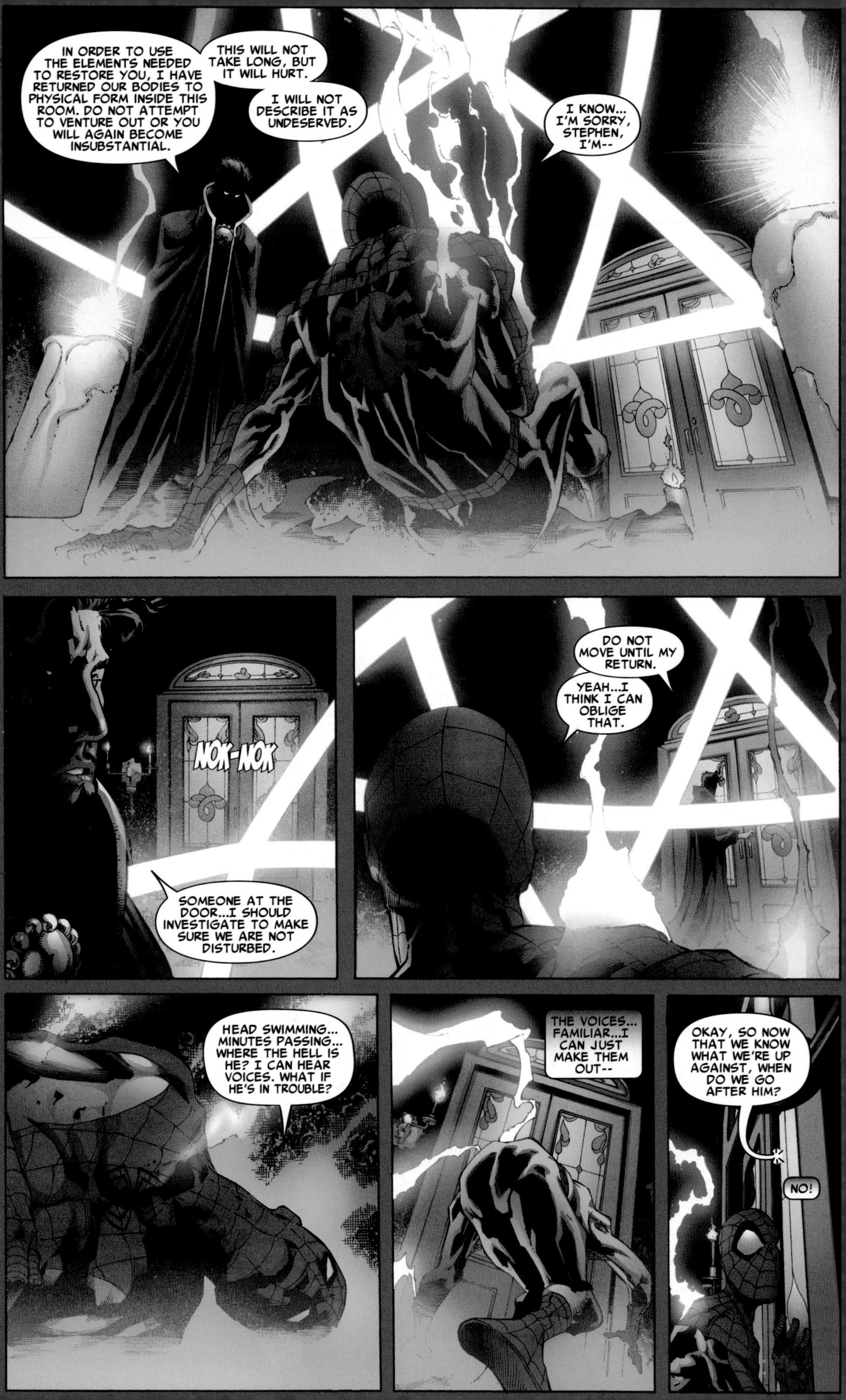
IN ORDER TO USE THE ELEMENTS NEEDED TO RESTORE YOU, I HAVE RETURNED OUR BODIES TO PHYSICAL FORM INSIDE THIS ROOM. DO NOT ATTEMPT TO VENTURE OUT OR YOU WILL AGAIN BECOME INSUBSTANTIAL.
THIS WILL NOT TAKE LONG, BUT IT WILL HURT.
I WILL NOT DESCRIBE IT AS UNDESERVED.
I KNOW... I'M SORRY, STEPHEN, I'M--
NOK-NOK
SOMEONE AT THE DOOR...I SHOULD INVESTIGATE TO MAKE SURE WE ARE NOT DISTURBED.
DO NOT MOVE UNTIL MY RETURN.
YEAH...I THINK I CAN OBLIGE THAT.
HEAD SWIMMING... MINUTES PASSING... WHERE THE HELL IS HE? I CAN HEAR VOICES. WHAT IF HE'S IN TROUBLE?
THE VOICES... FAMILIAR...I CAN JUST MAKE THEM OUT--
OKAY, SO NOW THAT WE KNOW WHAT WE'RE UP AGAINST, WHEN DO WE GO AFTER HIM?
NO!

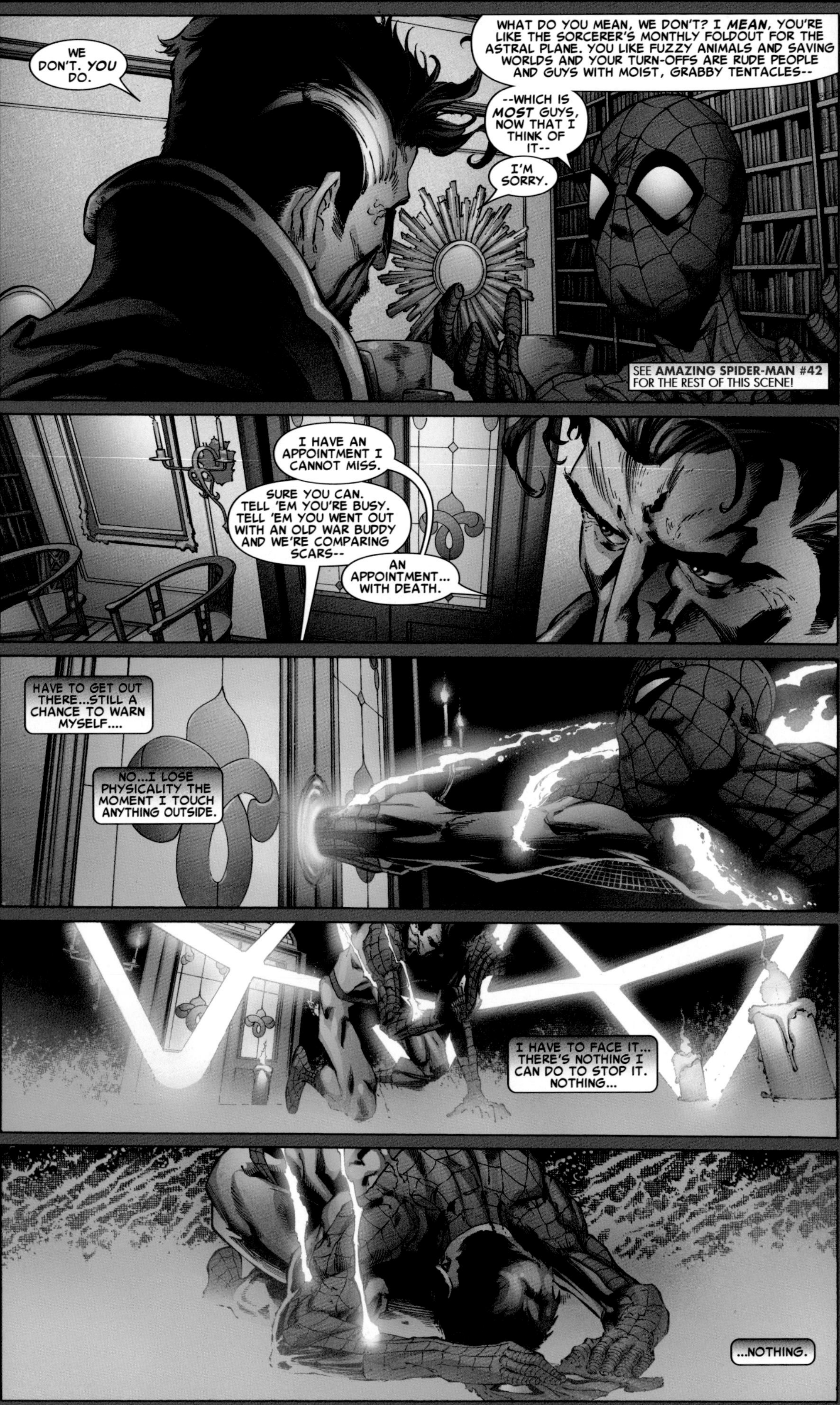

WE DON'T. YOU DO.
WHAT DO YOU MEAN, WE DON'T? I MEAN, YOU'RE LIKE THE SORCERER'S MONTHLY FOLDOUT FOR THE ASTRAL PLANE. YOU LIKE FUZZY ANIMALS AND SAVING WORLDS AND YOUR TURN-OFFS ARE RUDE PEOPLE AND GUYS WITH MOIST, GRABBY TENTACLES--
--WHICH IS MOST GUYS, NOW THAT I THINK OF IT--
I'M SORRY.
SEE AMAZING SPIDER-MAN #42 FOR THE REST OF THIS SCENE!
I HAVE AN APPOINTMENT I CANNOT MISS.
SURE YOU CAN. TELL 'EM YOU'RE BUSY. TELL 'EM YOU WENT OUT WITH AN OLD WAR BUDDY AND WE'RE COMPARING SCARS--
AN APPOINTMENT... WITH DEATH.
HAVE TO GET OUT THERE...STILL A CHANCE TO WARN MYSELF....
NO...I LOSE PHYSICALITY THE MOMENT I TOUCH ANYTHING OUTSIDE.
I HAVE TO FACE IT... THERE'S NOTHING I CAN DO TO STOP IT. NOTHING...
...NOTHING.

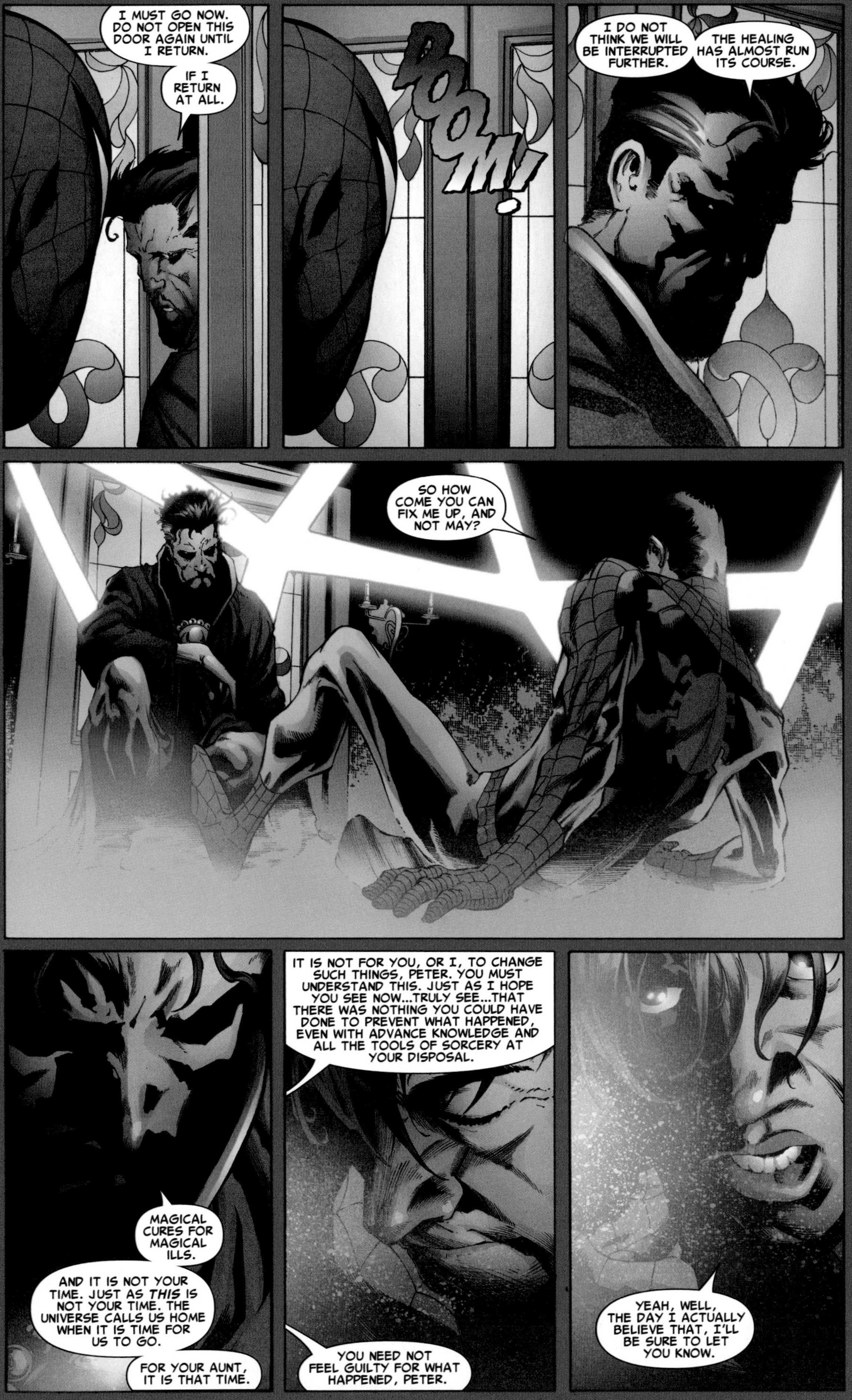
I MUST GO NOW. DO NOT OPEN THIS DOOR AGAIN UNTIL I RETURN.
IF I RETURN AT ALL.
BOOOM!
I DO NOT THINK WE WILL BE INTERRUPTED FURTHER.
THE HEALING HAS ALMOST RUN ITS COURSE.
SO HOW COME YOU CAN FIX ME UP, AND NOT MAY?
MAGICAL CURES FOR MAGICAL ILLS.
AND IT IS NOT YOUR TIME. JUST AS *THIS* IS NOT YOUR TIME. THE UNIVERSE CALLS US HOME WHEN IT IS TIME FOR US TO GO.
FOR YOUR AUNT, IT IS THAT TIME.
IT IS NOT FOR YOU, OR I, TO CHANGE SUCH THINGS, PETER. YOU MUST UNDERSTAND THIS. JUST AS I HOPE YOU SEE NOW...TRULY SEE...THAT THERE WAS NOTHING YOU COULD HAVE DONE TO PREVENT WHAT HAPPENED, EVEN WITH ADVANCE KNOWLEDGE AND ALL THE TOOLS OF SORCERY AT YOUR DISPOSAL.
YOU NEED NOT FEEL GUILTY FOR WHAT HAPPENED, PETER.
YEAH, WELL, THE DAY I ACTUALLY BELIEVE THAT, I'LL BE SURE TO LET YOU KNOW.

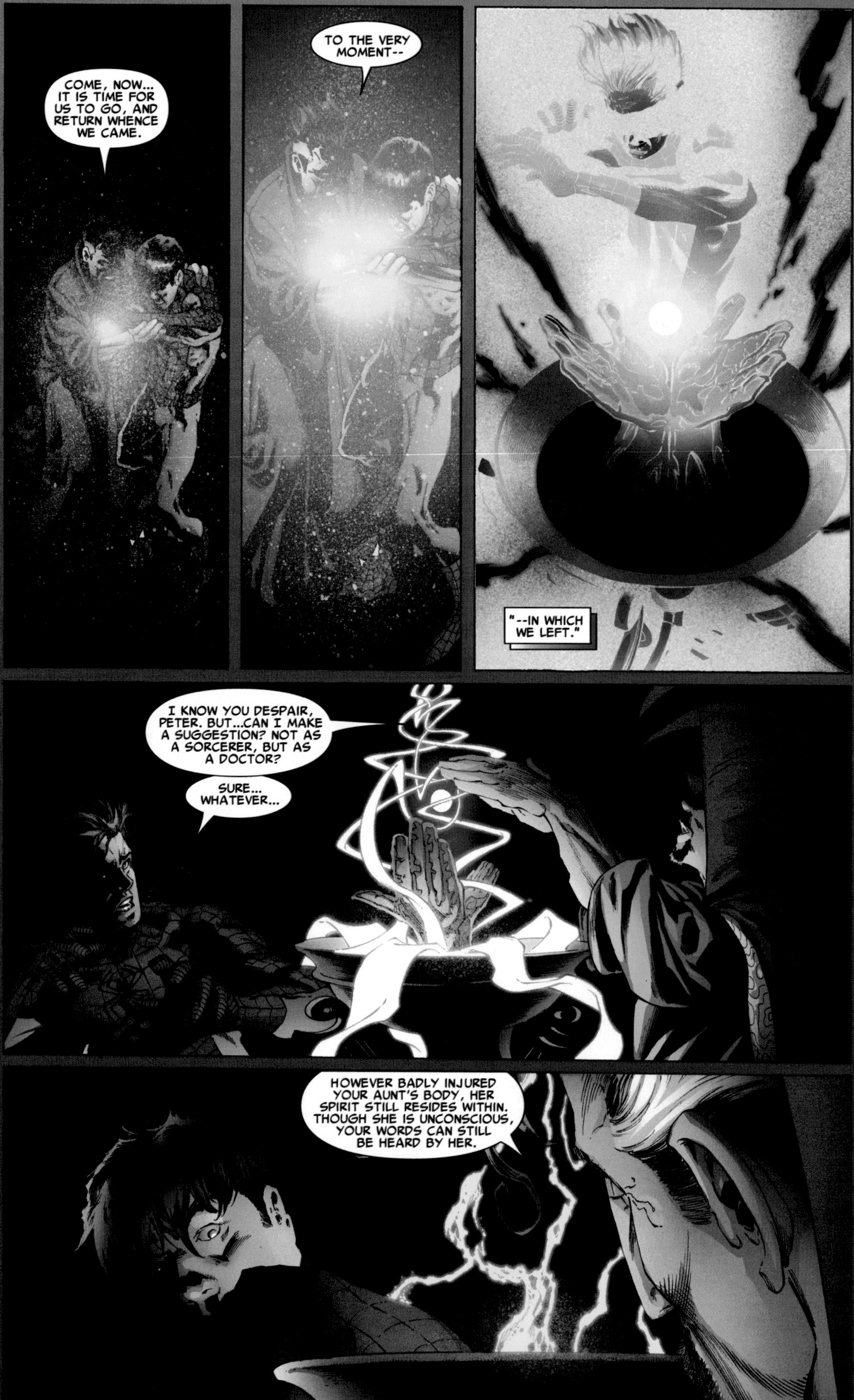
COME, NOW... IT IS TIME FOR US TO GO, AND RETURN WHENCE WE CAME.
TO THE VERY MOMENT--
"--IN WHICH WE LEFT."
I KNOW YOU DESPAIR, PETER. BUT...CAN I MAKE A SUGGESTION? NOT AS A SORCERER, BUT AS A DOCTOR?
SURE... WHATEVER...
HOWEVER BADLY INJURED YOUR AUNT'S BODY, HER SPIRIT STILL RESIDES WITHIN. THOUGH SHE IS UNCONSCIOUS, YOUR WORDS CAN STILL BE HEARD BY HER.

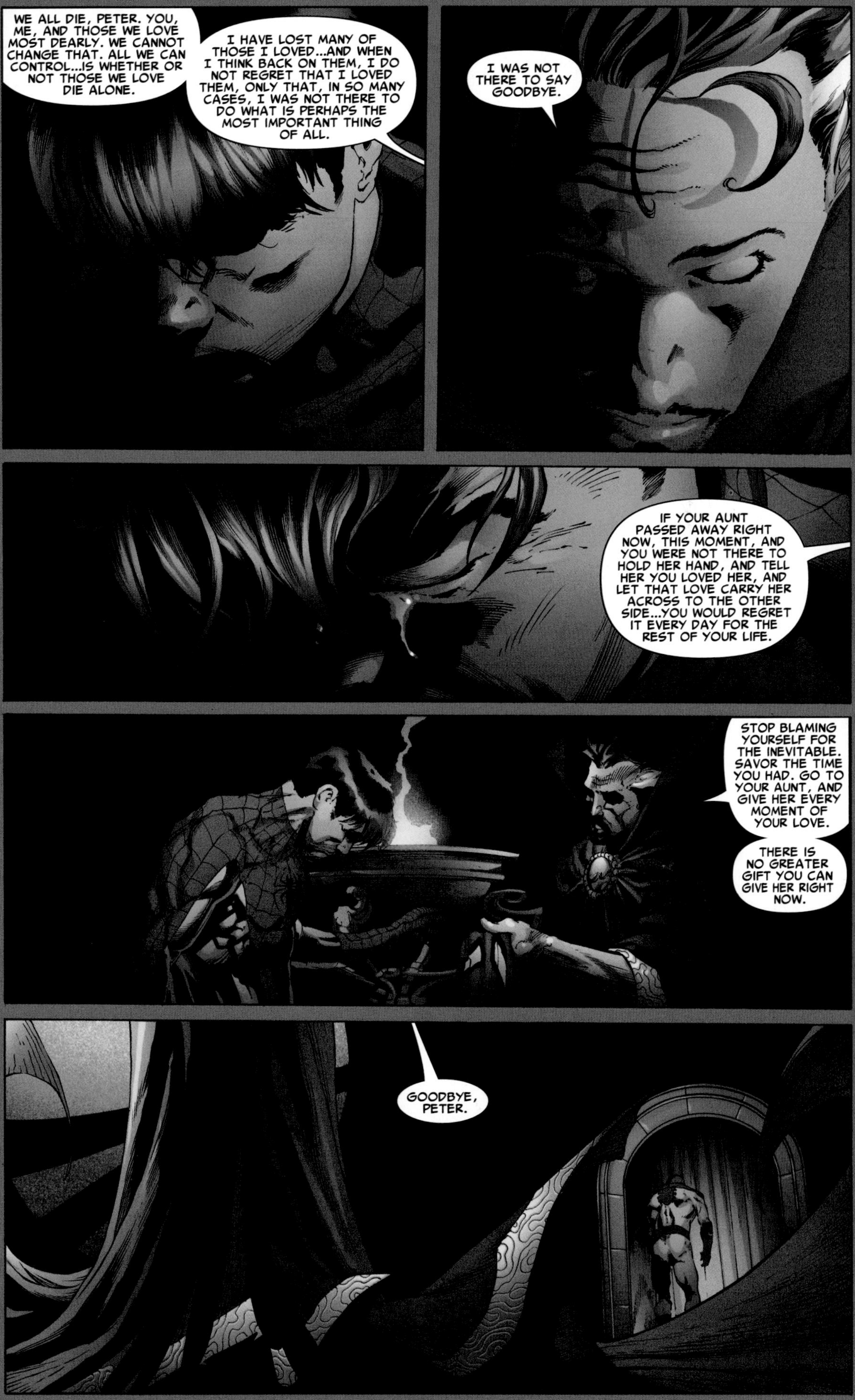
WE ALL DIE, PETER. YOU, ME, AND THOSE WE LOVE MOST DEARLY. WE CANNOT CHANGE THAT. ALL WE CAN CONTROL...IS WHETHER OR NOT THOSE WE LOVE DIE ALONE.
I HAVE LOST MANY OF THOSE I LOVED...AND WHEN I THINK BACK ON THEM, I DO NOT REGRET THAT I LOVED THEM, ONLY THAT, IN SO MANY CASES, I WAS NOT THERE TO DO WHAT IS PERHAPS THE MOST IMPORTANT THING OF ALL.
I WAS NOT THERE TO SAY GOODBYE.
IF YOUR AUNT PASSED AWAY RIGHT NOW, THIS MOMENT, AND YOU WERE NOT THERE TO HOLD HER HAND, AND TELL HER YOU LOVED HER, AND LET THAT LOVE CARRY HER ACROSS TO THE OTHER SIDE...YOU WOULD REGRET IT EVERY DAY FOR THE REST OF YOUR LIFE.
STOP BLAMING YOURSELF FOR THE INEVITABLE. SAVOR THE TIME YOU HAD. GO TO YOUR AUNT, AND GIVE HER EVERY MOMENT OF YOUR LOVE.
THERE IS NO GREATER GIFT YOU CAN GIVE HER RIGHT NOW.
GOODBYE, PETER.

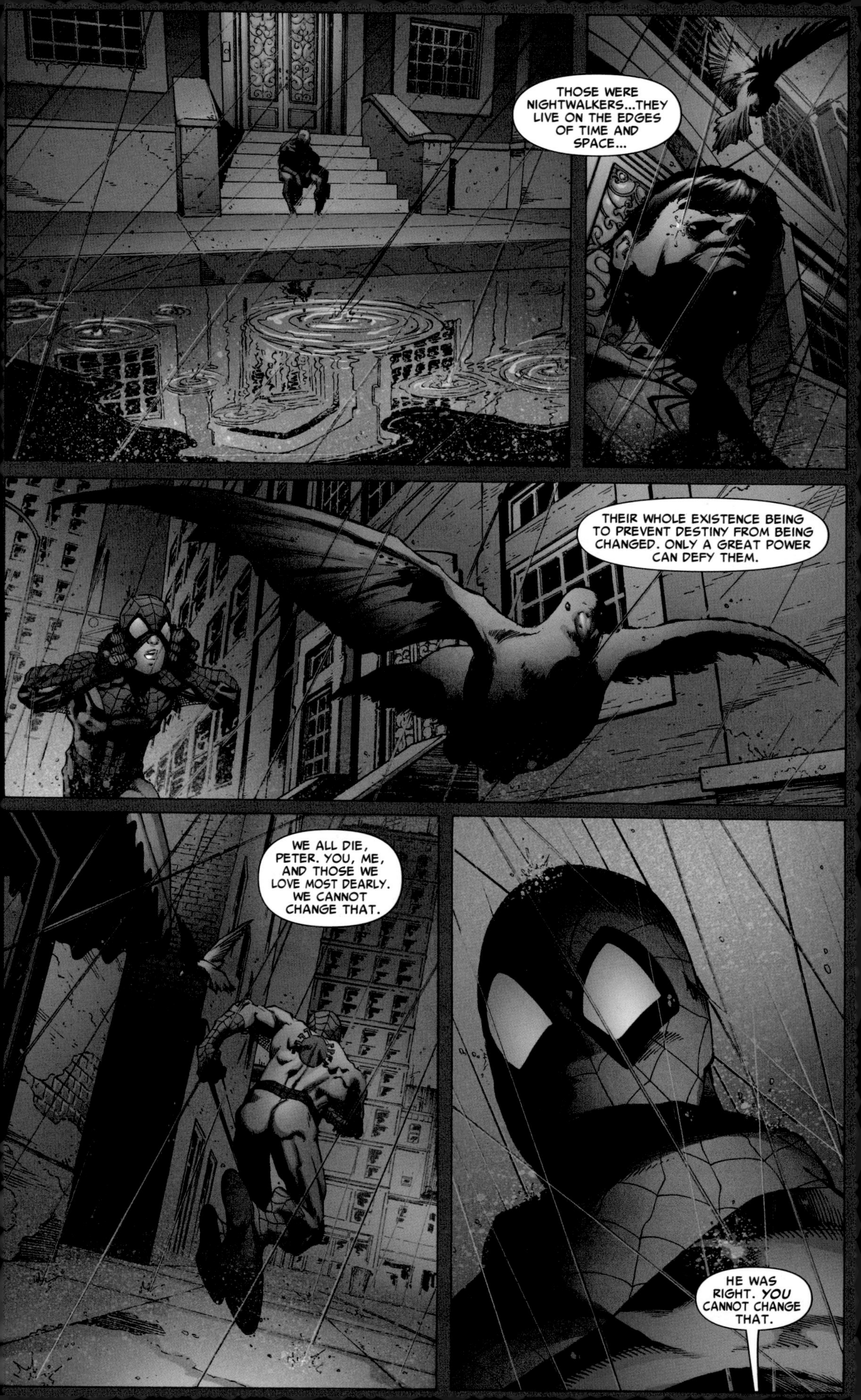
THOSE WERE NIGHTWALKERS...THEY LIVE ON THE EDGES OF TIME AND SPACE...
THEIR WHOLE EXISTENCE BEING TO PREVENT DESTINY FROM BEING CHANGED. ONLY A GREAT POWER CAN DEFY THEM.
WE ALL DIE, PETER. YOU, ME, AND THOSE WE LOVE MOST DEARLY. WE CANNOT CHANGE THAT.
HE WAS RIGHT. *YOU* CANNOT CHANGE THAT.

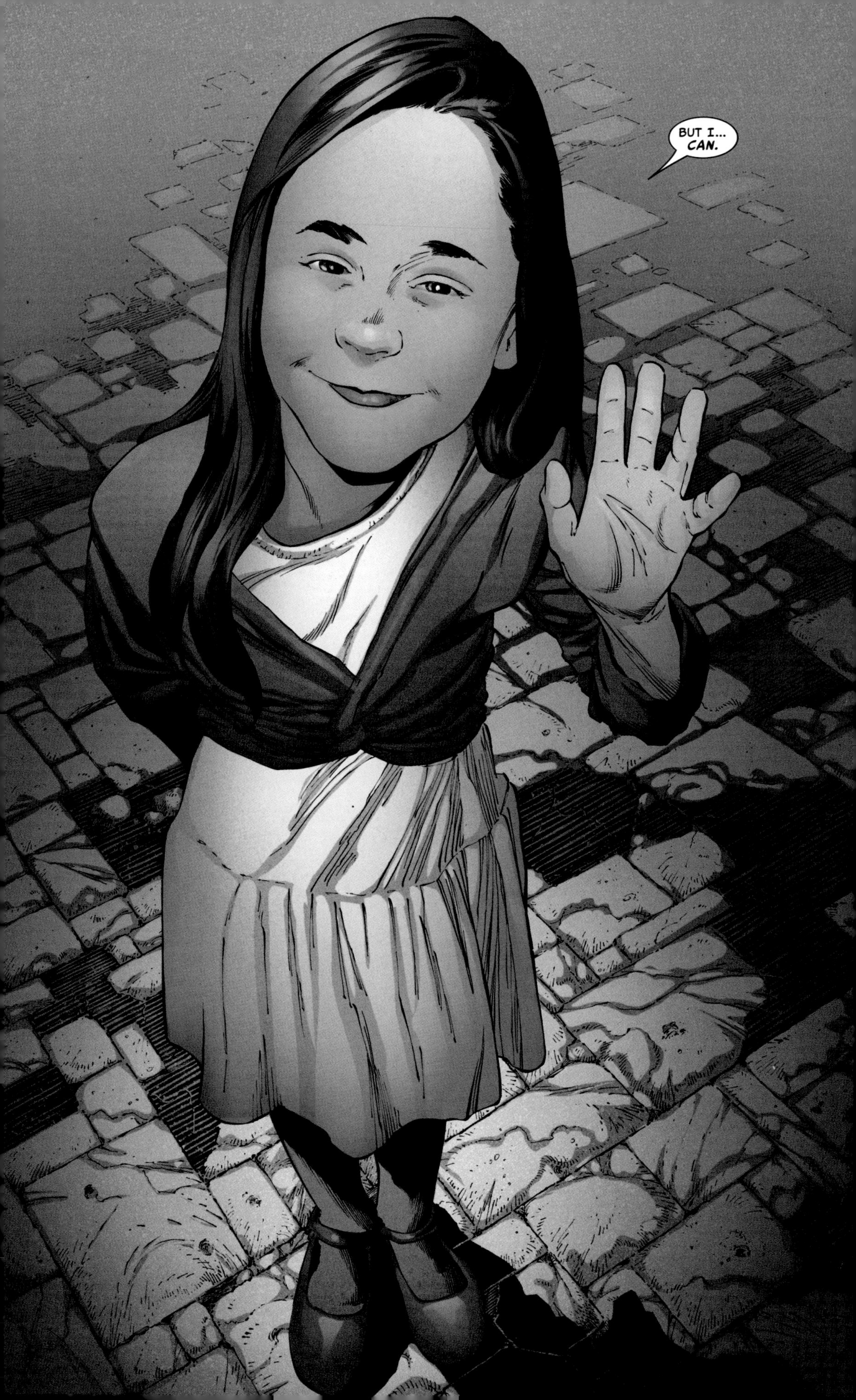
BUT I... CAN.

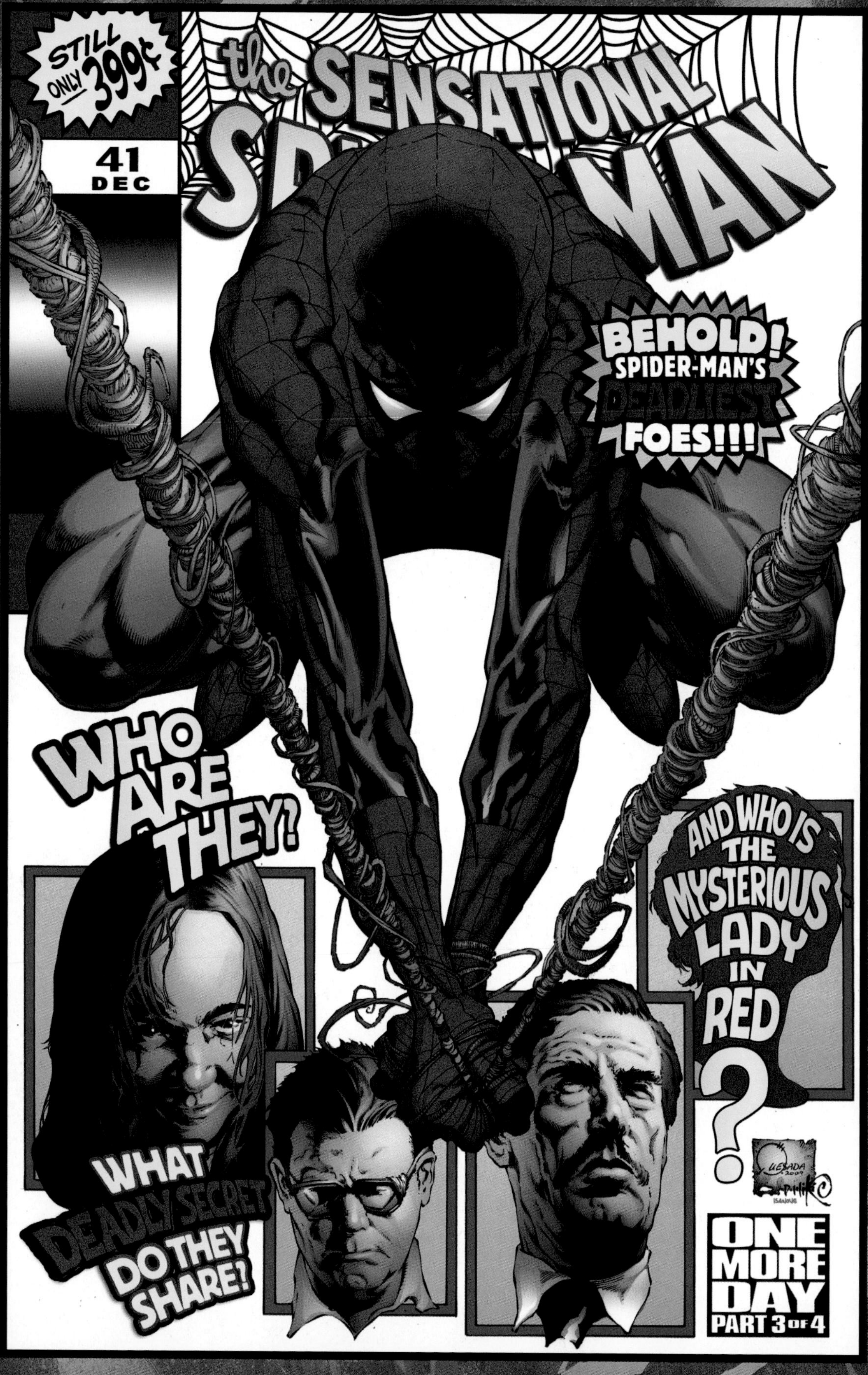
STILL ONLY 399¢
the SENSATIONAL SPIDER-MAN
41 DEC
BEHOLD! SPIDER-MAN'S DEADLIEST FOES!!!
WHO ARE THEY?
AND WHO IS THE MYSTERIOUS LADY IN RED ?
WHAT DEADLY SECRET DO THEY SHARE?
ONE MORE DAY PART 3 OF 4

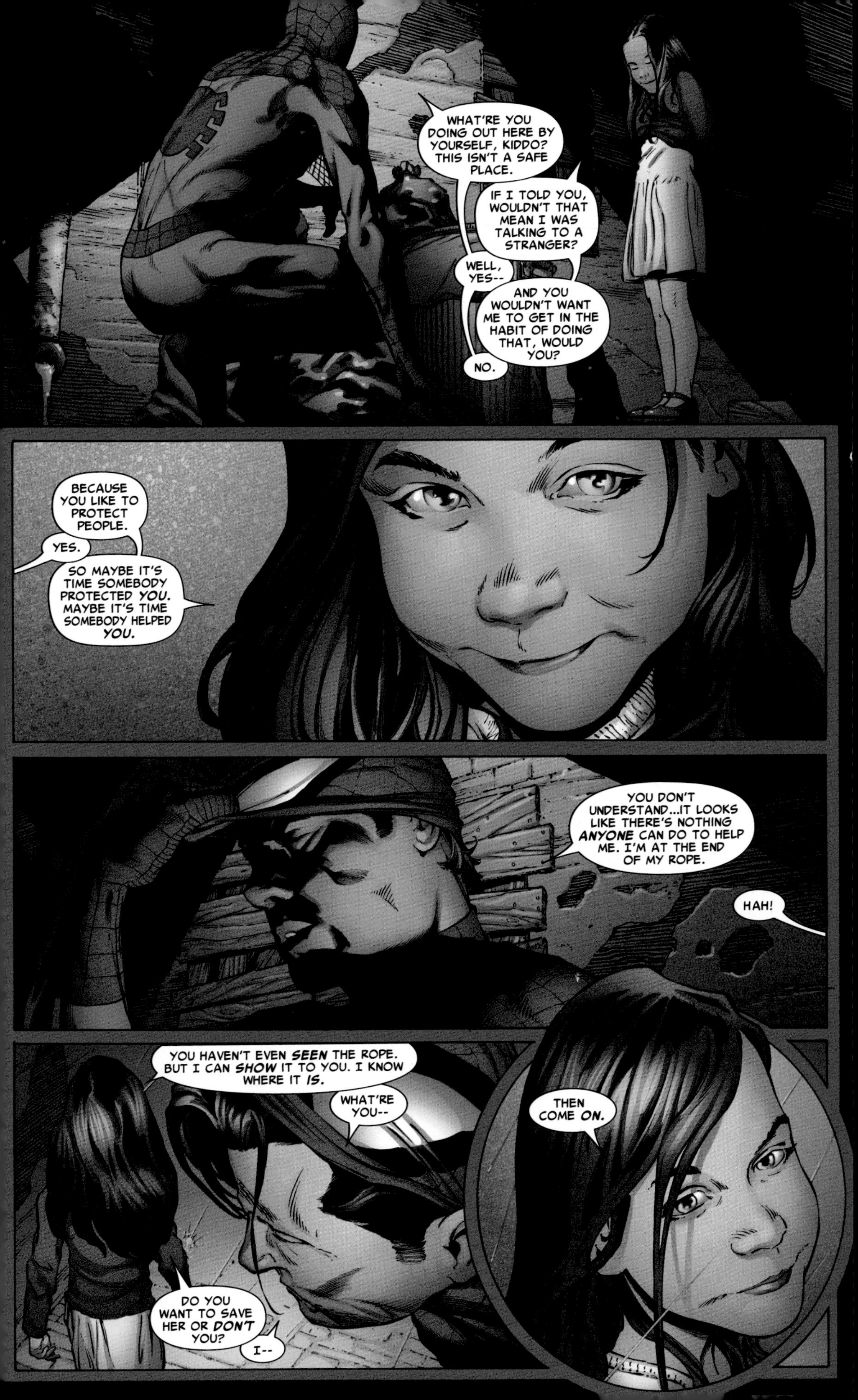
WHAT'RE YOU DOING OUT HERE BY YOURSELF, KIDDO? THIS ISN'T A SAFE PLACE.
IF I TOLD YOU, WOULDN'T THAT MEAN I WAS TALKING TO A STRANGER?
WELL, YES--
AND YOU WOULDN'T WANT ME TO GET IN THE HABIT OF DOING THAT, WOULD YOU?
NO.
BECAUSE YOU LIKE TO PROTECT PEOPLE.
YES.
SO MAYBE IT'S TIME SOMEBODY PROTECTED YOU. MAYBE IT'S TIME SOMEBODY HELPED YOU.
YOU DON'T UNDERSTAND...IT LOOKS LIKE THERE'S NOTHING ANYONE CAN DO TO HELP ME. I'M AT THE END OF MY ROPE.
HAH!
YOU HAVEN'T EVEN SEEN THE ROPE. BUT I CAN SHOW IT TO YOU. I KNOW WHERE IT IS.
WHAT'RE YOU--
THEN COME ON.
DO YOU WANT TO SAVE HER OR DON'T YOU?
I--

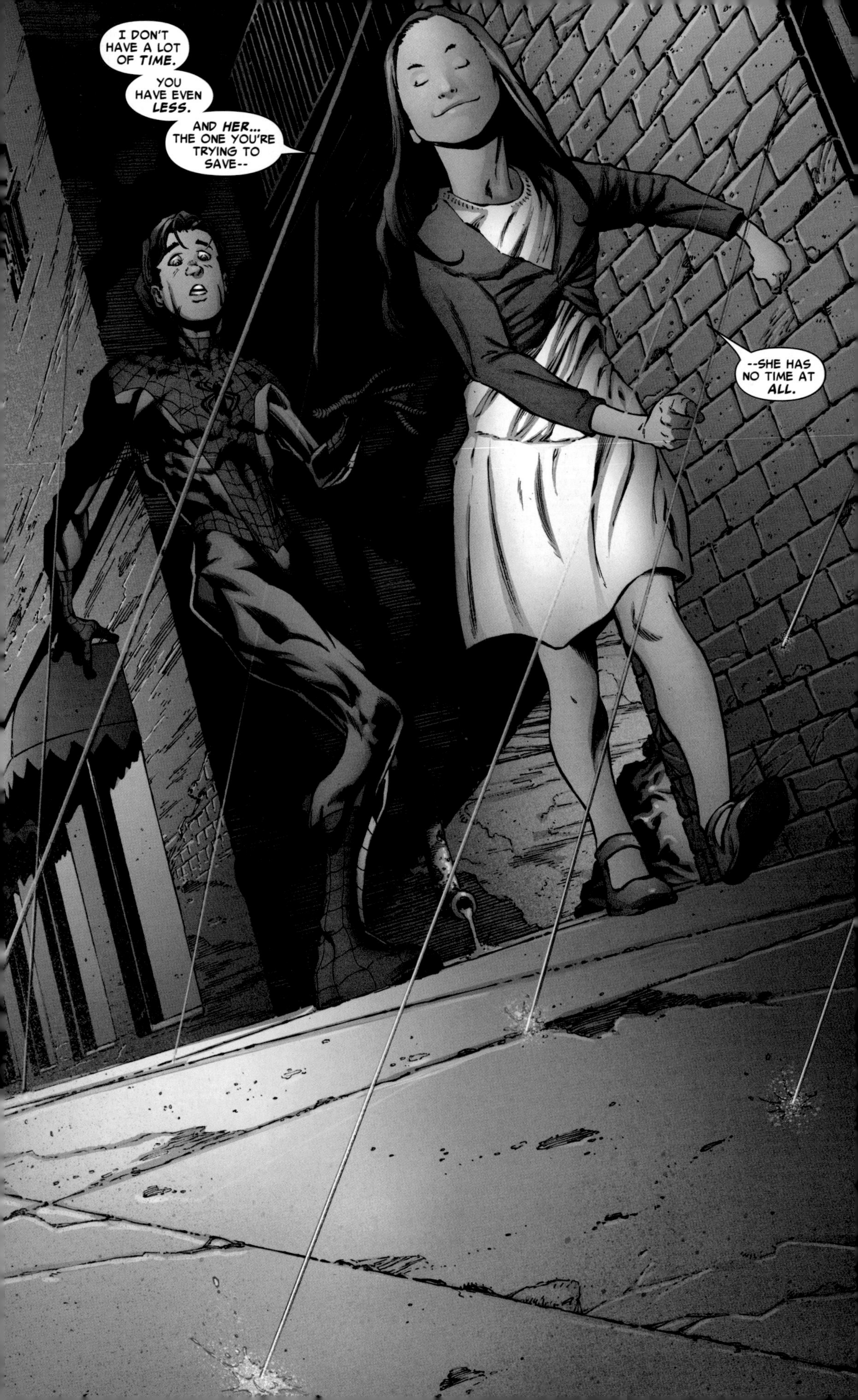
I DON'T HAVE A LOT OF TIME.
YOU HAVE EVEN LESS.
AND HER... THE ONE YOU'RE TRYING TO SAVE--
--SHE HAS NO TIME AT ALL.

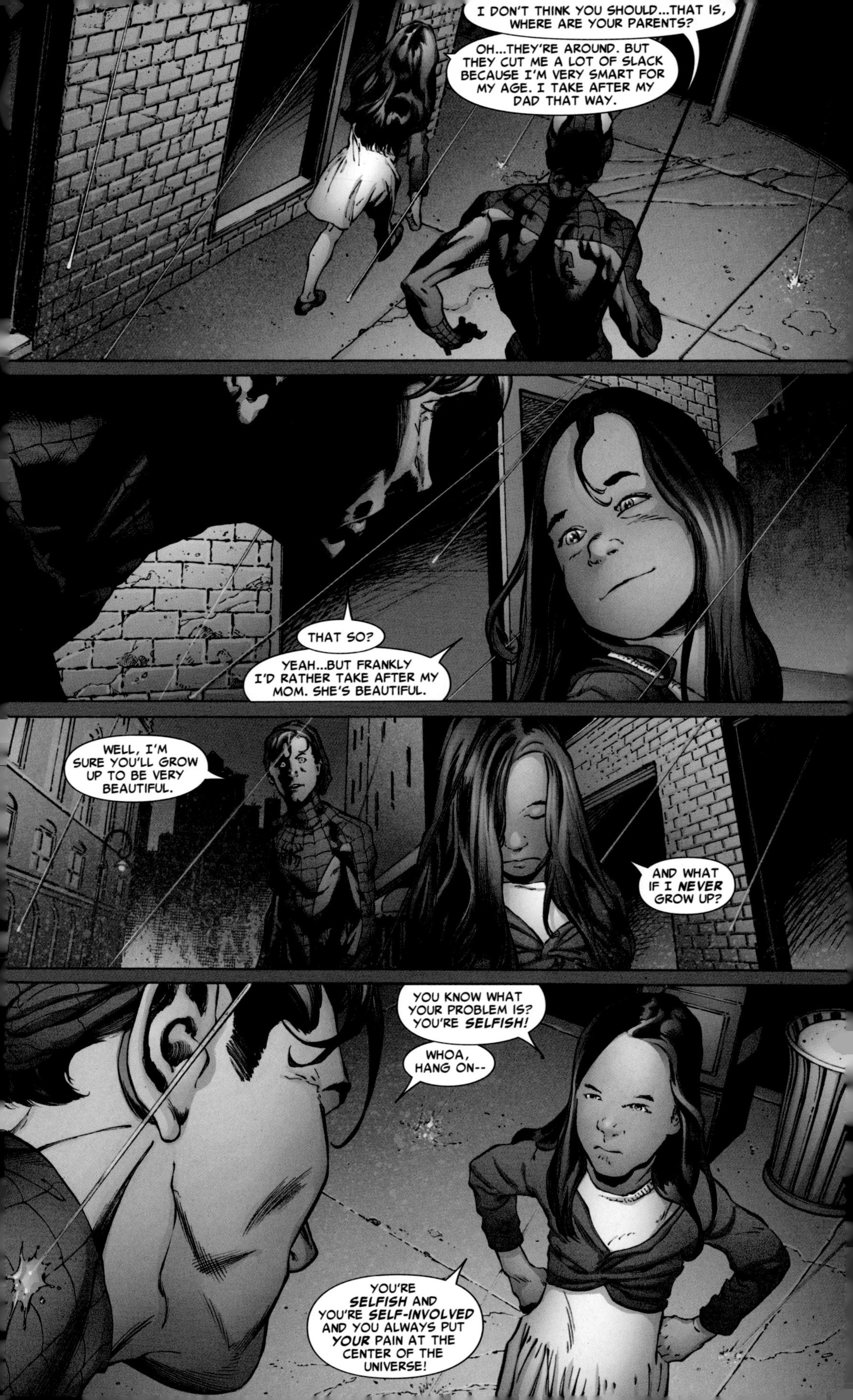
I DON'T THINK YOU SHOULD...THAT IS, WHERE ARE YOUR PARENTS?
OH...THEY'RE AROUND. BUT THEY CUT ME A LOT OF SLACK BECAUSE I'M VERY SMART FOR MY AGE. I TAKE AFTER MY DAD THAT WAY.
THAT SO?
YEAH...BUT FRANKLY I'D RATHER TAKE AFTER MY MOM. SHE'S BEAUTIFUL.
WELL, I'M SURE YOU'LL GROW UP TO BE VERY BEAUTIFUL.
AND WHAT IF I *NEVER* GROW UP?
YOU KNOW WHAT YOUR PROBLEM IS? YOU'RE *SELFISH!*
WHOA, HANG ON--
YOU'RE *SELFISH* AND YOU'RE *SELF-INVOLVED* AND YOU ALWAYS PUT *YOUR* PAIN AT THE CENTER OF THE UNIVERSE!

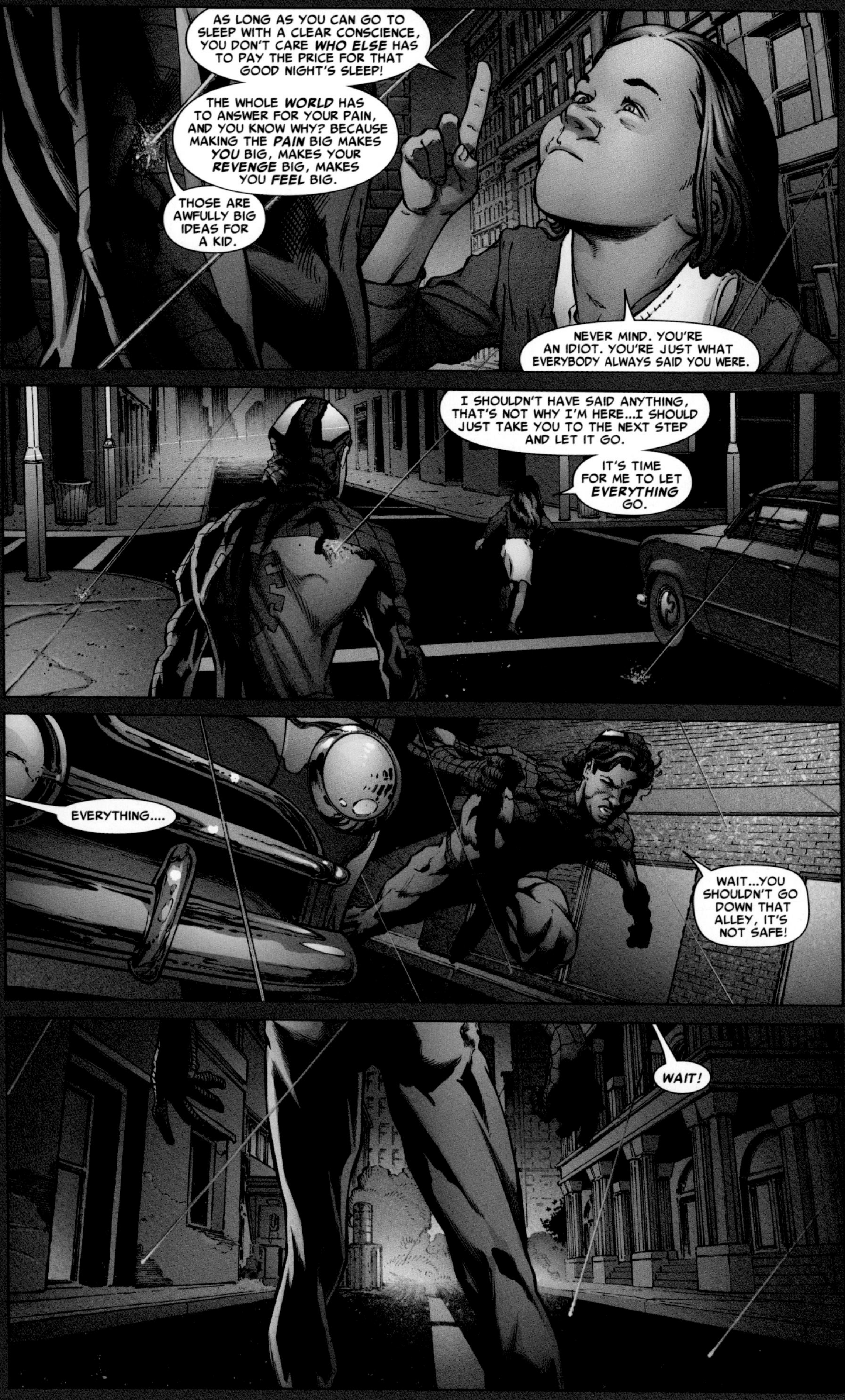
AS LONG AS YOU CAN GO TO SLEEP WITH A CLEAR CONSCIENCE, YOU DON'T CARE WHO ELSE HAS TO PAY THE PRICE FOR THAT GOOD NIGHT'S SLEEP!
THE WHOLE WORLD HAS TO ANSWER FOR YOUR PAIN, AND YOU KNOW WHY? BECAUSE MAKING THE PAIN BIG MAKES YOU BIG, MAKES YOUR REVENGE BIG, MAKES YOU FEEL BIG.
THOSE ARE AWFULLY BIG IDEAS FOR A KID.
NEVER MIND. YOU'RE AN IDIOT. YOU'RE JUST WHAT EVERYBODY ALWAYS SAID YOU WERE.
I SHOULDN'T HAVE SAID ANYTHING, THAT'S NOT WHY I'M HERE...I SHOULD JUST TAKE YOU TO THE NEXT STEP AND LET IT GO.
IT'S TIME FOR ME TO LET EVERYTHING GO.
EVERYTHING....
WAIT...YOU SHOULDN'T GO DOWN THAT ALLEY, IT'S NOT SAFE!
WAIT!

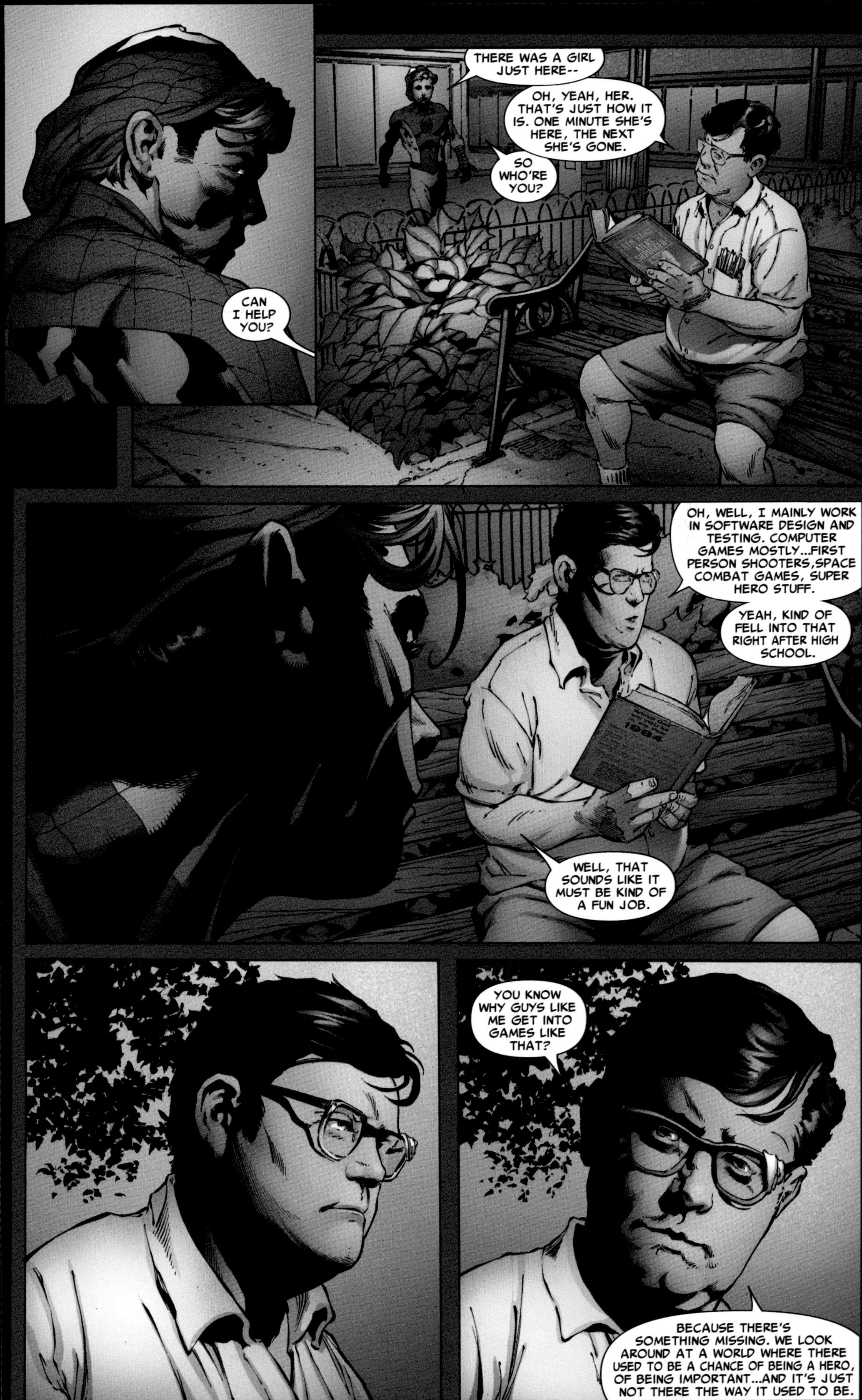

CAN I HELP YOU?
THERE WAS A GIRL JUST HERE--
OH, YEAH, HER. THAT'S JUST HOW IT IS. ONE MINUTE SHE'S HERE, THE NEXT SHE'S GONE.
SO WHO'RE YOU?
OH, WELL, I MAINLY WORK IN SOFTWARE DESIGN AND TESTING. COMPUTER GAMES MOSTLY...FIRST PERSON SHOOTERS,SPACE COMBAT GAMES, SUPER HERO STUFF.
YEAH, KIND OF FELL INTO THAT RIGHT AFTER HIGH SCHOOL.
WELL, THAT SOUNDS LIKE IT MUST BE KIND OF A FUN JOB.
YOU KNOW WHY GUYS LIKE ME GET INTO GAMES LIKE THAT?
BECAUSE THERE'S SOMETHING MISSING. WE LOOK AROUND AT A WORLD WHERE THERE USED TO BE A CHANCE OF BEING A HERO, OF BEING IMPORTANT...AND IT'S JUST NOT THERE THE WAY IT USED TO BE.

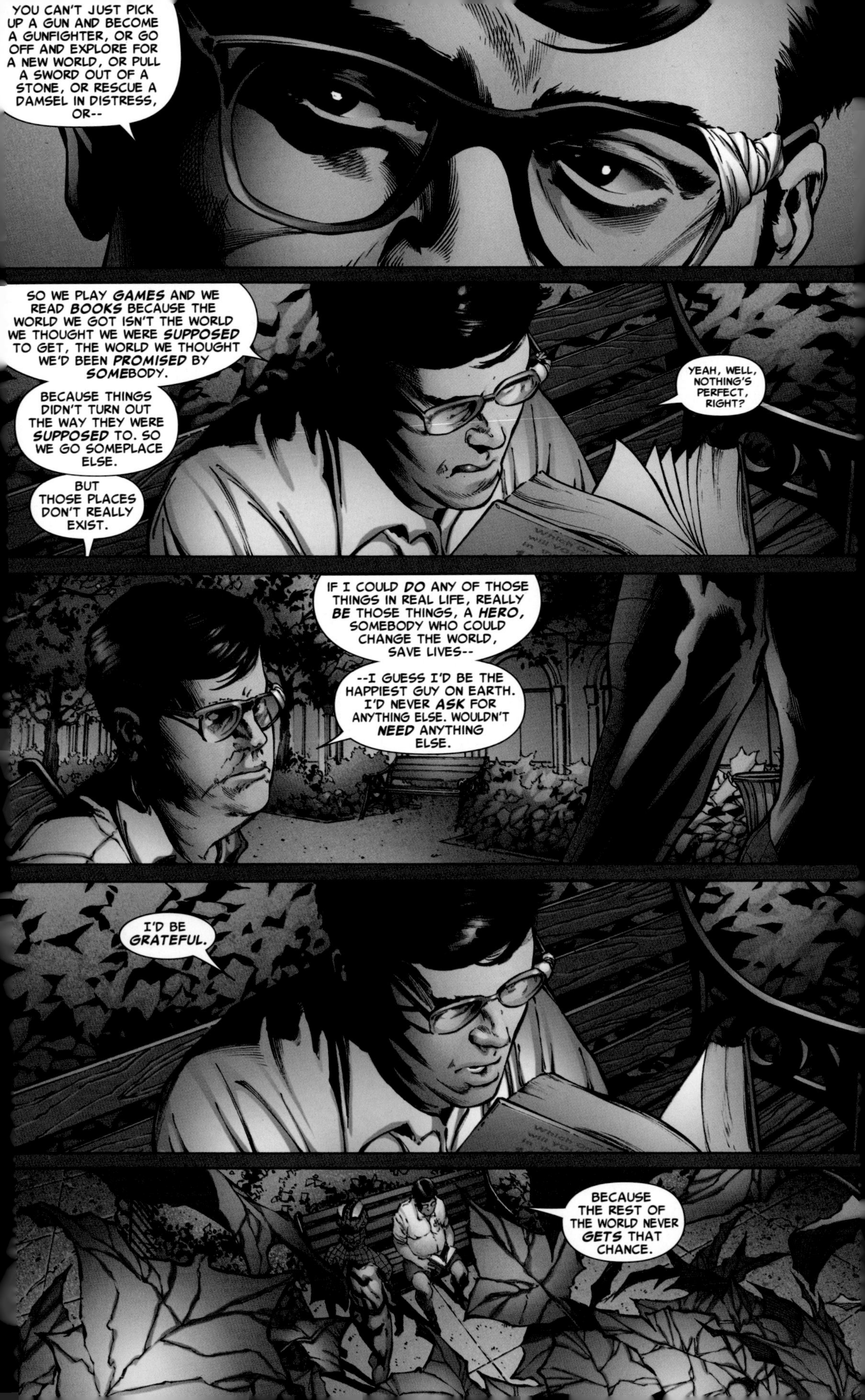
YOU CAN'T JUST PICK UP A GUN AND BECOME A GUNFIGHTER, OR GO OFF AND EXPLORE FOR A NEW WORLD, OR PULL A SWORD OUT OF A STONE, OR RESCUE A DAMSEL IN DISTRESS, OR--
SO WE PLAY GAMES AND WE READ BOOKS BECAUSE THE WORLD WE GOT ISN'T THE WORLD WE THOUGHT WE WERE SUPPOSED TO GET, THE WORLD WE THOUGHT WE'D BEEN PROMISED BY SOMEBODY.
BECAUSE THINGS DIDN'T TURN OUT THE WAY THEY WERE SUPPOSED TO. SO WE GO SOMEPLACE ELSE.
BUT THOSE PLACES DON'T REALLY EXIST.
YEAH, WELL, NOTHING'S PERFECT, RIGHT?
IF I COULD DO ANY OF THOSE THINGS IN REAL LIFE, REALLY BE THOSE THINGS, A HERO, SOMEBODY WHO COULD CHANGE THE WORLD, SAVE LIVES--
--I GUESS I'D BE THE HAPPIEST GUY ON EARTH. I'D NEVER ASK FOR ANYTHING ELSE. WOULDN'T NEED ANYTHING ELSE.
I'D BE GRATEFUL.
BECAUSE THE REST OF THE WORLD NEVER GETS THAT CHANCE.

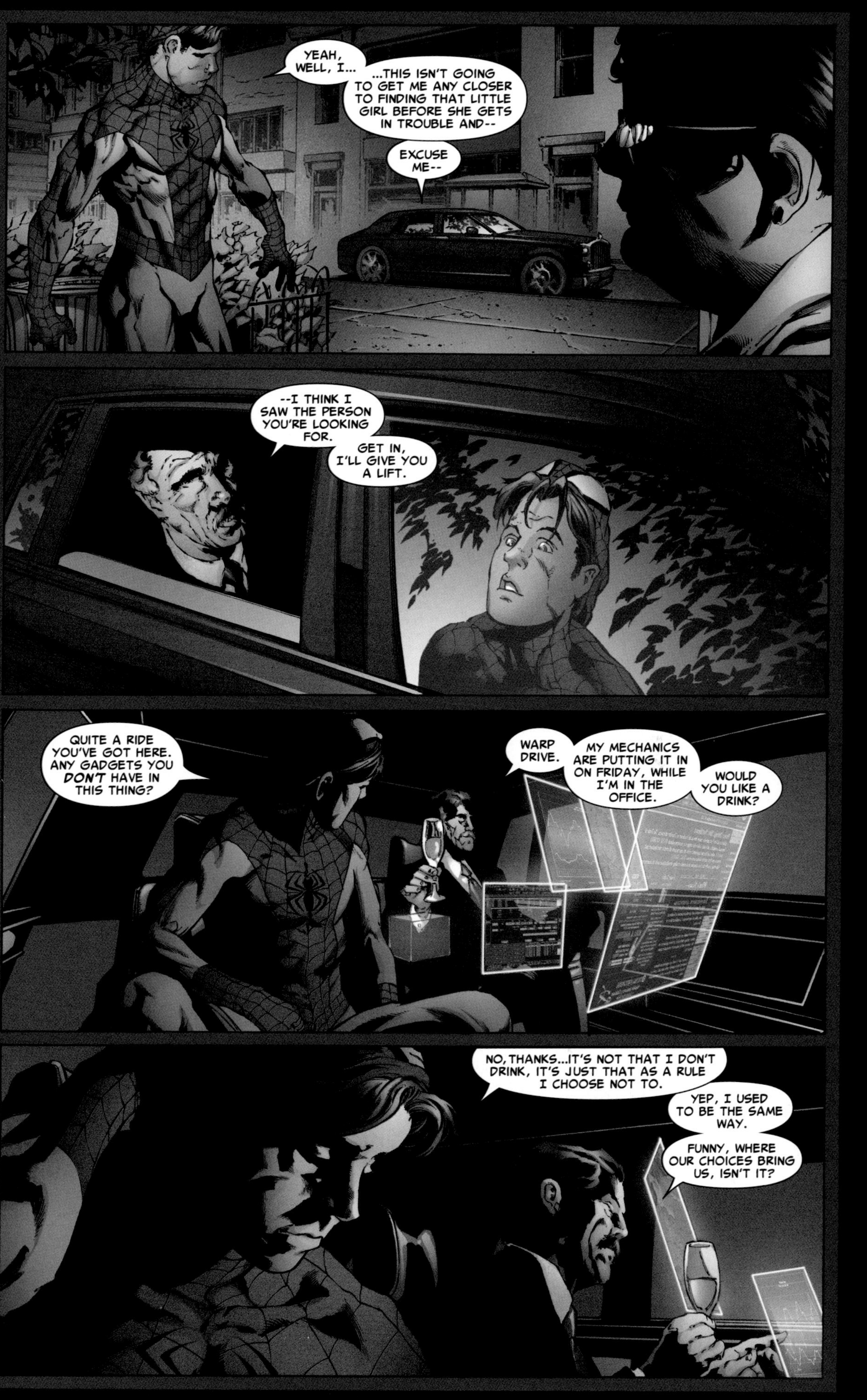
YEAH, WELL, I...
...THIS ISN'T GOING TO GET ME ANY CLOSER TO FINDING THAT LITTLE GIRL BEFORE SHE GETS IN TROUBLE AND--
EXCUSE ME--
--I THINK I SAW THE PERSON YOU'RE LOOKING FOR.
GET IN, I'LL GIVE YOU A LIFT.
QUITE A RIDE YOU'VE GOT HERE. ANY GADGETS YOU DON'T HAVE IN THIS THING?
WARP DRIVE.
MY MECHANICS ARE PUTTING IT IN ON FRIDAY, WHILE I'M IN THE OFFICE.
WOULD YOU LIKE A DRINK?
NO, THANKS...IT'S NOT THAT I DON'T DRINK, IT'S JUST THAT AS A RULE I CHOOSE NOT TO.
YEP, I USED TO BE THE SAME WAY.
FUNNY, WHERE OUR CHOICES BRING US, ISN'T IT?

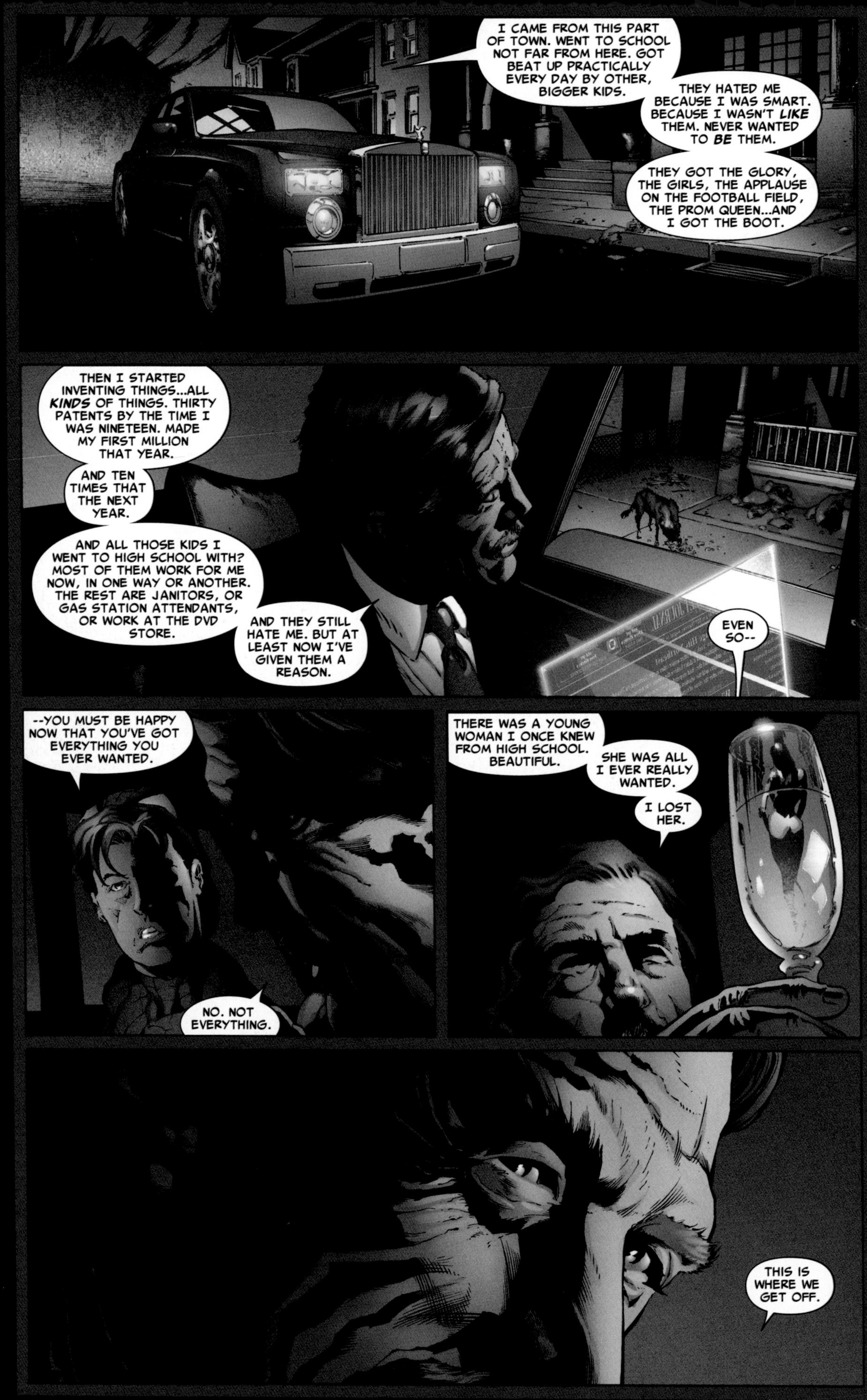
I CAME FROM THIS PART OF TOWN. WENT TO SCHOOL NOT FAR FROM HERE. GOT BEAT UP PRACTICALLY EVERY DAY BY OTHER, BIGGER KIDS.
THEY HATED ME BECAUSE I WAS SMART. BECAUSE I WASN'T *LIKE* THEM. NEVER WANTED TO *BE* THEM.
THEY GOT THE GLORY, THE GIRLS, THE APPLAUSE ON THE FOOTBALL FIELD, THE PROM QUEEN...AND I GOT THE BOOT.
THEN I STARTED INVENTING THINGS...ALL *KINDS* OF THINGS. THIRTY PATENTS BY THE TIME I WAS NINETEEN. MADE MY FIRST MILLION THAT YEAR.
AND TEN TIMES THAT THE NEXT YEAR.
AND ALL THOSE KIDS I WENT TO HIGH SCHOOL WITH? MOST OF THEM WORK FOR ME NOW, IN ONE WAY OR ANOTHER. THE REST ARE JANITORS, OR GAS STATION ATTENDANTS, OR WORK AT THE DVD STORE.
AND THEY STILL HATE ME. BUT AT LEAST NOW I'VE GIVEN THEM A REASON.
EVEN SO--
--YOU MUST BE HAPPY NOW THAT YOU'VE GOT EVERYTHING YOU EVER WANTED.
NO. NOT EVERYTHING.
THERE WAS A YOUNG WOMAN I ONCE KNEW FROM HIGH SCHOOL. BEAUTIFUL.
SHE WAS ALL I EVER REALLY WANTED.
I LOST HER.
THIS IS WHERE WE GET OFF.

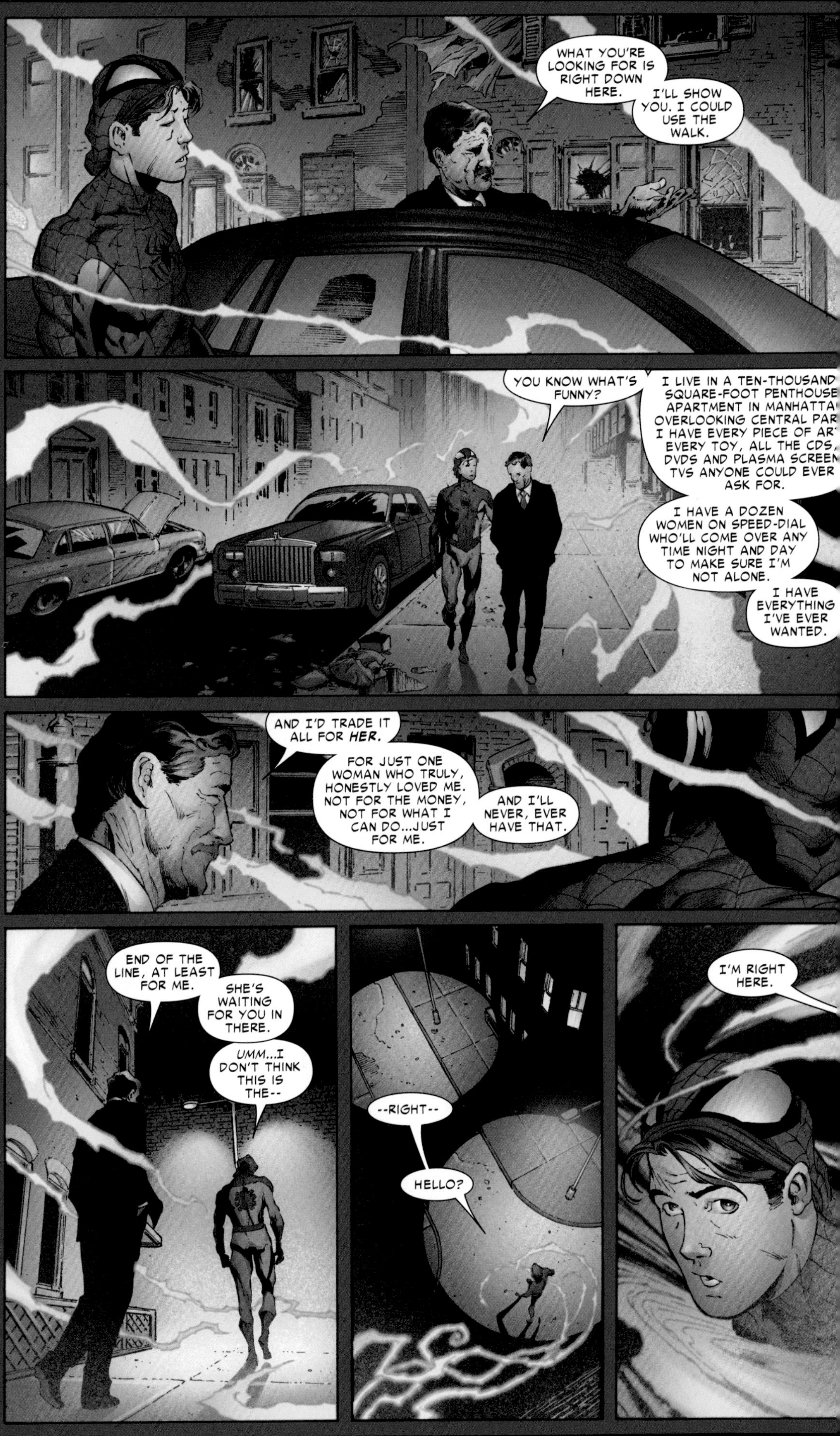

WHAT YOU'RE LOOKING FOR IS RIGHT DOWN HERE.
I'LL SHOW YOU. I COULD USE THE WALK.
YOU KNOW WHAT'S FUNNY?
I LIVE IN A TEN-THOUSAND SQUARE-FOOT PENTHOUSE APARTMENT IN MANHATTA OVERLOOKING CENTRAL PAR I HAVE EVERY PIECE OF AR EVERY TOY, ALL THE CDS, DVDS AND PLASMA SCREEN TVS ANYONE COULD EVER ASK FOR.
I HAVE A DOZEN WOMEN ON SPEED-DIAL WHO'LL COME OVER ANY TIME NIGHT AND DAY TO MAKE SURE I'M NOT ALONE.
I HAVE EVERYTHING I'VE EVER WANTED.
AND I'D TRADE IT ALL FOR *HER*.
FOR JUST ONE WOMAN WHO TRULY, HONESTLY LOVED ME. NOT FOR THE MONEY, NOT FOR WHAT I CAN DO...JUST FOR ME.
AND I'LL NEVER, EVER HAVE THAT.
END OF THE LINE, AT LEAST FOR ME.
SHE'S WAITING FOR YOU IN THERE.
UMM...I DON'T THINK THIS IS THE--
--RIGHT--
HELLO?
I'M RIGHT HERE.

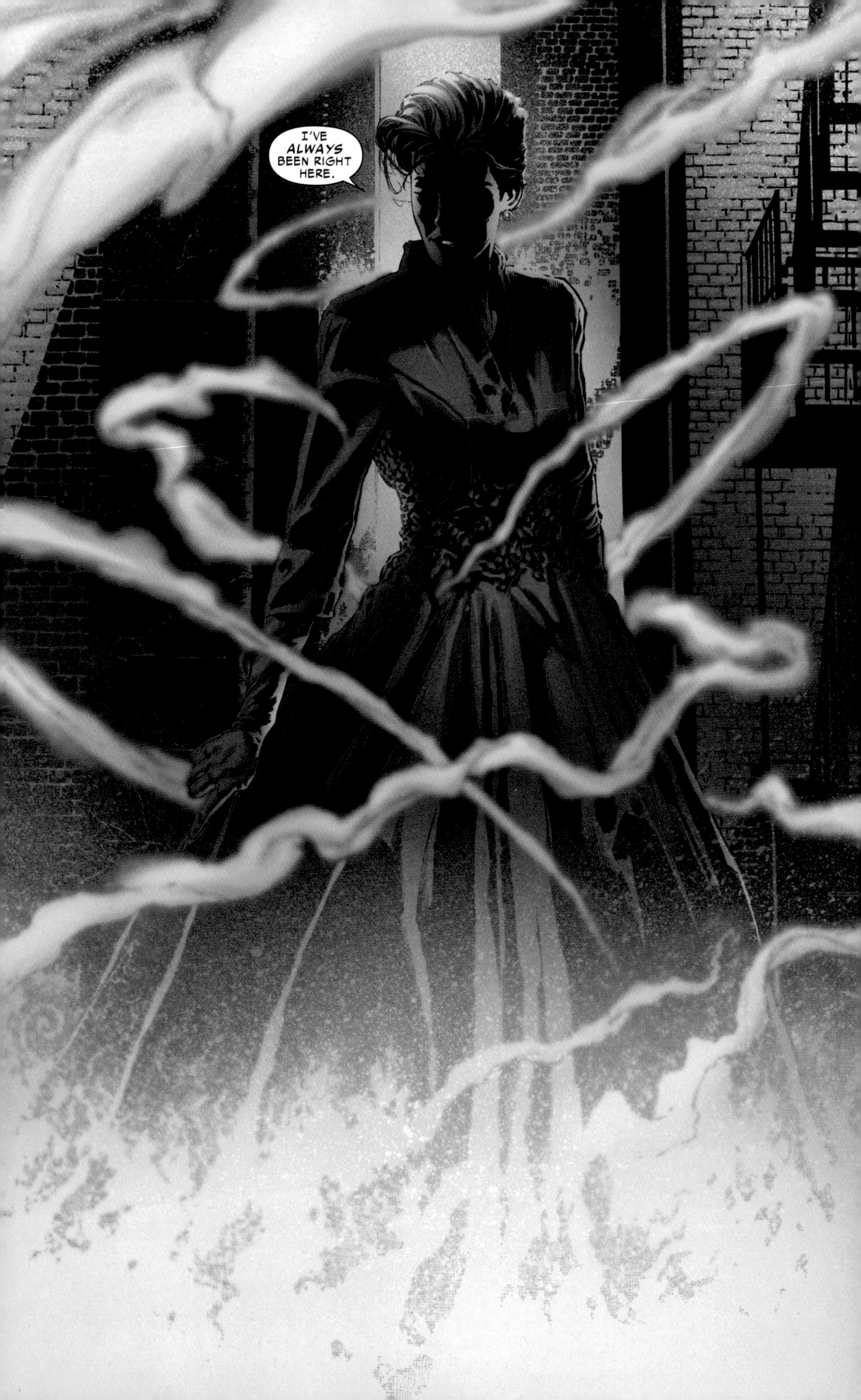
I'VE ALWAYS BEEN RIGHT HERE.

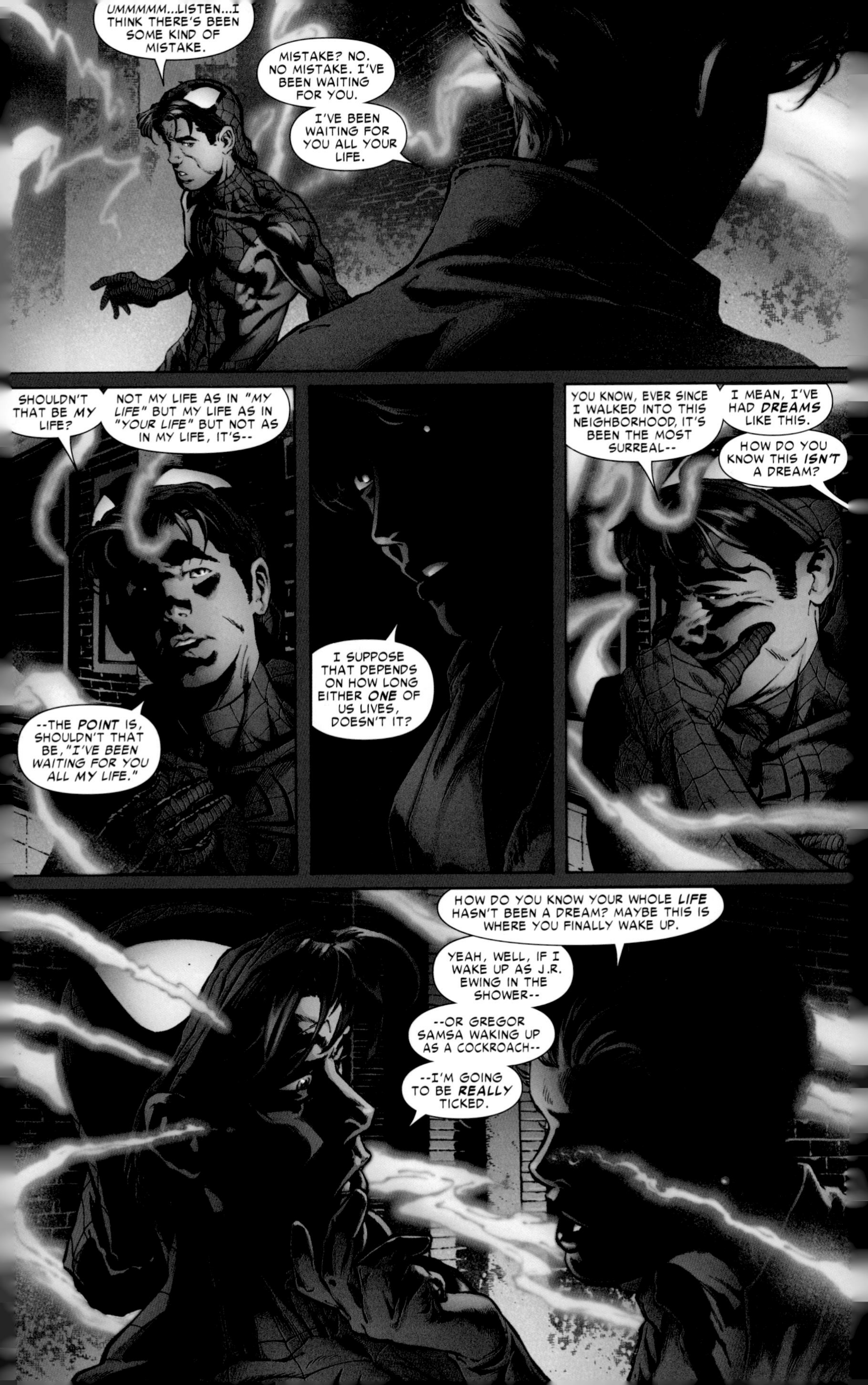
UMMMMM...LISTEN...I THINK THERE'S BEEN SOME KIND OF MISTAKE.
MISTAKE? NO. NO MISTAKE. I'VE BEEN WAITING FOR YOU.
I'VE BEEN WAITING FOR YOU ALL YOUR LIFE.
SHOULDN'T THAT BE MY LIFE?
NOT MY LIFE AS IN "MY LIFE" BUT MY LIFE AS IN "YOUR LIFE" BUT NOT AS IN MY LIFE, IT'S--
--THE POINT IS, SHOULDN'T THAT BE, "I'VE BEEN WAITING FOR YOU ALL MY LIFE."
I SUPPOSE THAT DEPENDS ON HOW LONG EITHER ONE OF US LIVES, DOESN'T IT?
YOU KNOW, EVER SINCE I WALKED INTO THIS NEIGHBORHOOD, IT'S BEEN THE MOST SURREAL--
I MEAN, I'VE HAD DREAMS LIKE THIS.
HOW DO YOU KNOW THIS ISN'T A DREAM?
HOW DO YOU KNOW YOUR WHOLE LIFE HASN'T BEEN A DREAM? MAYBE THIS IS WHERE YOU FINALLY WAKE UP.
YEAH, WELL, IF I WAKE UP AS J.R. EWING IN THE SHOWER--
--OR GREGOR SAMSA WAKING UP AS A COCKROACH--
--I'M GOING TO BE REALLY TICKED.

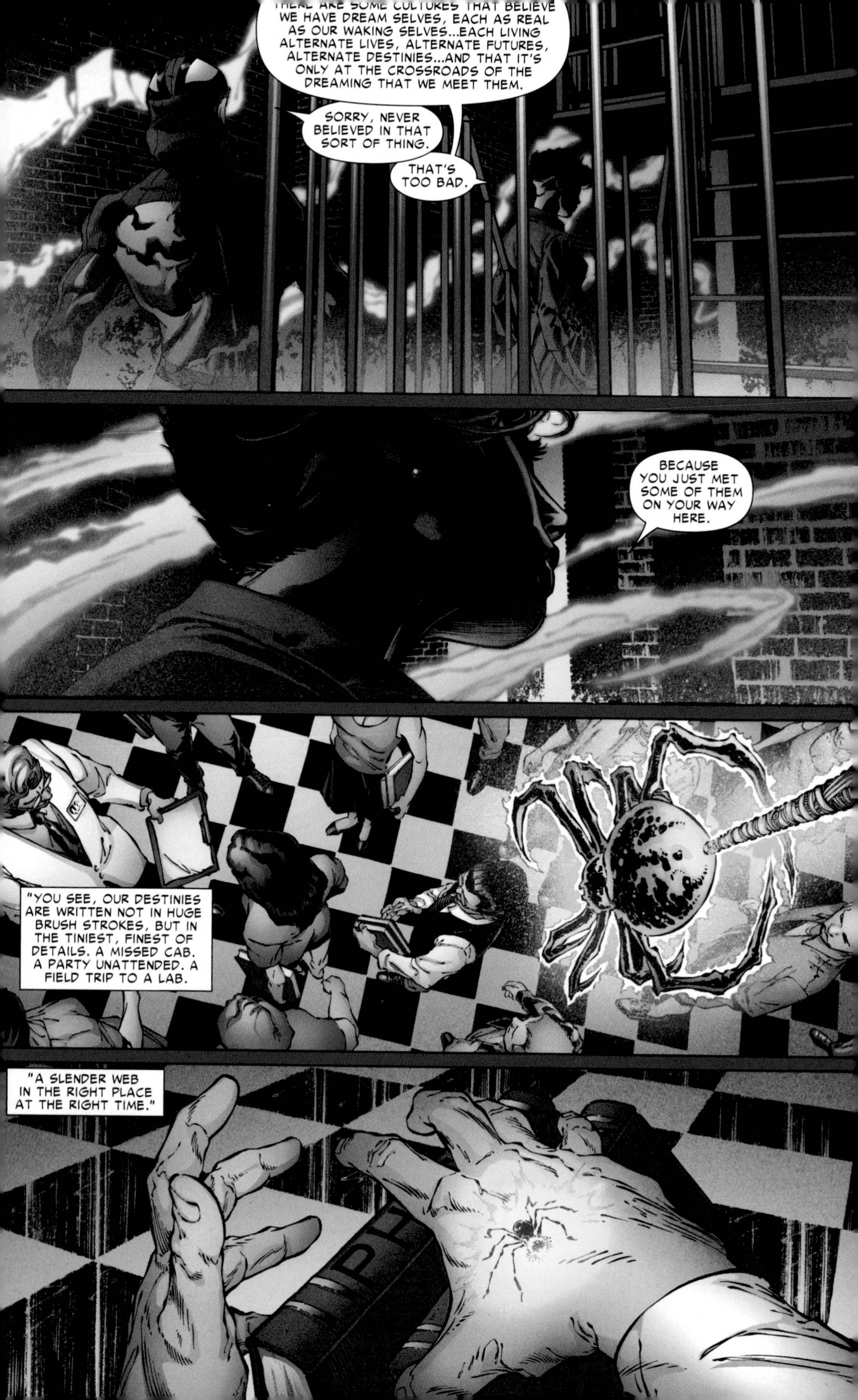
THERE ARE SOME CULTURES THAT BELIEVE WE HAVE DREAM SELVES, EACH AS REAL AS OUR WAKING SELVES...EACH LIVING ALTERNATE LIVES, ALTERNATE FUTURES, ALTERNATE DESTINIES...AND THAT IT'S ONLY AT THE CROSSROADS OF THE DREAMING THAT WE MEET THEM.
SORRY, NEVER BELIEVED IN THAT SORT OF THING.
THAT'S TOO BAD.
BECAUSE YOU JUST MET SOME OF THEM ON YOUR WAY HERE.
"YOU SEE, OUR DESTINIES ARE WRITTEN NOT IN HUGE BRUSH STROKES, BUT IN THE TINIEST, FINEST OF DETAILS. A MISSED CAB. A PARTY UNATTENDED. A FIELD TRIP TO A LAB.
"A SLENDER WEB IN THE RIGHT PLACE AT THE RIGHT TIME."

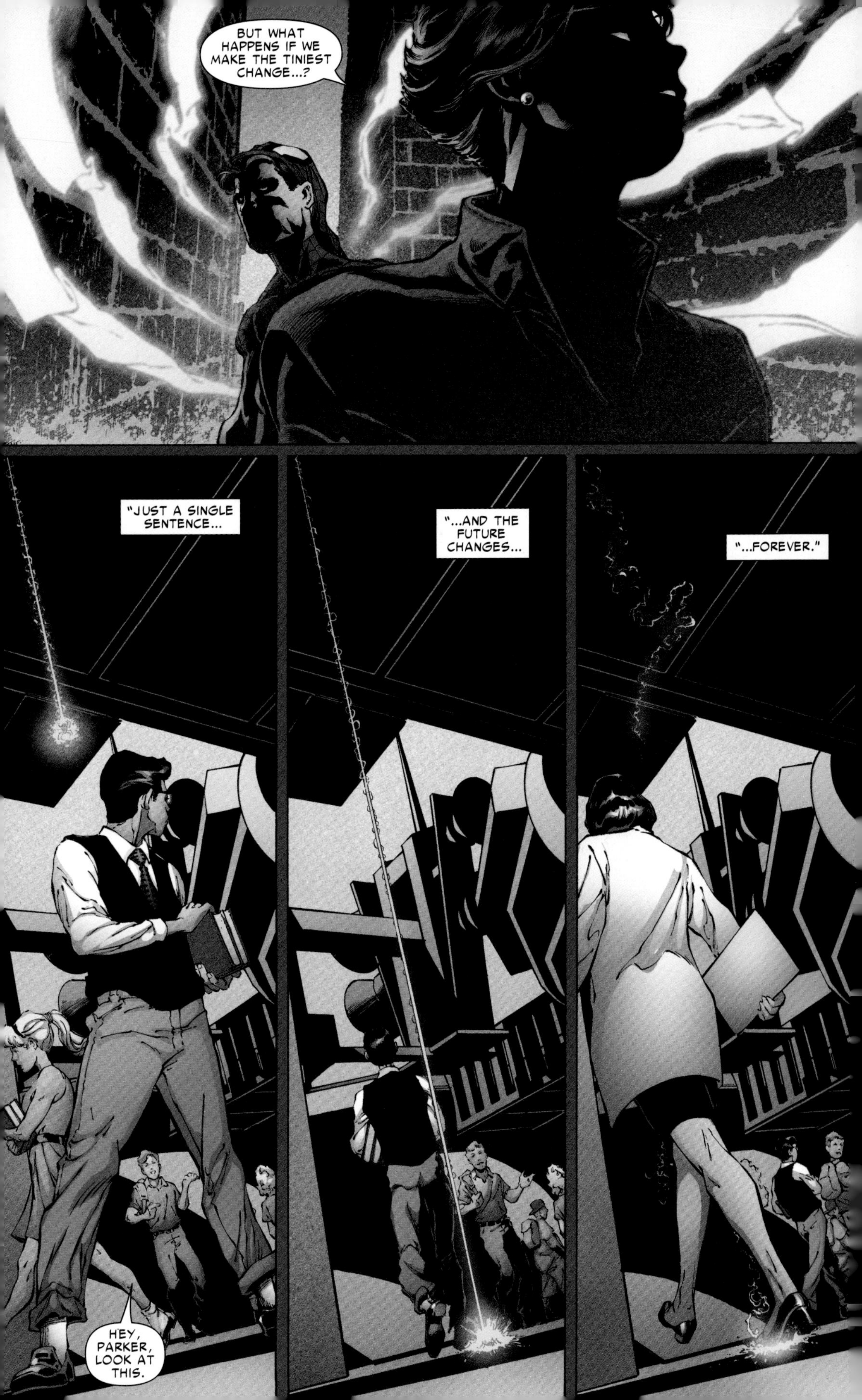

BUT WHAT HAPPENS IF WE MAKE THE TINIEST CHANGE...?
"JUST A SINGLE SENTENCE...
HEY, PARKER, LOOK AT THIS.
"...AND THE FUTURE CHANGES...
"...FOREVER."

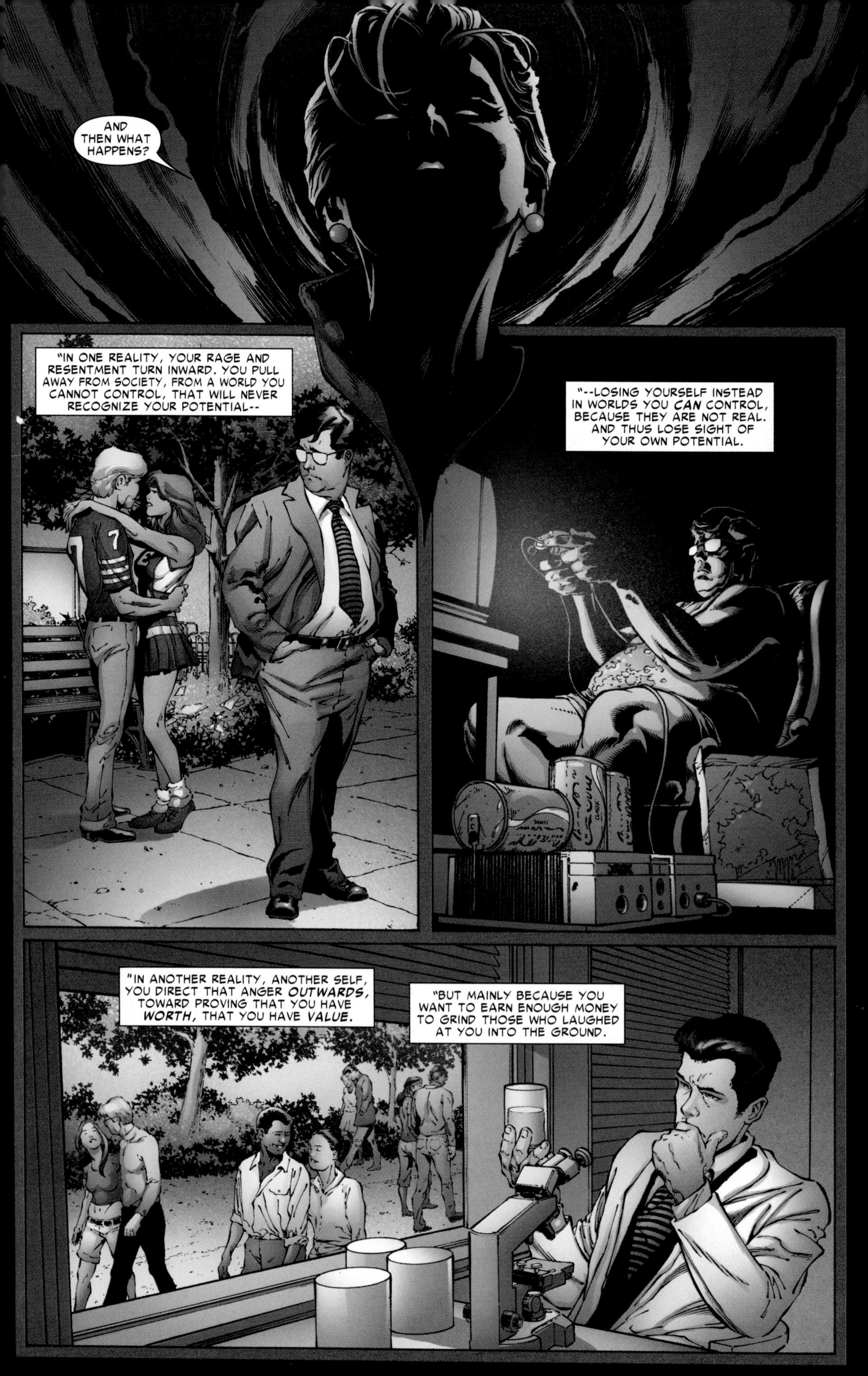
AND THEN WHAT HAPPENS?
"IN ONE REALITY, YOUR RAGE AND RESENTMENT TURN INWARD. YOU PULL AWAY FROM SOCIETY, FROM A WORLD YOU CANNOT CONTROL, THAT WILL NEVER RECOGNIZE YOUR POTENTIAL--
"--LOSING YOURSELF INSTEAD IN WORLDS YOU CAN CONTROL, BECAUSE THEY ARE NOT REAL. AND THUS LOSE SIGHT OF YOUR OWN POTENTIAL.
"IN ANOTHER REALITY, ANOTHER SELF, YOU DIRECT THAT ANGER OUTWARDS, TOWARD PROVING THAT YOU HAVE WORTH, THAT YOU HAVE VALUE.
"BUT MAINLY BECAUSE YOU WANT TO EARN ENOUGH MONEY TO GRIND THOSE WHO LAUGHED AT YOU INTO THE GROUND.

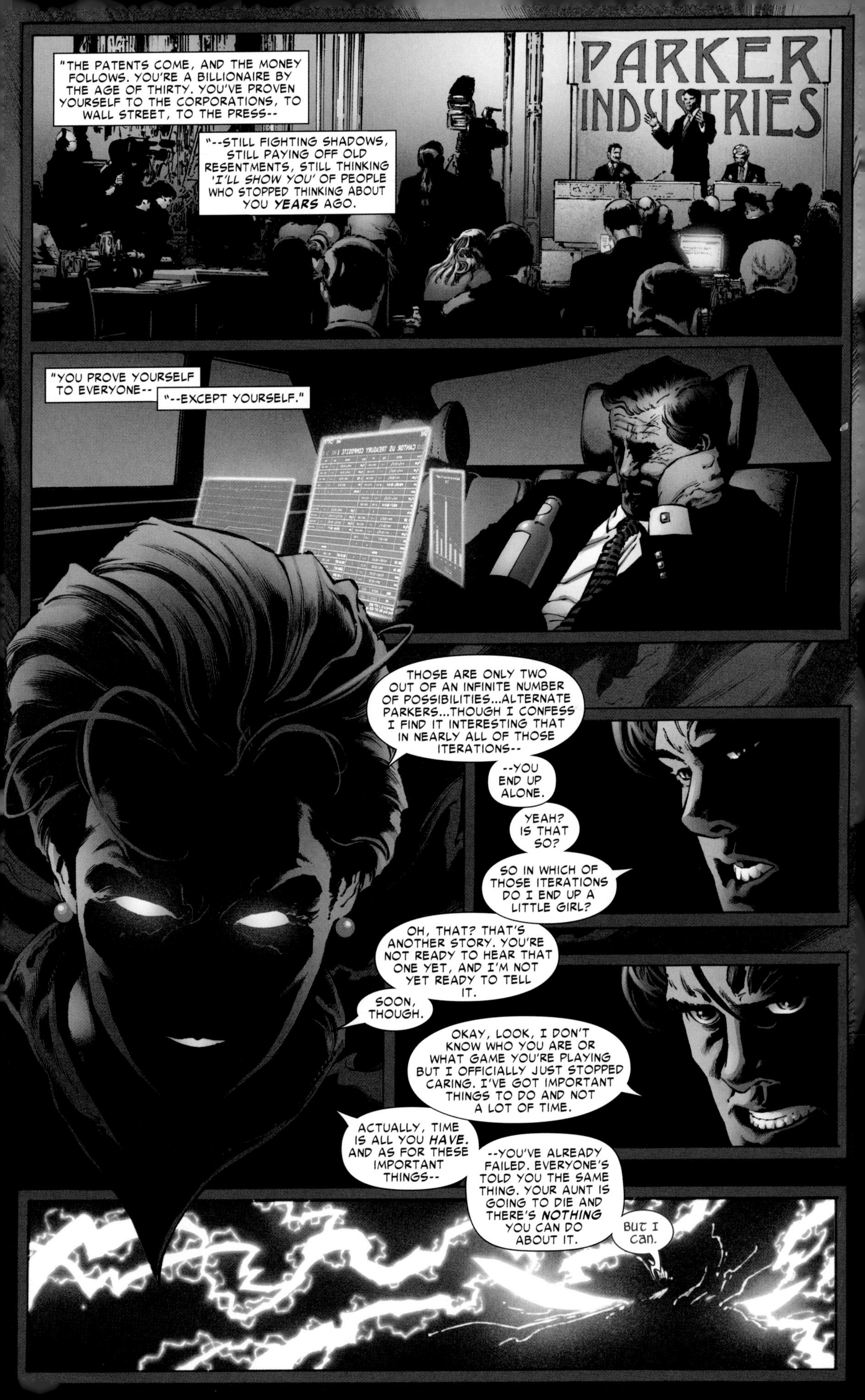
"THE PATENTS COME, AND THE MONEY FOLLOWS. YOU'RE A BILLIONAIRE BY THE AGE OF THIRTY. YOU'VE PROVEN YOURSELF TO THE CORPORATIONS, TO WALL STREET, TO THE PRESS--
PARKER INDUSTRIES
"--STILL FIGHTING SHADOWS, STILL PAYING OFF OLD RESENTMENTS, STILL THINKING *'I'LL SHOW YOU'* OF PEOPLE WHO STOPPED THINKING ABOUT YOU ***YEARS*** AGO.
"YOU PROVE YOURSELF TO EVERYONE--
"--EXCEPT YOURSELF."
THOSE ARE ONLY TWO OUT OF AN INFINITE NUMBER OF POSSIBILITIES...ALTERNATE PARKERS...THOUGH I CONFESS I FIND IT INTERESTING THAT IN NEARLY ALL OF THOSE ITERATIONS--
--YOU END UP ALONE.
YEAH? IS THAT SO?
SO IN WHICH OF THOSE ITERATIONS DO I END UP A *LITTLE GIRL?*
OH, THAT? THAT'S ANOTHER STORY. YOU'RE NOT READY TO HEAR THAT ONE YET, AND I'M NOT YET READY TO TELL IT.
SOON, THOUGH.
OKAY, LOOK, I DON'T KNOW WHO YOU ARE OR WHAT GAME YOU'RE PLAYING BUT I OFFICIALLY JUST STOPPED CARING. I'VE GOT IMPORTANT THINGS TO DO AND NOT A LOT OF TIME.
ACTUALLY, TIME IS ALL YOU *HAVE.* AND AS FOR THESE IMPORTANT THINGS--
--YOU'VE ALREADY FAILED. EVERYONE'S TOLD YOU THE SAME THING. YOUR AUNT IS GOING TO DIE AND THERE'S ***NOTHING*** YOU CAN DO ABOUT IT.
But I can.

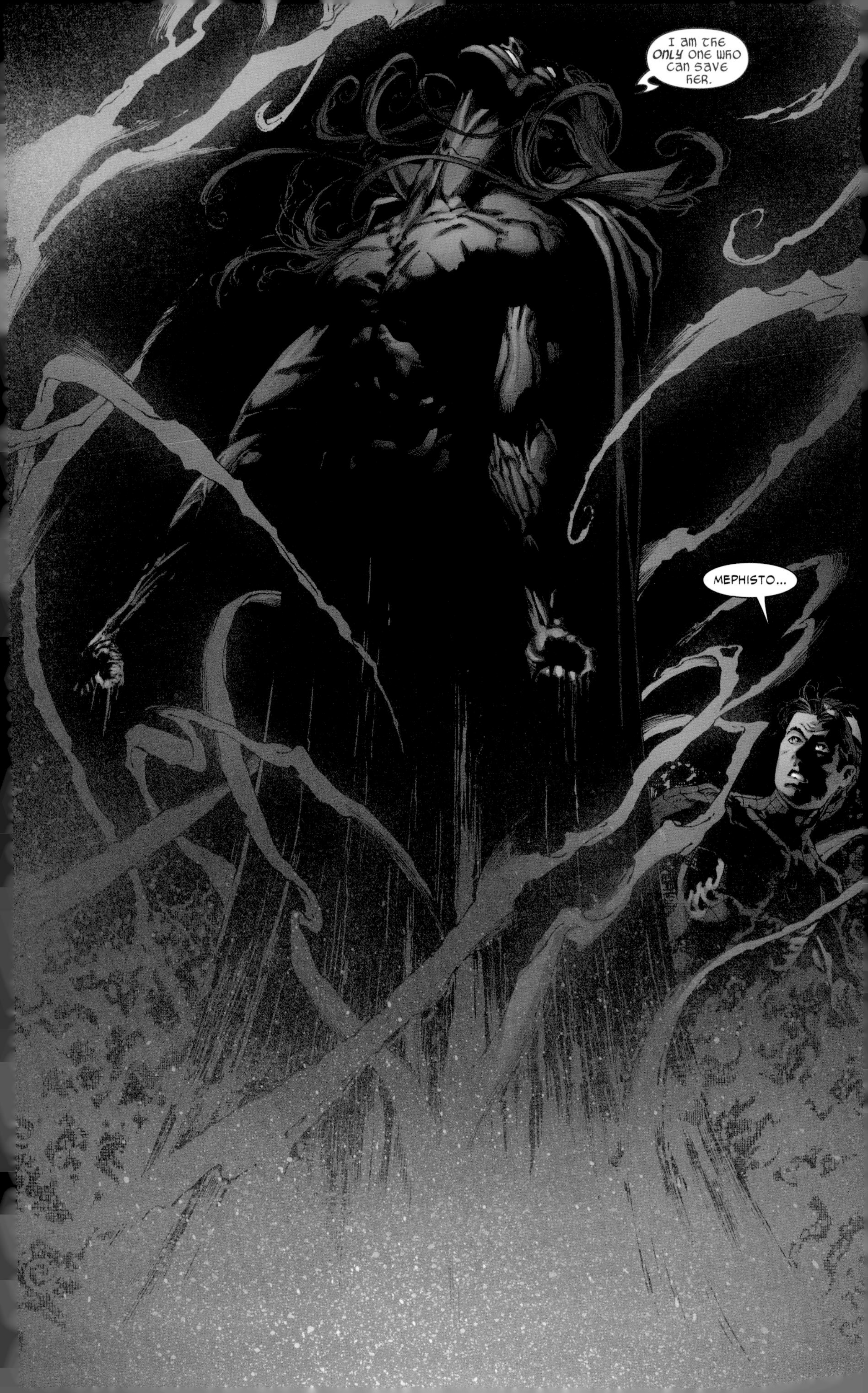
I AM THE ONLY ONE WHO CAN SAVE HER.
MEPHISTO...

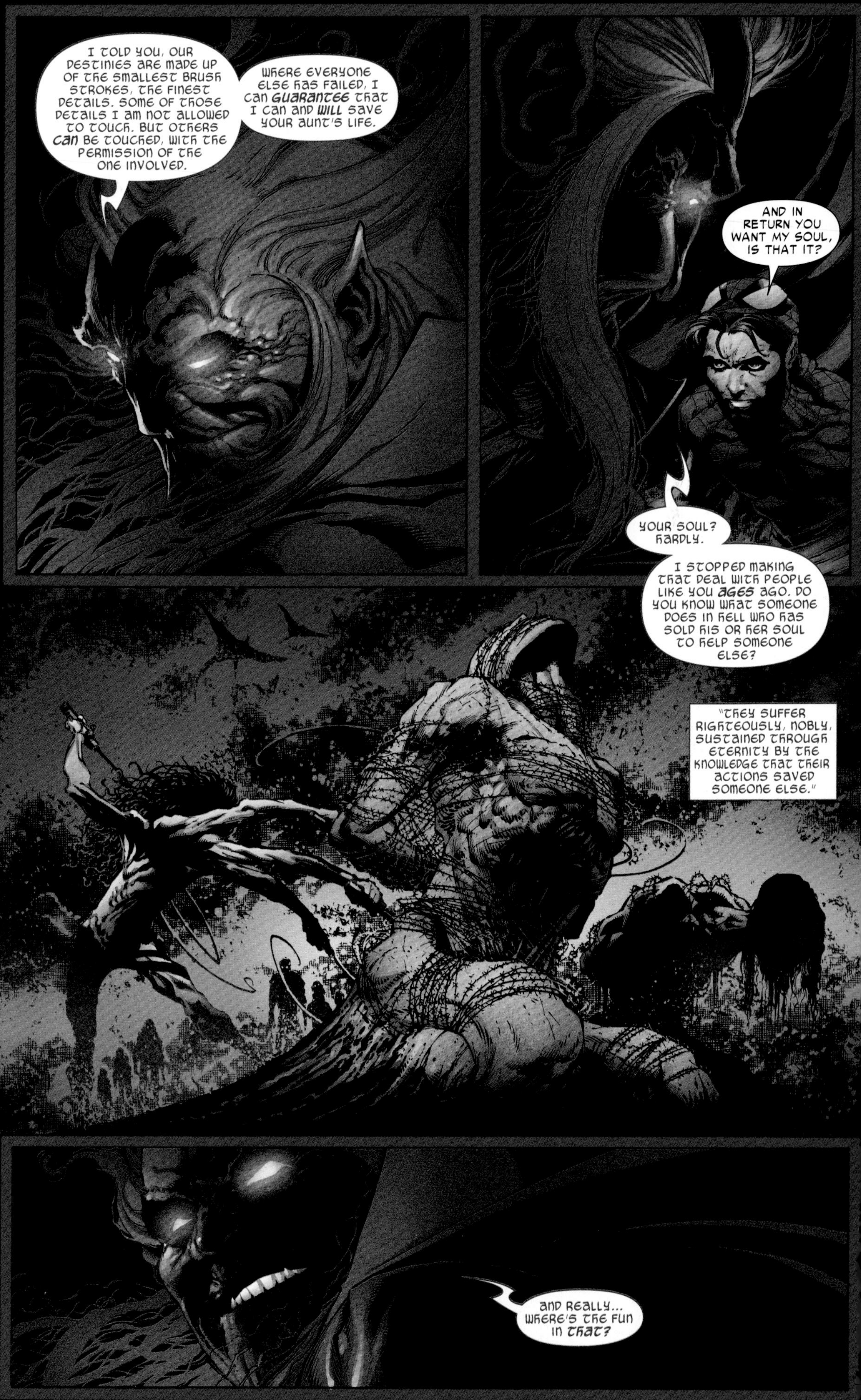
I TOLD YOU, OUR DESTINIES ARE MADE UP OF THE SMALLEST BRUSH STROKES, THE FINEST DETAILS. SOME OF THOSE DETAILS I AM NOT ALLOWED TO TOUCH. BUT OTHERS CAN BE TOUCHED, WITH THE PERMISSION OF THE ONE INVOLVED.
WHERE EVERYONE ELSE HAS FAILED, I CAN GUARANTEE THAT I CAN AND WILL SAVE YOUR AUNT'S LIFE.
AND IN RETURN YOU WANT MY SOUL, IS THAT IT?
YOUR SOUL? HARDLY.
I STOPPED MAKING THAT DEAL WITH PEOPLE LIKE YOU AGES AGO. DO YOU KNOW WHAT SOMEONE DOES IN HELL WHO HAS SOLD HIS OR HER SOUL TO HELP SOMEONE ELSE?
"THEY SUFFER RIGHTEOUSLY, NOBLY, SUSTAINED THROUGH ETERNITY BY THE KNOWLEDGE THAT THEIR ACTIONS SAVED SOMEONE ELSE."
AND REALLY... WHERE'S THE FUN IN THAT?

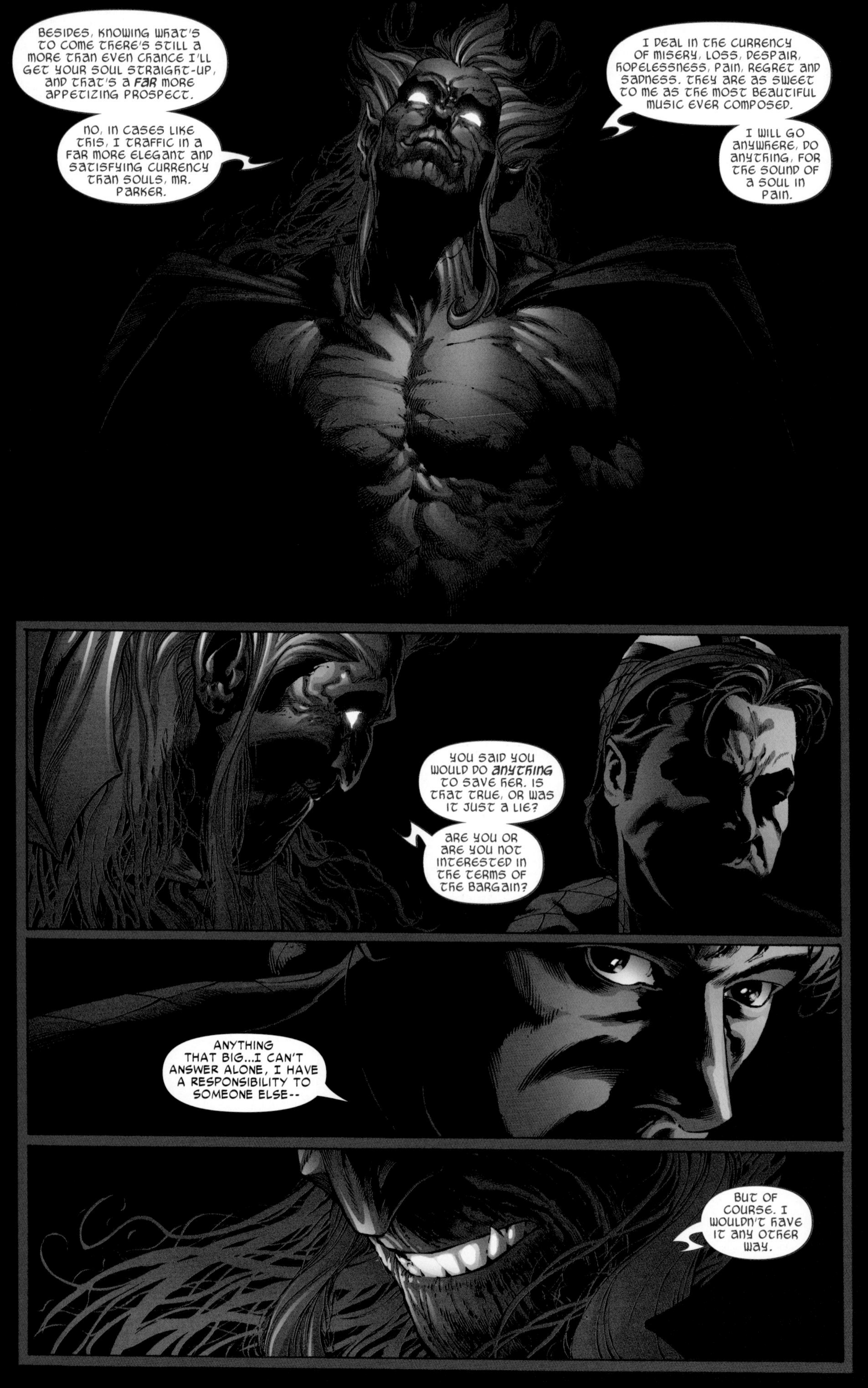
BESIDES, KNOWING WHAT'S TO COME THERE'S STILL A MORE THAN EVEN CHANCE I'LL GET YOUR SOUL STRAIGHT-UP, AND THAT'S A FAR MORE APPETIZING PROSPECT.
NO, IN CASES LIKE THIS, I TRAFFIC IN A FAR MORE ELEGANT AND SATISFYING CURRENCY THAN SOULS, MR. PARKER.
I DEAL IN THE CURRENCY OF MISERY, LOSS, DESPAIR, HOPELESSNESS, PAIN, REGRET AND SADNESS. THEY ARE AS SWEET TO ME AS THE MOST BEAUTIFUL MUSIC EVER COMPOSED.
I WILL GO ANYWHERE, DO ANYTHING, FOR THE SOUND OF A SOUL IN PAIN.
YOU SAID YOU WOULD DO ANYTHING TO SAVE HER. IS THAT TRUE, OR WAS IT JUST A LIE?
ARE YOU OR ARE YOU NOT INTERESTED IN THE TERMS OF THE BARGAIN?
ANYTHING THAT BIG...I CAN'T ANSWER ALONE, I HAVE A RESPONSIBILITY TO SOMEONE ELSE--
BUT OF COURSE. I WOULDN'T HAVE IT ANY OTHER WAY.

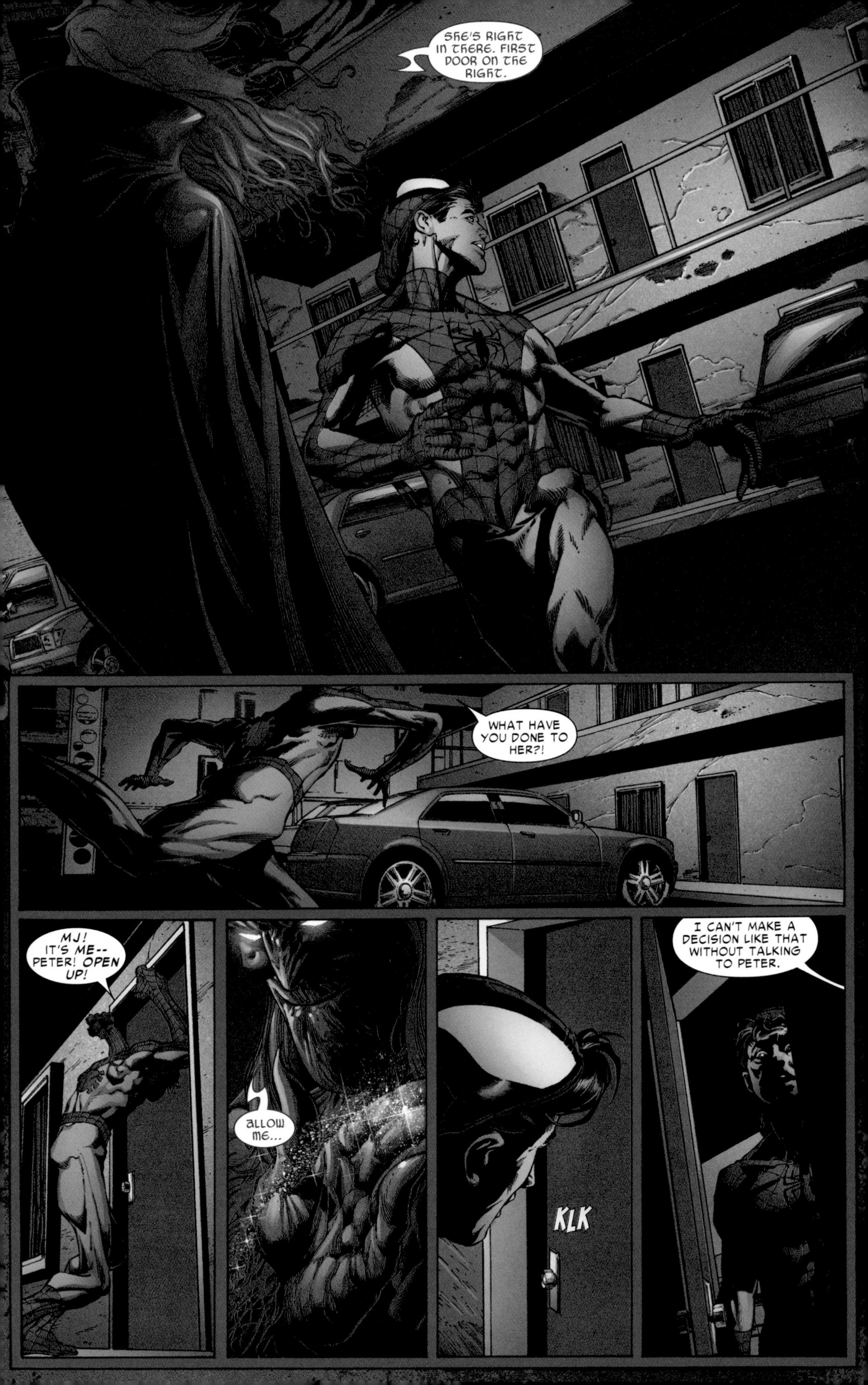
SHE'S RIGHT IN THERE. FIRST DOOR ON THE RIGHT.
WHAT HAVE YOU DONE TO HER?!
MJ! IT'S ME-- PETER! OPEN UP!
ALLOW ME...
KLK
I CAN'T MAKE A DECISION LIKE THAT WITHOUT TALKING TO PETER.

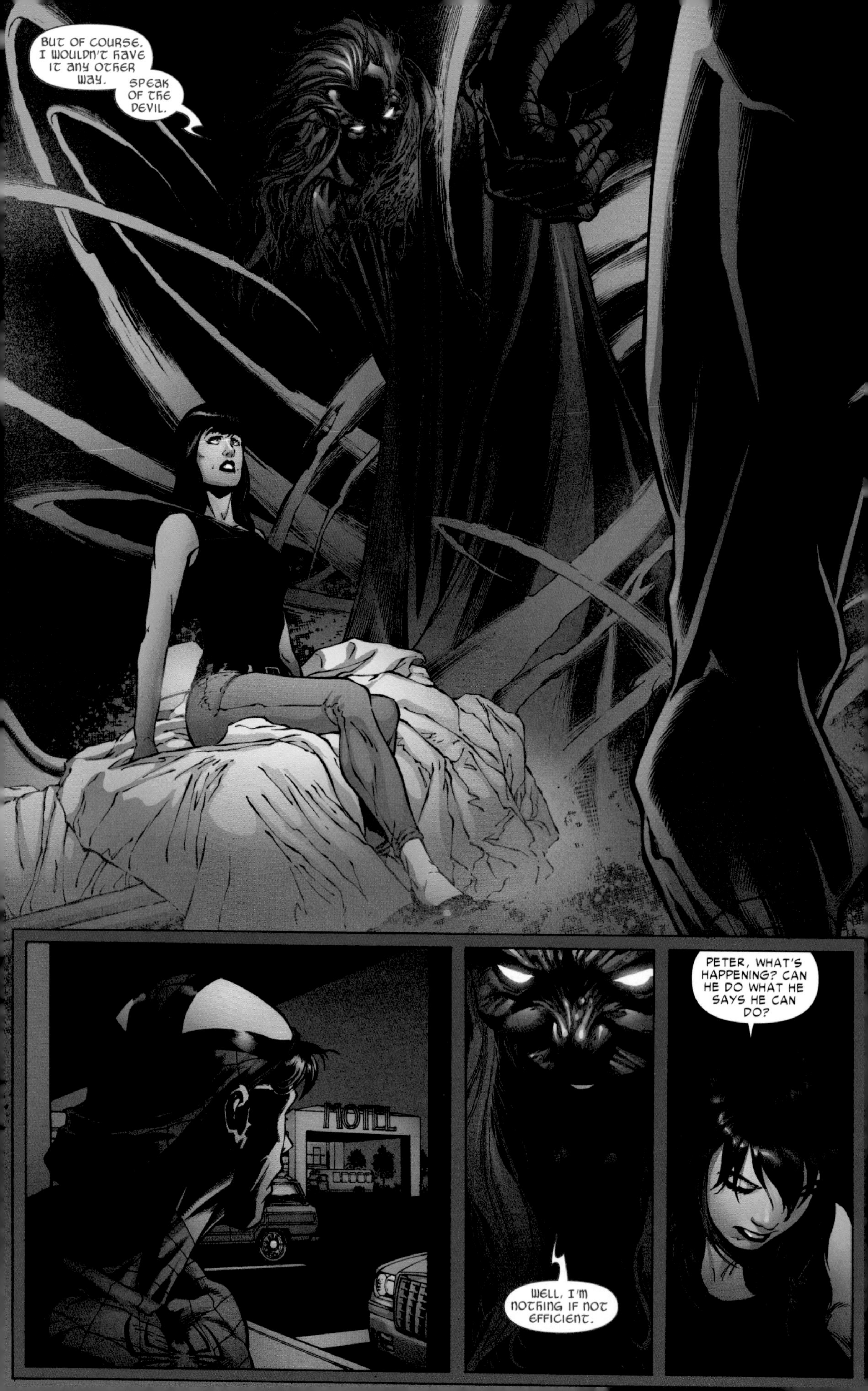
BUT OF COURSE. I WOULDN'T HAVE IT ANY OTHER WAY.
SPEAK OF THE DEVIL.
WELL, I'M NOTHING IF NOT EFFICIENT.
PETER, WHAT'S HAPPENING? CAN HE DO WHAT HE SAYS HE CAN DO?

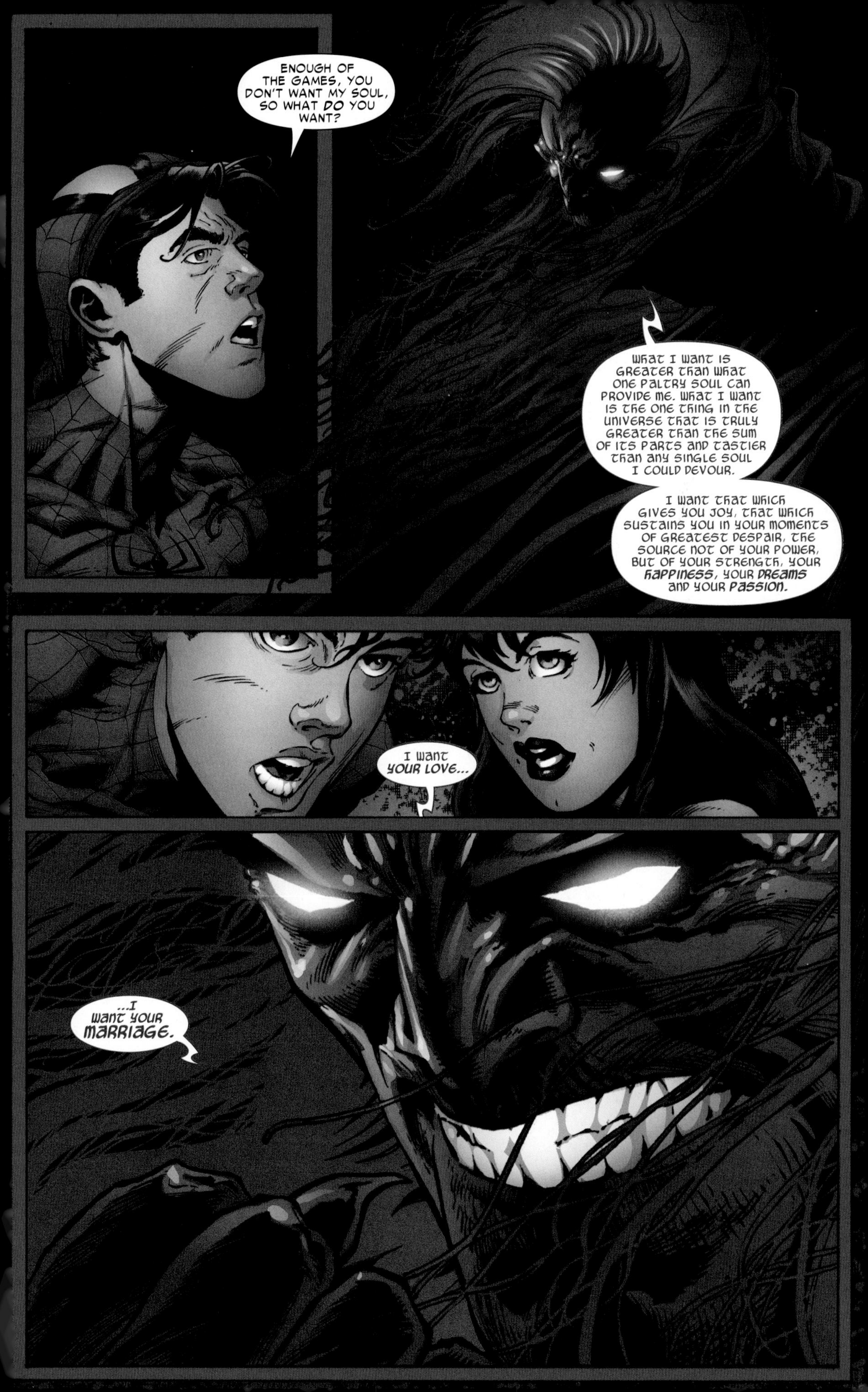
ENOUGH OF THE GAMES, YOU DON'T WANT MY SOUL, SO WHAT DO YOU WANT?
WHAT I WANT IS GREATER THAN WHAT ONE PALTRY SOUL CAN PROVIDE ME. WHAT I WANT IS THE ONE THING IN THE UNIVERSE THAT IS TRULY GREATER THAN THE SUM OF ITS PARTS AND TASTIER THAN ANY SINGLE SOUL I COULD DEVOUR.
I WANT THAT WHICH GIVES YOU JOY, THAT WHICH SUSTAINS YOU IN YOUR MOMENTS OF GREATEST DESPAIR, THE SOURCE NOT OF YOUR POWER, BUT OF YOUR STRENGTH, YOUR HAPPINESS, YOUR DREAMS AND YOUR PASSION.
I WANT YOUR LOVE...
...I WANT YOUR MARRIAGE.

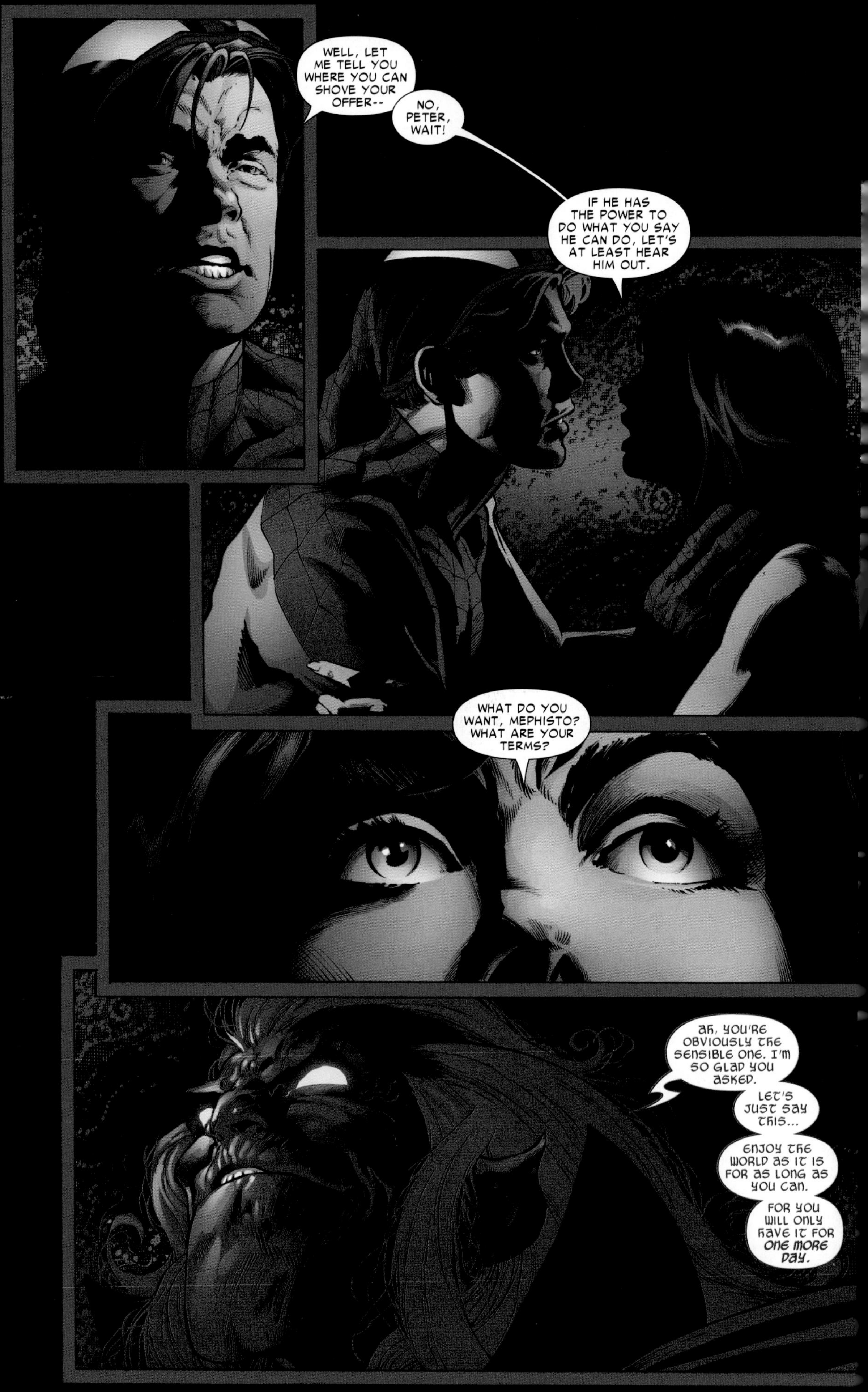
WELL, LET ME TELL YOU WHERE YOU CAN SHOVE YOUR OFFER--
NO, PETER, WAIT!
IF HE HAS THE POWER TO DO WHAT YOU SAY HE CAN DO, LET'S AT LEAST HEAR HIM OUT.
WHAT DO YOU WANT, MEPHISTO? WHAT ARE YOUR TERMS?
AH, YOU'RE OBVIOUSLY THE SENSIBLE ONE. I'M SO GLAD YOU ASKED.
LET'S JUST SAY THIS...
ENJOY THE WORLD AS IT IS FOR AS LONG AS YOU CAN.
FOR YOU WILL ONLY HAVE IT FOR ONE MORE DAY.

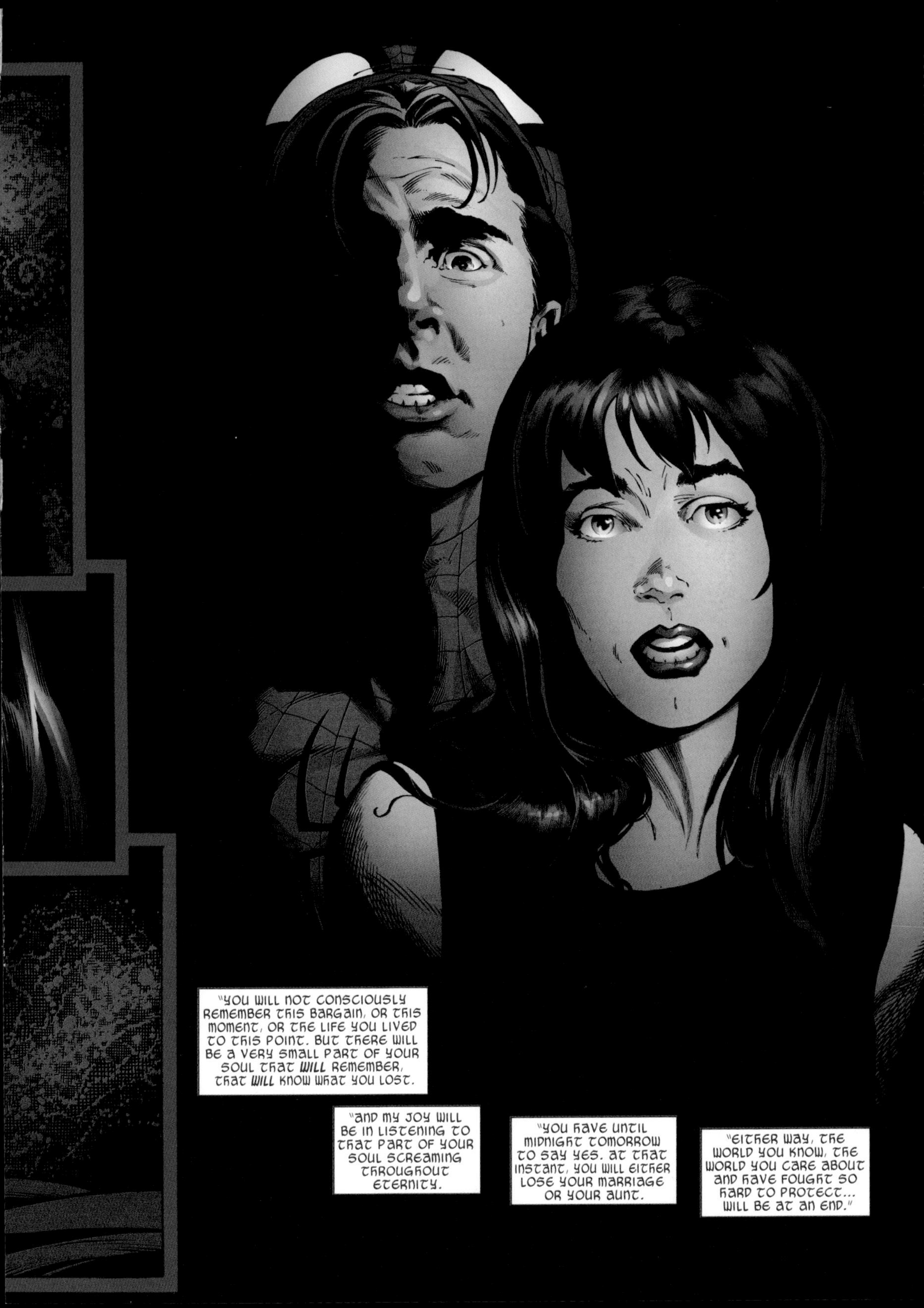
"YOU WILL NOT CONSCIOUSLY REMEMBER THIS BARGAIN, OR THIS MOMENT, OR THE LIFE YOU LIVED TO THIS POINT. BUT THERE WILL BE A VERY SMALL PART OF YOUR SOUL THAT WILL REMEMBER, THAT WILL KNOW WHAT YOU LOST.
"AND MY JOY WILL BE IN LISTENING TO THAT PART OF YOUR SOUL SCREAMING THROUGHOUT ETERNITY.
"YOU HAVE UNTIL MIDNIGHT TOMORROW TO SAY YES. AT THAT INSTANT, YOU WILL EITHER LOSE YOUR MARRIAGE OR YOUR AUNT.
"EITHER WAY, THE WORLD YOU KNOW, THE WORLD YOU CARE ABOUT AND HAVE FOUGHT SO HARD TO PROTECT... WILL BE AT AN END."

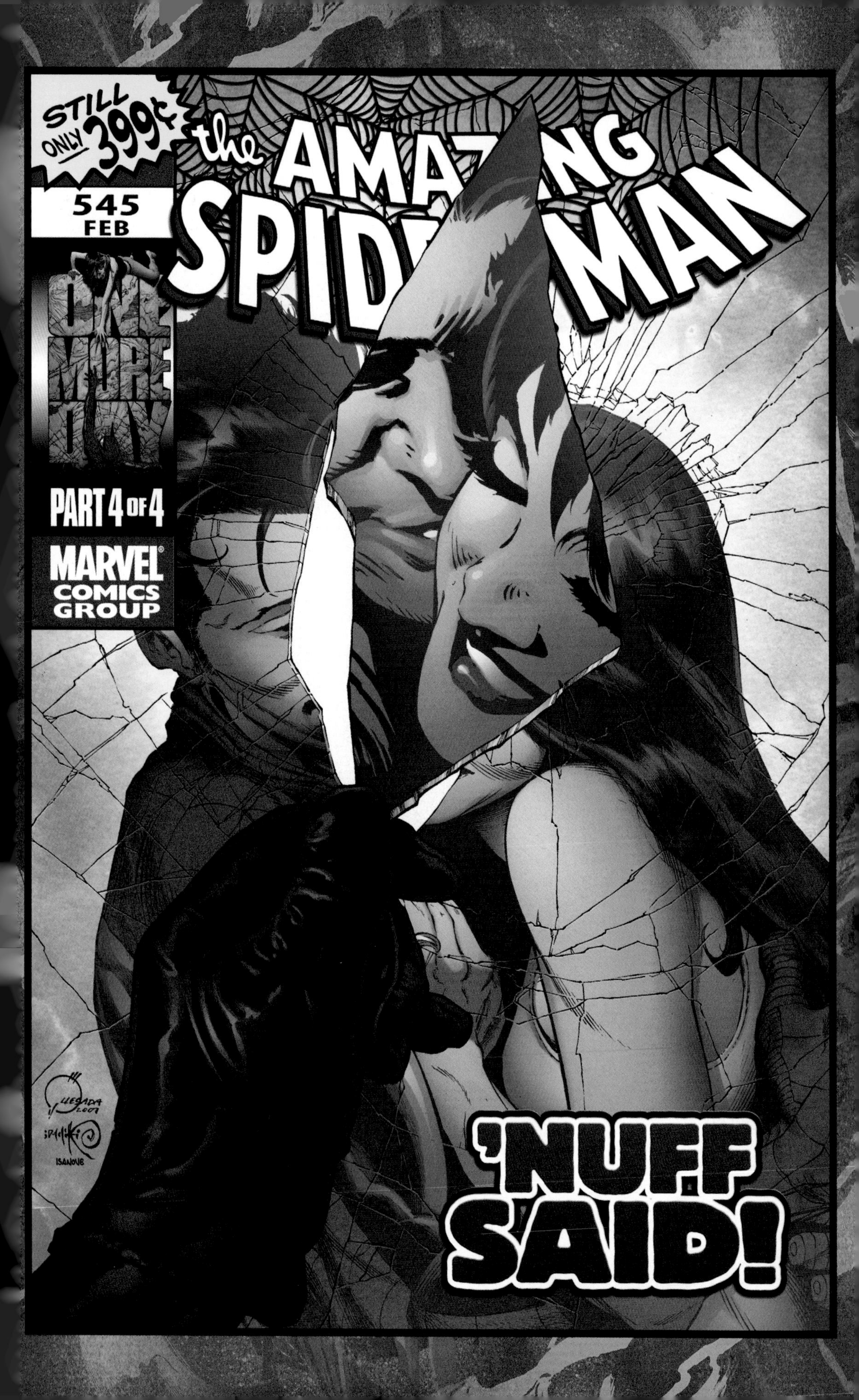
STILL ONLY 399¢
the AMAZING SPIDER-MAN
545
FEB
ONE MORE DAY
PART 4 OF 4
MARVEL COMICS GROUP
'NUFF SAID!

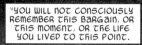

"YOU WILL NOT CONSCIOUSLY REMEMBER THIS BARGAIN, OR THIS MOMENT, OR THE LIFE YOU LIVED TO THIS POINT.
BEEEEEEEEEEEEEEE
"BUT THERE WILL BE A VERY SMALL PART OF YOUR SOUL THAT WILL REMEMBER, THAT WILL KNOW WHAT YOU LOST.
PAPER EMPTY
NOISE COUPLET
14:23
FREEZE
KAMATAKI OSAMU
00
SETTING
PERSONAL DISP
BED DISP
BED-000001
BED-000002
BED-000003
BED-000004
BED-000005
BED-000006
BED-000007
"AND MY JOY WILL BE IN LISTENING TO THAT PART OF YOUR SOUL SCREAMING THROUGHOUT ETERNITY.
"YOU HAVE UNTIL MIDNIGHT TOMORROW TO SAY YES. AT THAT INSTANT, YOU WILL EITHER LOSE YOUR MARRIAGE OR YOUR AUNT.

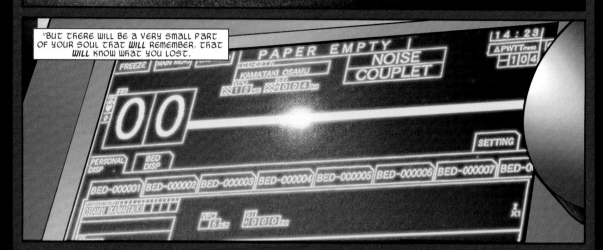

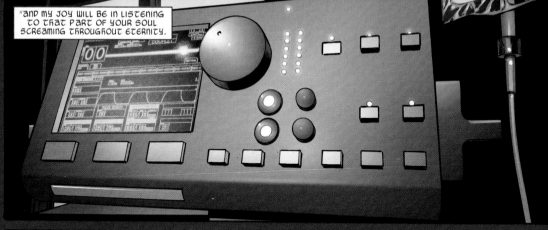

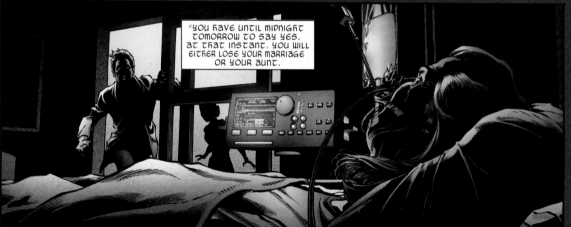

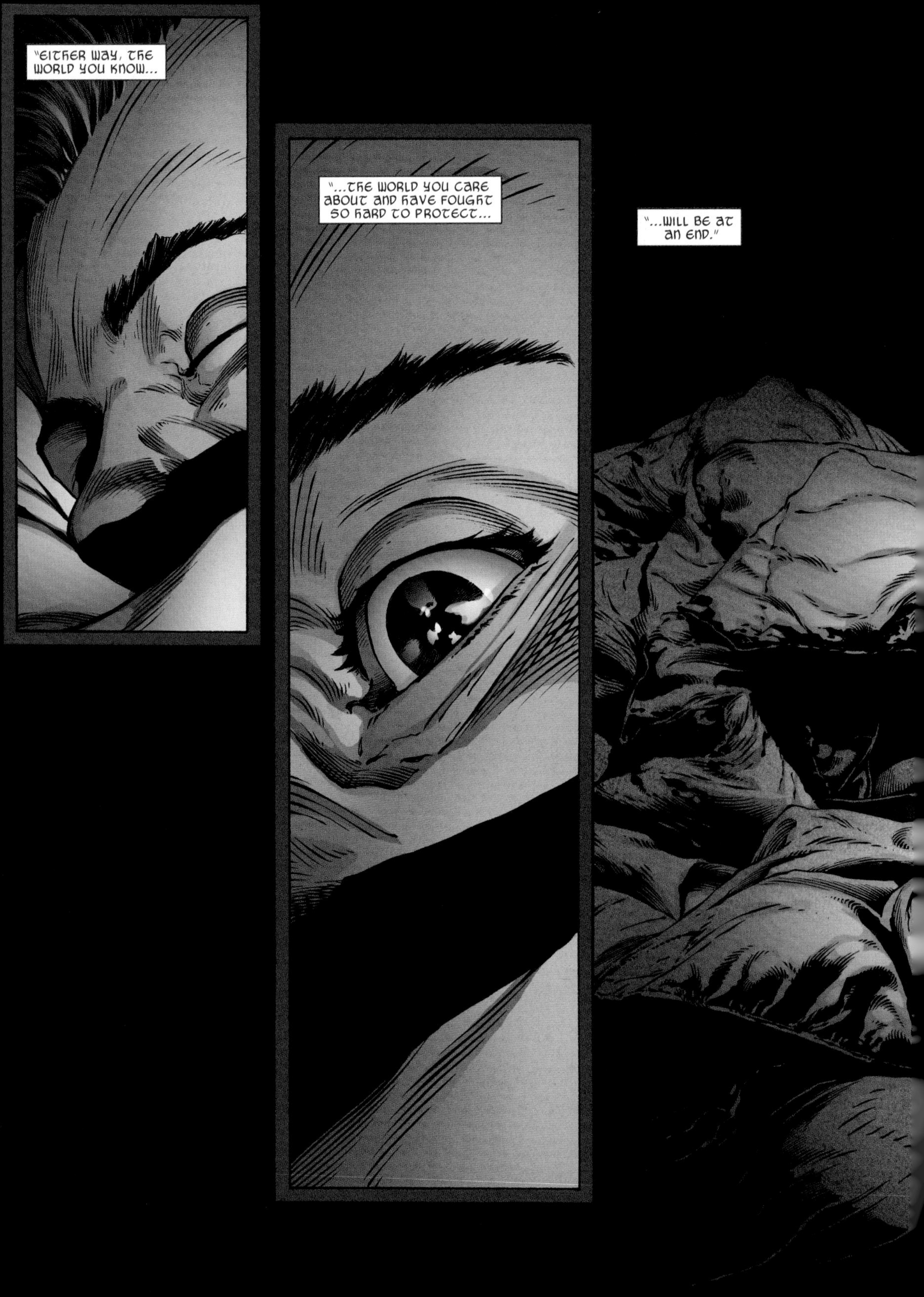
"EITHER WAY, THE WORLD YOU KNOW...
"...THE WORLD YOU CARE ABOUT AND HAVE FOUGHT SO HARD TO PROTECT...
"...WILL BE AT AN END."

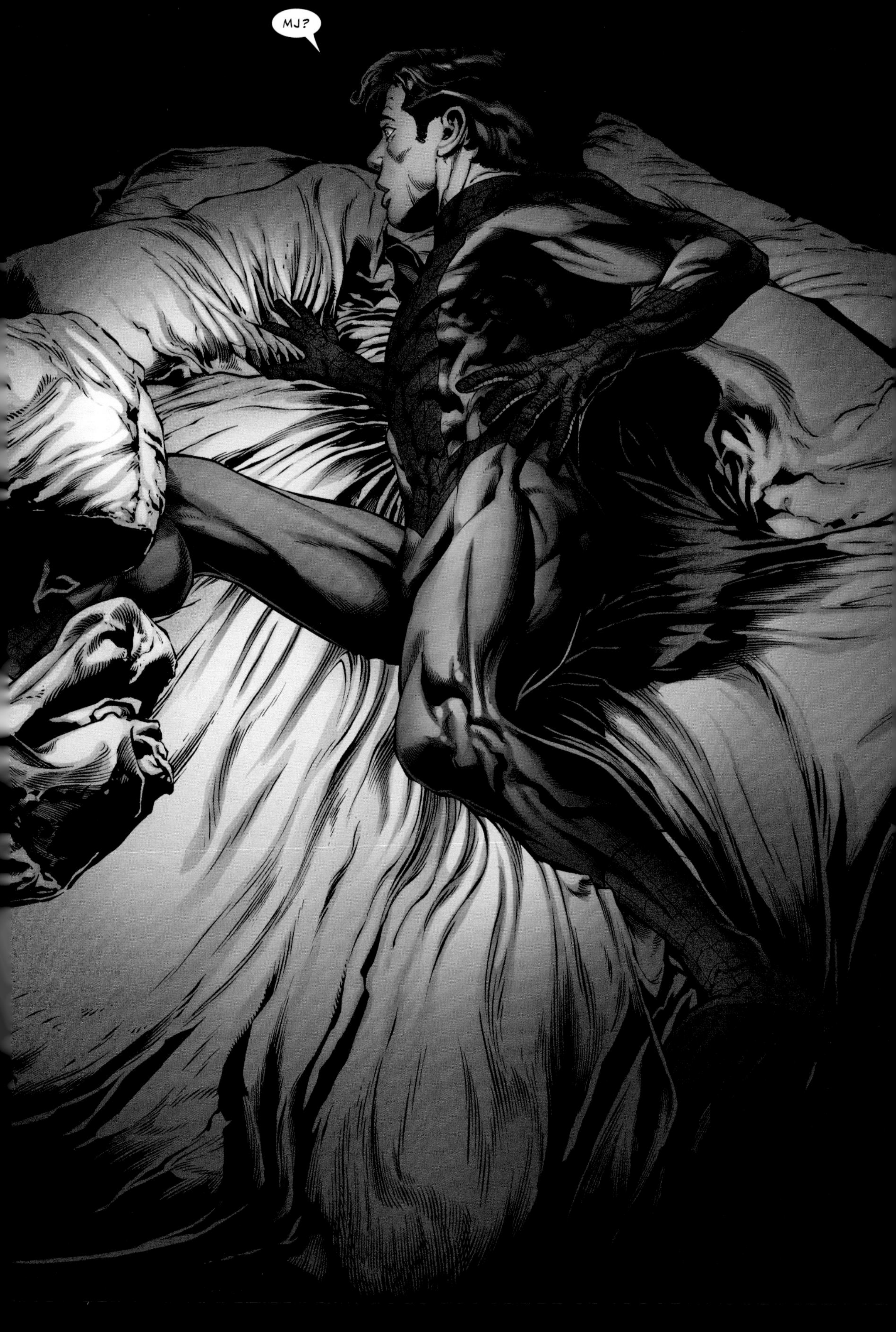
MJ?

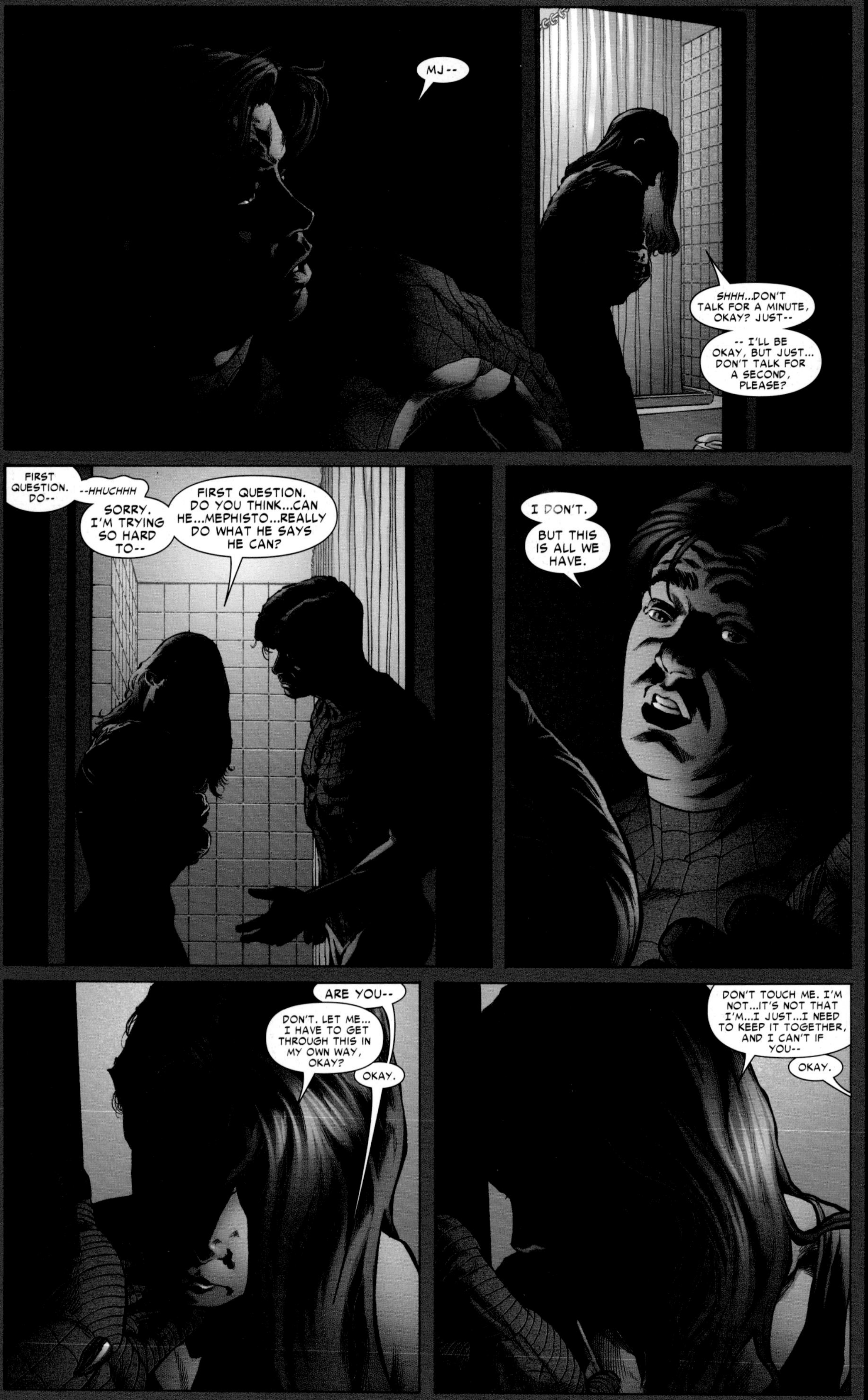
MJ--
SHHH...DON'T TALK FOR A MINUTE, OKAY? JUST--
-- I'LL BE OKAY, BUT JUST... DON'T TALK FOR A SECOND, PLEASE?
FIRST QUESTION. DO--
--HHUCHHH
SORRY. I'M TRYING SO HARD TO--
FIRST QUESTION. DO YOU THINK...CAN HE...MEPHISTO...REALLY DO WHAT HE SAYS HE CAN?
I DON'T.
BUT THIS IS ALL WE HAVE.
ARE YOU--
DON'T. LET ME... I HAVE TO GET THROUGH THIS IN MY OWN WAY, OKAY?
OKAY.
DON'T TOUCH ME. I'M NOT...IT'S NOT THAT I'M...I JUST...I NEED TO KEEP IT TOGETHER, AND I CAN'T IF YOU--
OKAY.

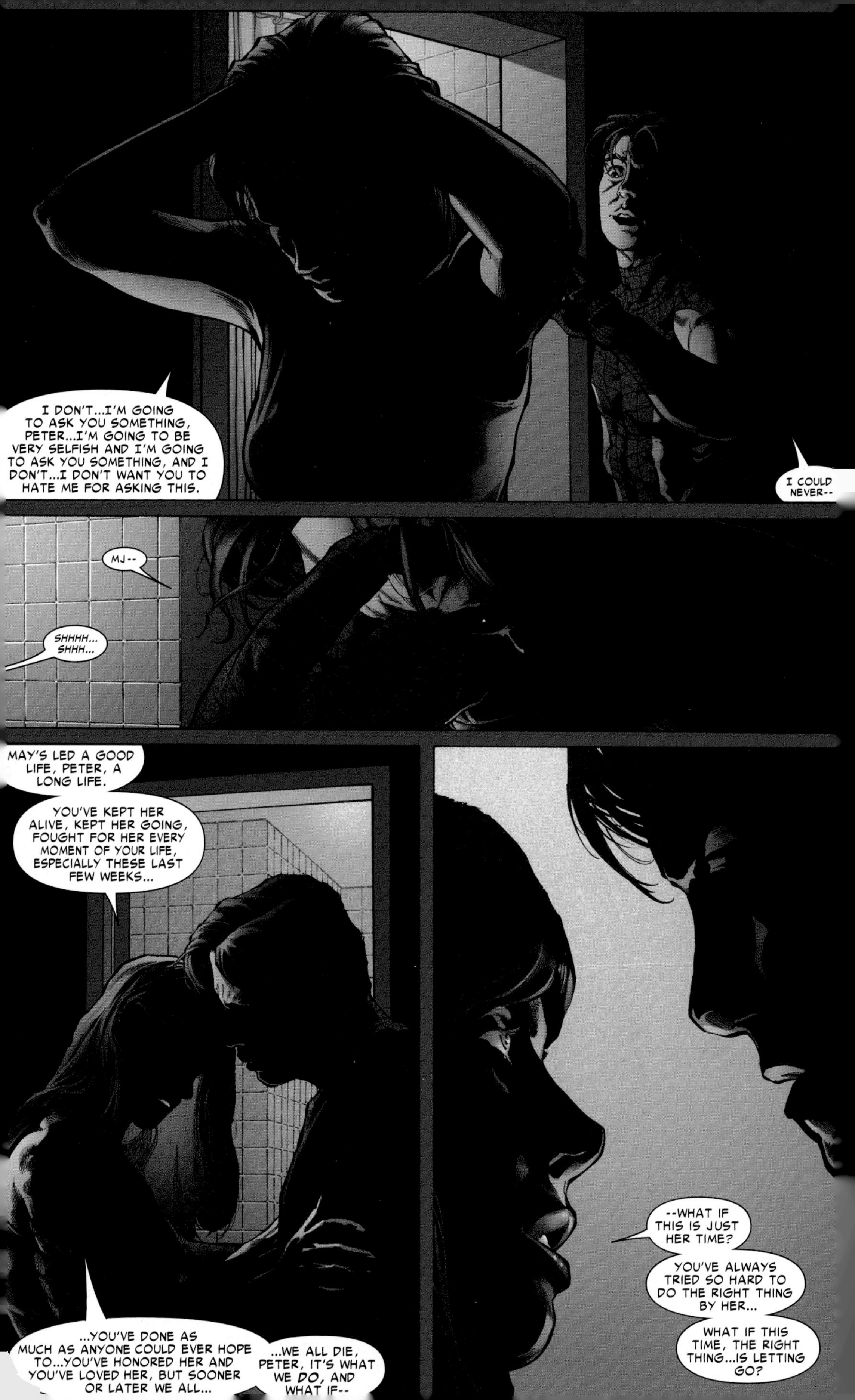
I DON'T...I'M GOING TO ASK YOU SOMETHING, PETER...I'M GOING TO BE VERY SELFISH AND I'M GOING TO ASK YOU SOMETHING, AND I DON'T...I DON'T WANT YOU TO HATE ME FOR ASKING THIS.
I COULD NEVER--
MJ--
SHHHH... SHHH...
MAY'S LED A GOOD LIFE, PETER, A LONG LIFE.
YOU'VE KEPT HER ALIVE, KEPT HER GOING, FOUGHT FOR HER EVERY MOMENT OF YOUR LIFE, ESPECIALLY THESE LAST FEW WEEKS...
...YOU'VE DONE AS MUCH AS ANYONE COULD EVER HOPE TO...YOU'VE HONORED HER AND YOU'VE LOVED HER, BUT SOONER OR LATER WE ALL...
...WE ALL DIE, PETER, IT'S WHAT WE DO, AND WHAT IF--
--WHAT IF THIS IS JUST HER TIME?
YOU'VE ALWAYS TRIED SO HARD TO DO THE RIGHT THING BY HER...
WHAT IF THIS TIME, THE RIGHT THING...IS LETTING GO?

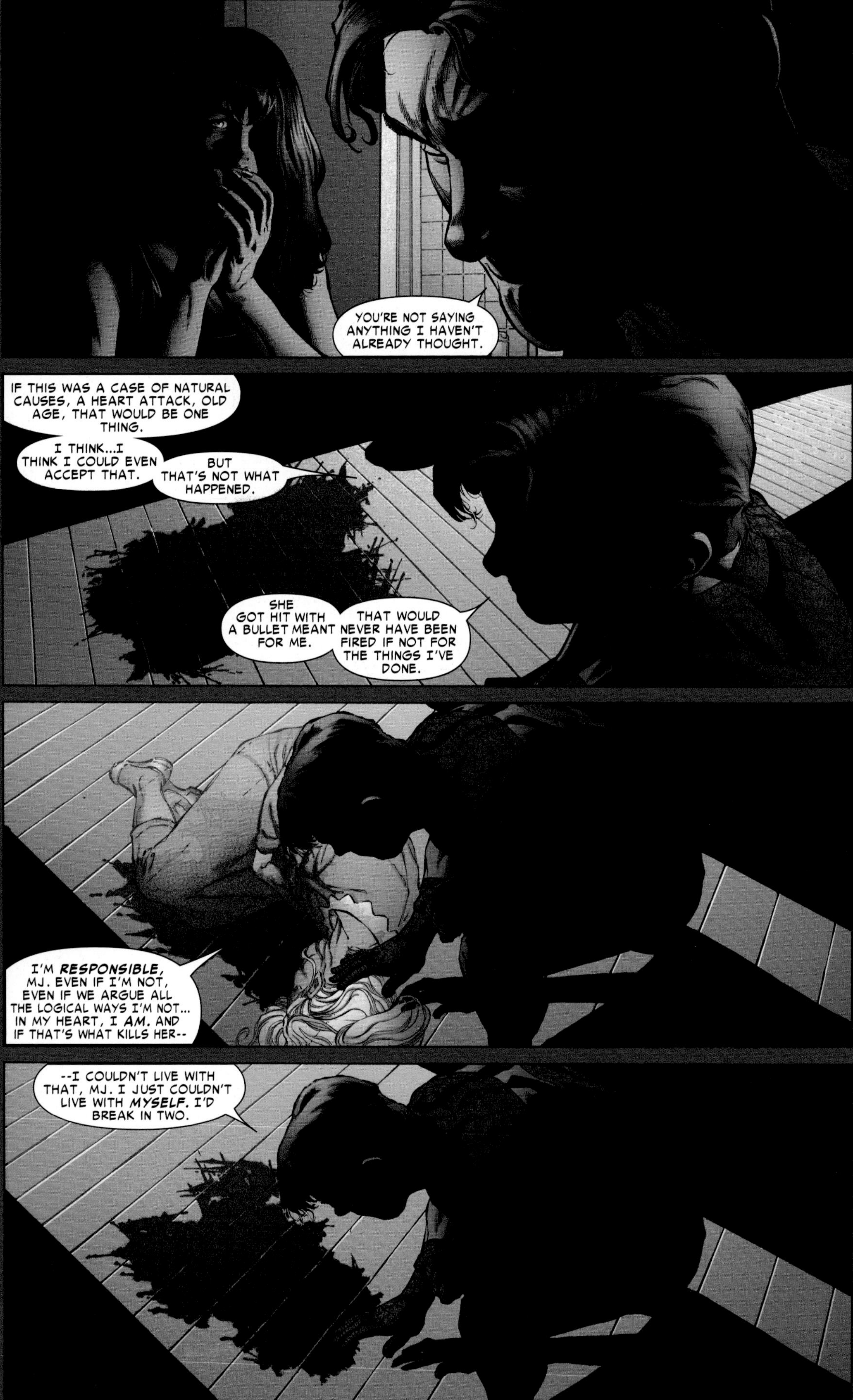
YOU'RE NOT SAYING ANYTHING I HAVEN'T ALREADY THOUGHT.
IF THIS WAS A CASE OF NATURAL CAUSES, A HEART ATTACK, OLD AGE, THAT WOULD BE ONE THING.
I THINK...I THINK I COULD EVEN ACCEPT THAT.
BUT THAT'S NOT WHAT HAPPENED.
SHE GOT HIT WITH A BULLET MEANT FOR ME.
THAT WOULD NEVER HAVE BEEN FIRED IF NOT FOR THE THINGS I'VE DONE.
I'M ***RESPONSIBLE,*** MJ. EVEN IF I'M NOT, EVEN IF WE ARGUE ALL THE LOGICAL WAYS I'M NOT... IN MY HEART, I ***AM.*** AND IF THAT'S WHAT KILLS HER--
--I COULDN'T LIVE WITH THAT, MJ. I JUST COULDN'T LIVE WITH ***MYSELF.*** I'D BREAK IN TWO.

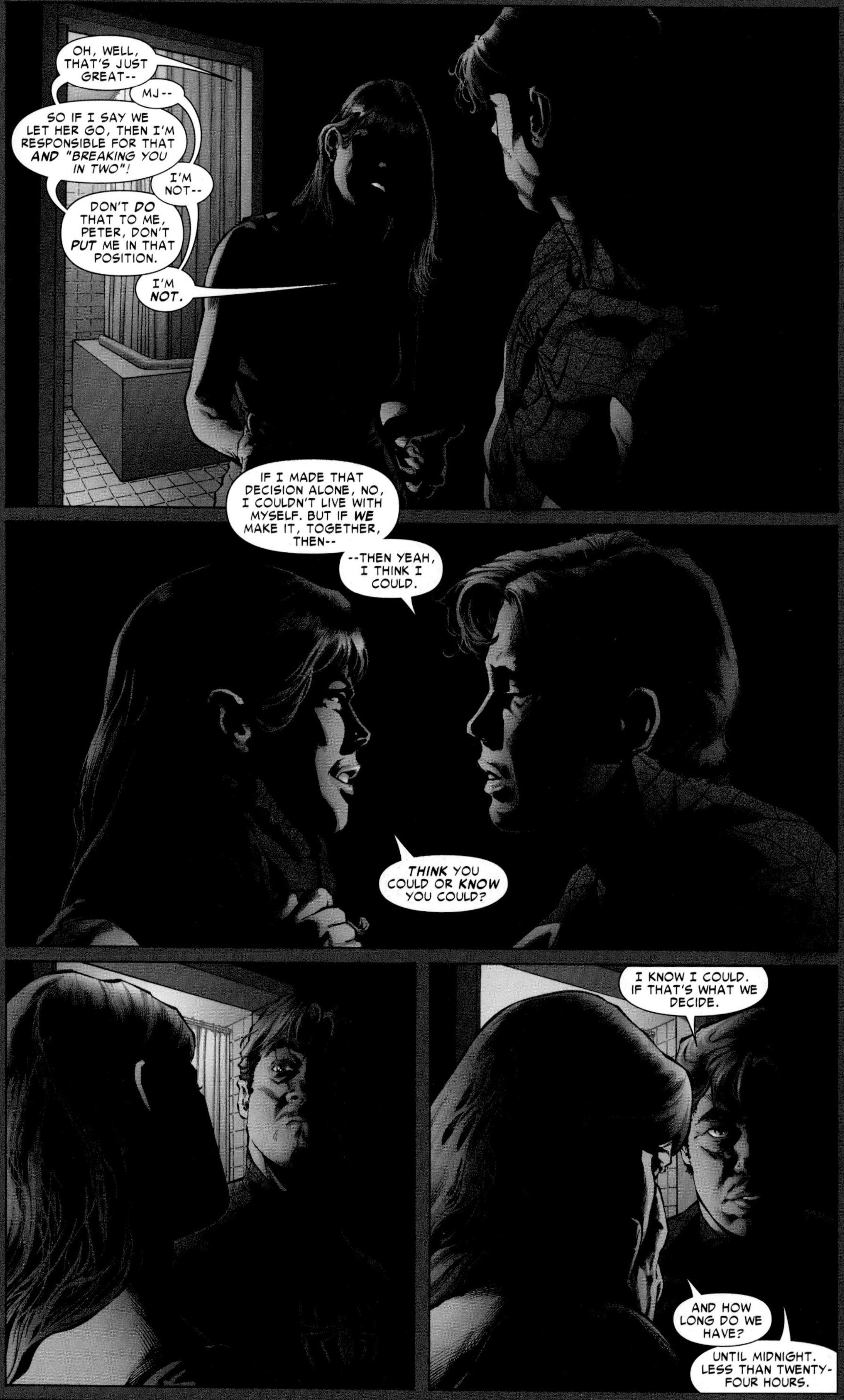
OH, WELL, THAT'S JUST GREAT--
MJ--
SO IF I SAY WE LET HER GO, THEN I'M RESPONSIBLE FOR THAT AND "BREAKING YOU IN TWO"!
I'M NOT--
DON'T DO THAT TO ME, PETER, DON'T PUT ME IN THAT POSITION.
I'M NOT.
IF I MADE THAT DECISION ALONE, NO, I COULDN'T LIVE WITH MYSELF. BUT IF WE MAKE IT, TOGETHER, THEN--
--THEN YEAH, I THINK I COULD.
THINK YOU COULD OR KNOW YOU COULD?
I KNOW I COULD. IF THAT'S WHAT WE DECIDE.
AND HOW LONG DO WE HAVE?
UNTIL MIDNIGHT. LESS THAN TWENTY-FOUR HOURS.

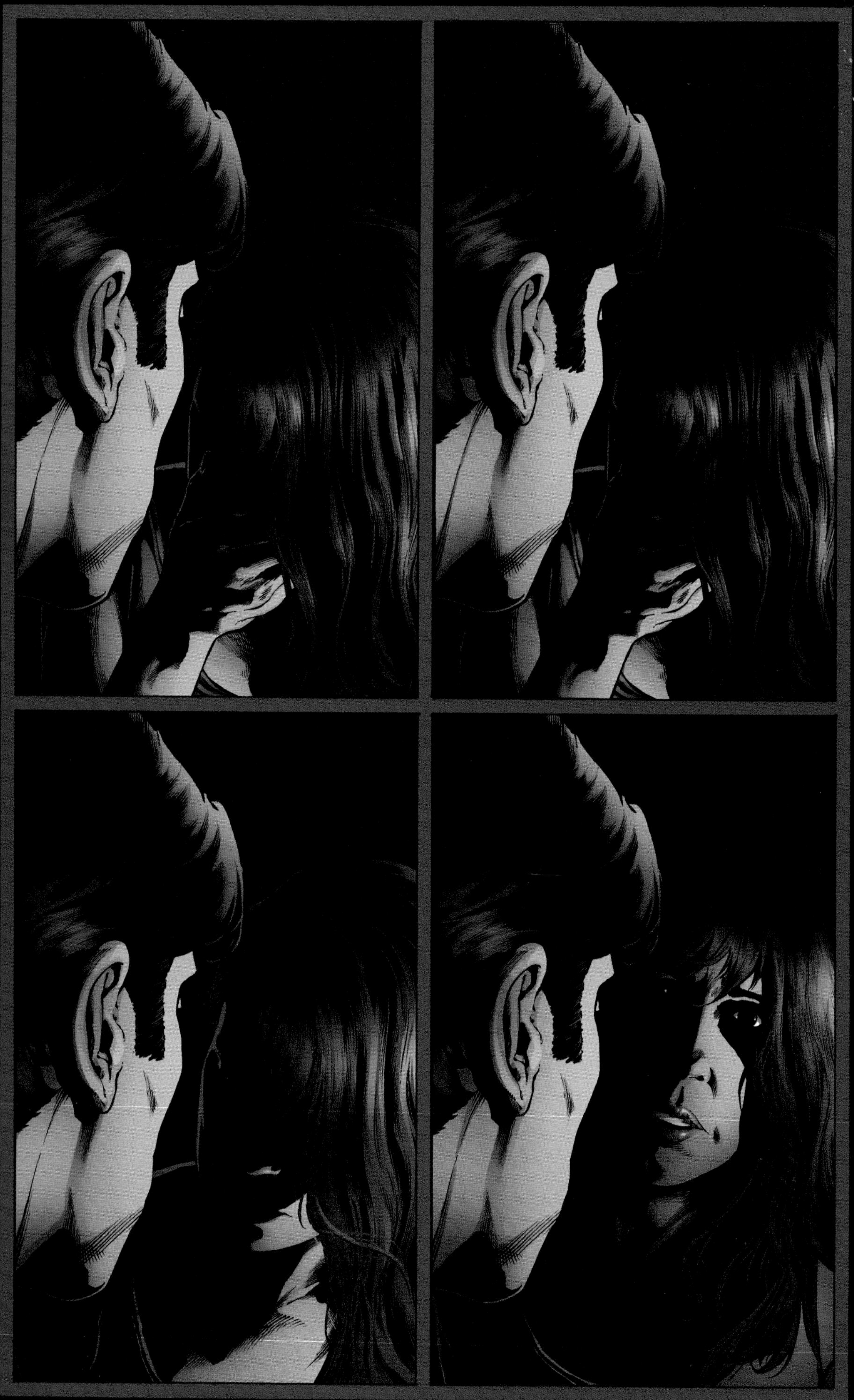

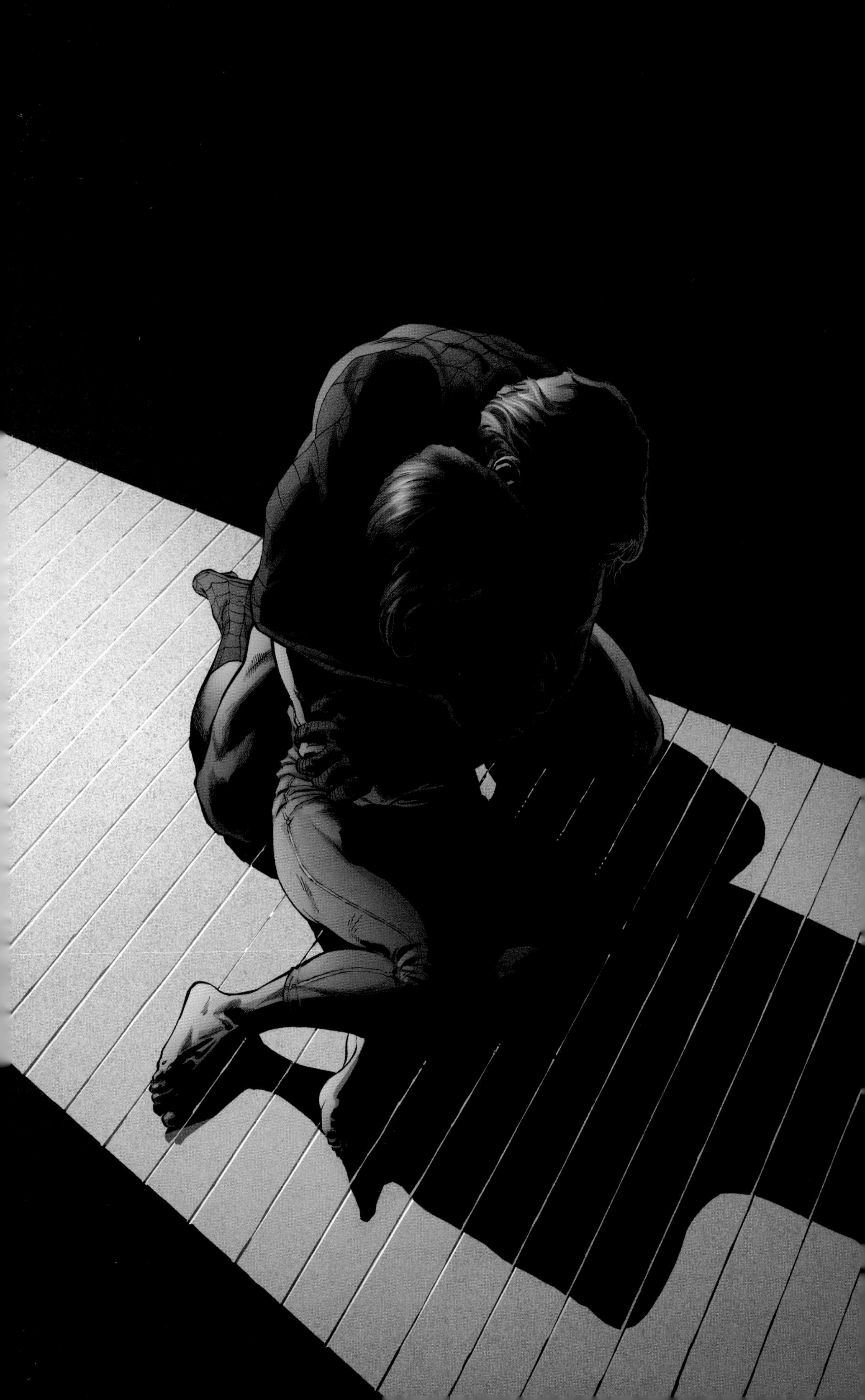

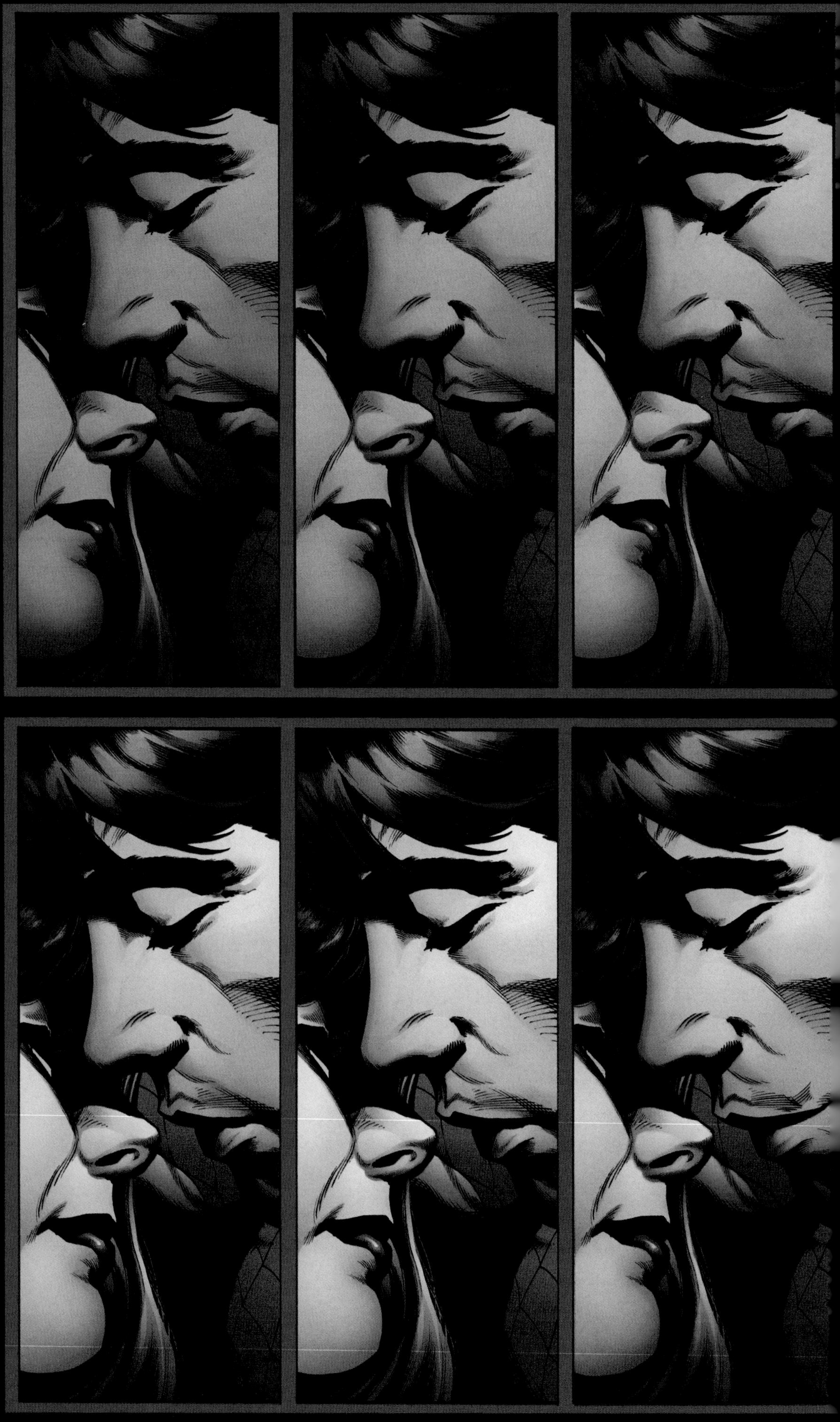

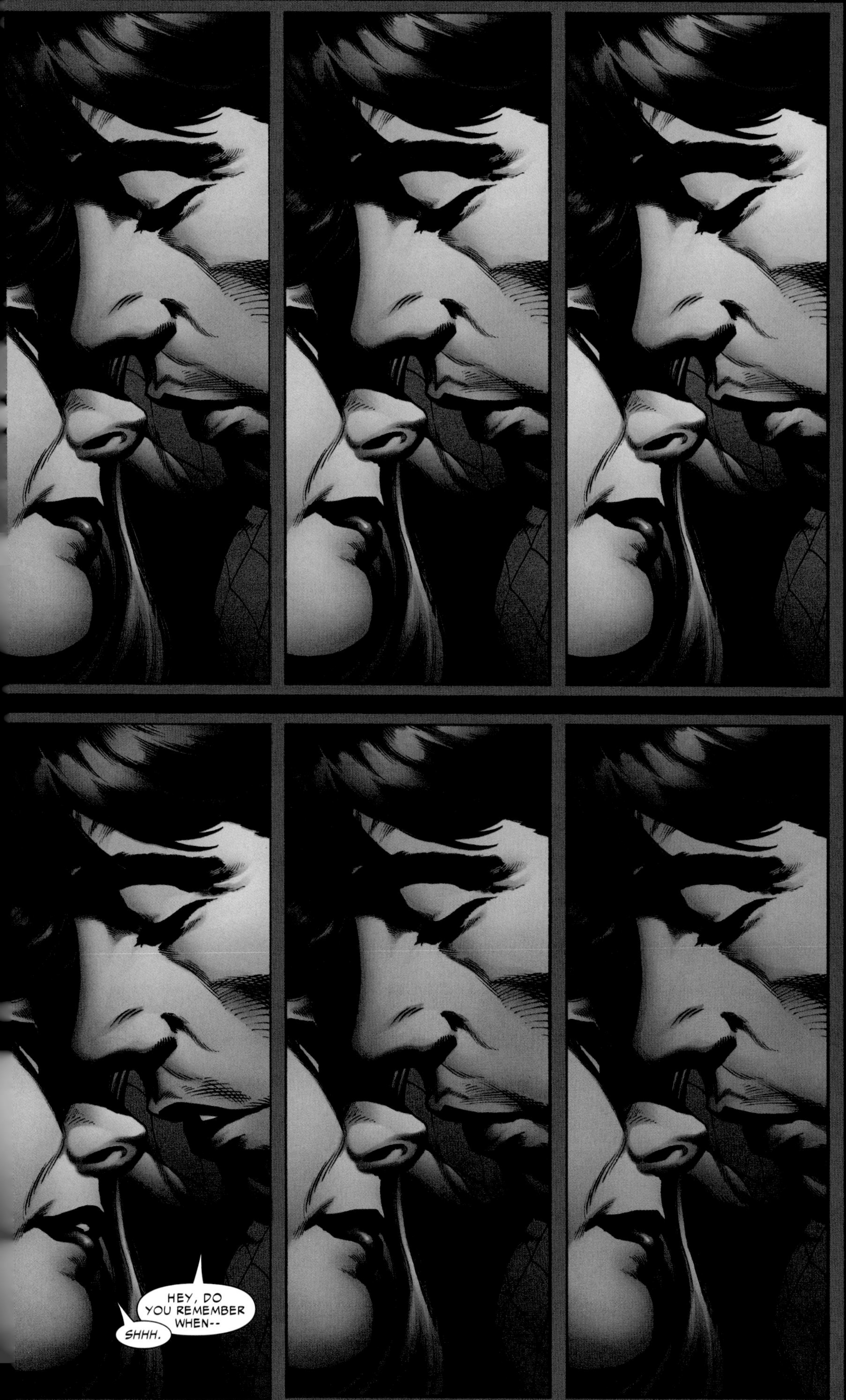
HEY, DO YOU REMEMBER WHEN--
SHHH.

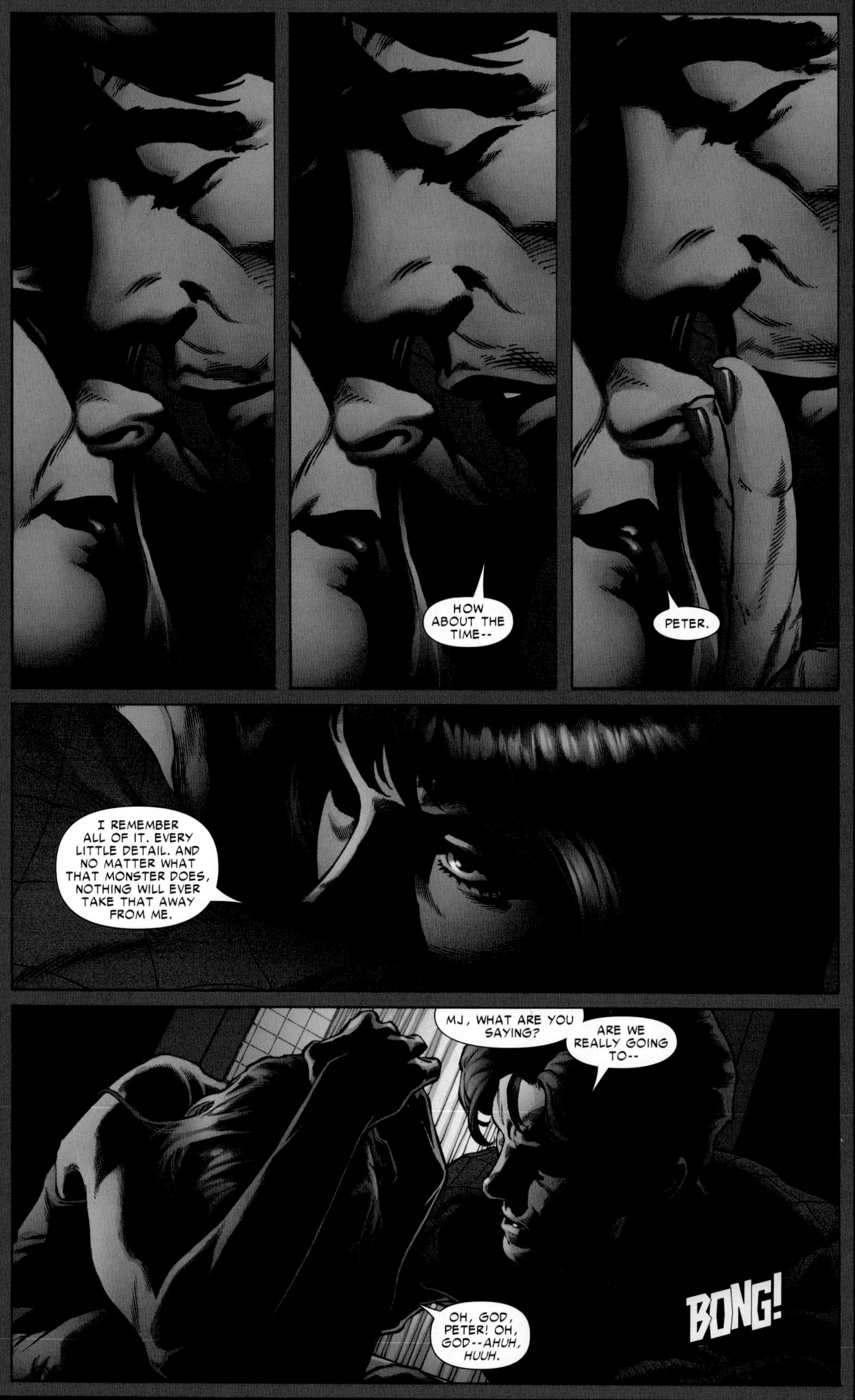
HOW ABOUT THE TIME--
PETER.
I REMEMBER ALL OF IT. EVERY LITTLE DETAIL. AND NO MATTER WHAT THAT MONSTER DOES, NOTHING WILL EVER TAKE THAT AWAY FROM ME.
MJ, WHAT ARE YOU SAYING?
ARE WE REALLY GOING TO--
OH, GOD, PETER! OH, GOD--AHUH, HUUH.
BONG!

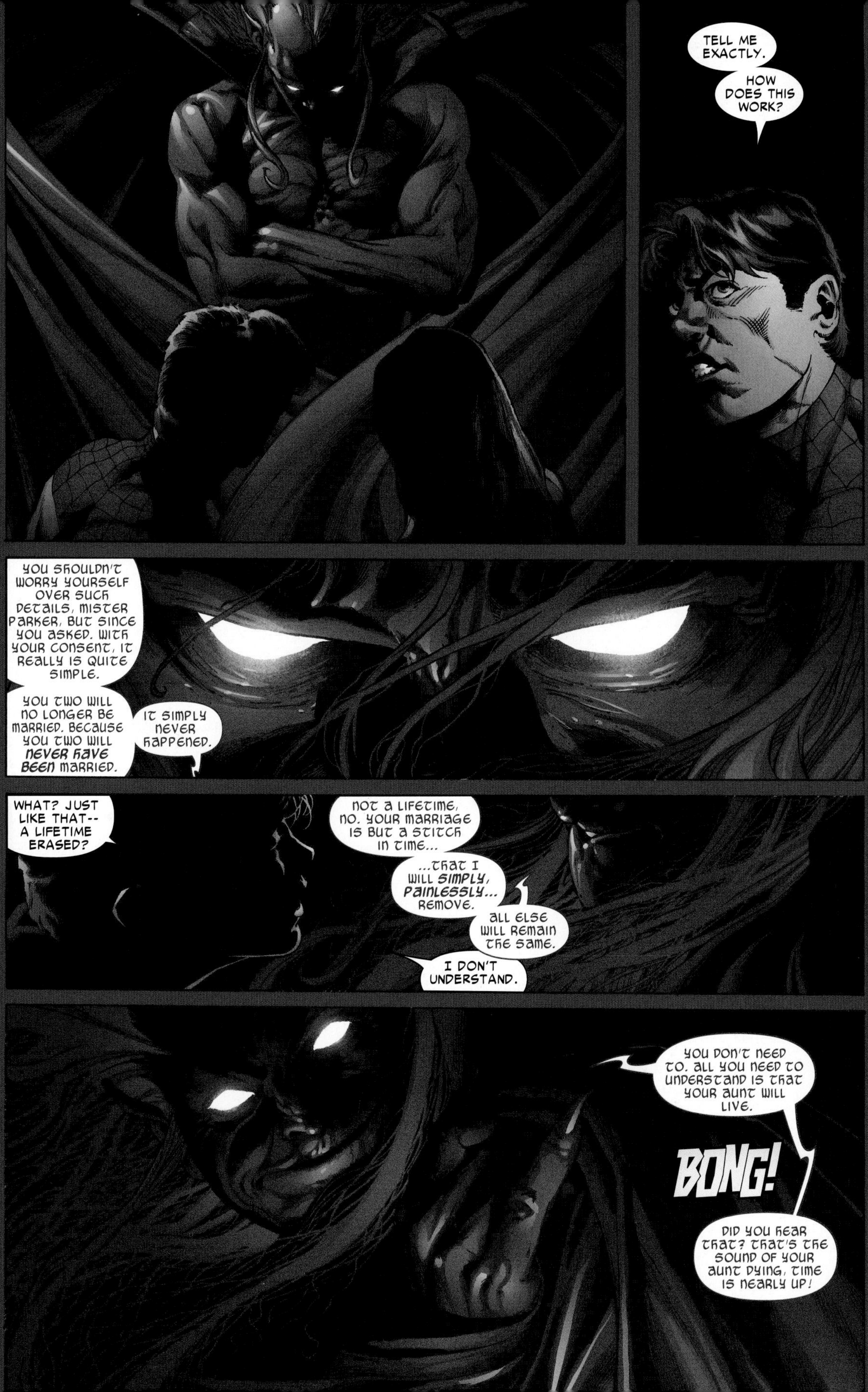
TELL ME EXACTLY.
HOW DOES THIS WORK?
YOU SHOULDN'T WORRY YOURSELF OVER SUCH DETAILS, MISTER PARKER, BUT SINCE YOU ASKED. WITH YOUR CONSENT, IT REALLY IS QUITE SIMPLE.
YOU TWO WILL NO LONGER BE MARRIED. BECAUSE YOU TWO WILL *NEVER HAVE BEEN* MARRIED.
IT SIMPLY NEVER HAPPENED.
WHAT? JUST LIKE THAT-- A LIFETIME ERASED?
NOT A LIFETIME, NO. YOUR MARRIAGE IS BUT A STITCH IN TIME...
...THAT I WILL *SIMPLY, PAINLESSLY...* REMOVE.
ALL ELSE WILL REMAIN THE SAME.
I DON'T UNDERSTAND.
YOU DON'T NEED TO. ALL YOU NEED TO UNDERSTAND IS THAT YOUR AUNT WILL LIVE.
BONG!
DID YOU HEAR THAT? THAT'S THE SOUND OF YOUR AUNT DYING. TIME IS NEARLY UP!

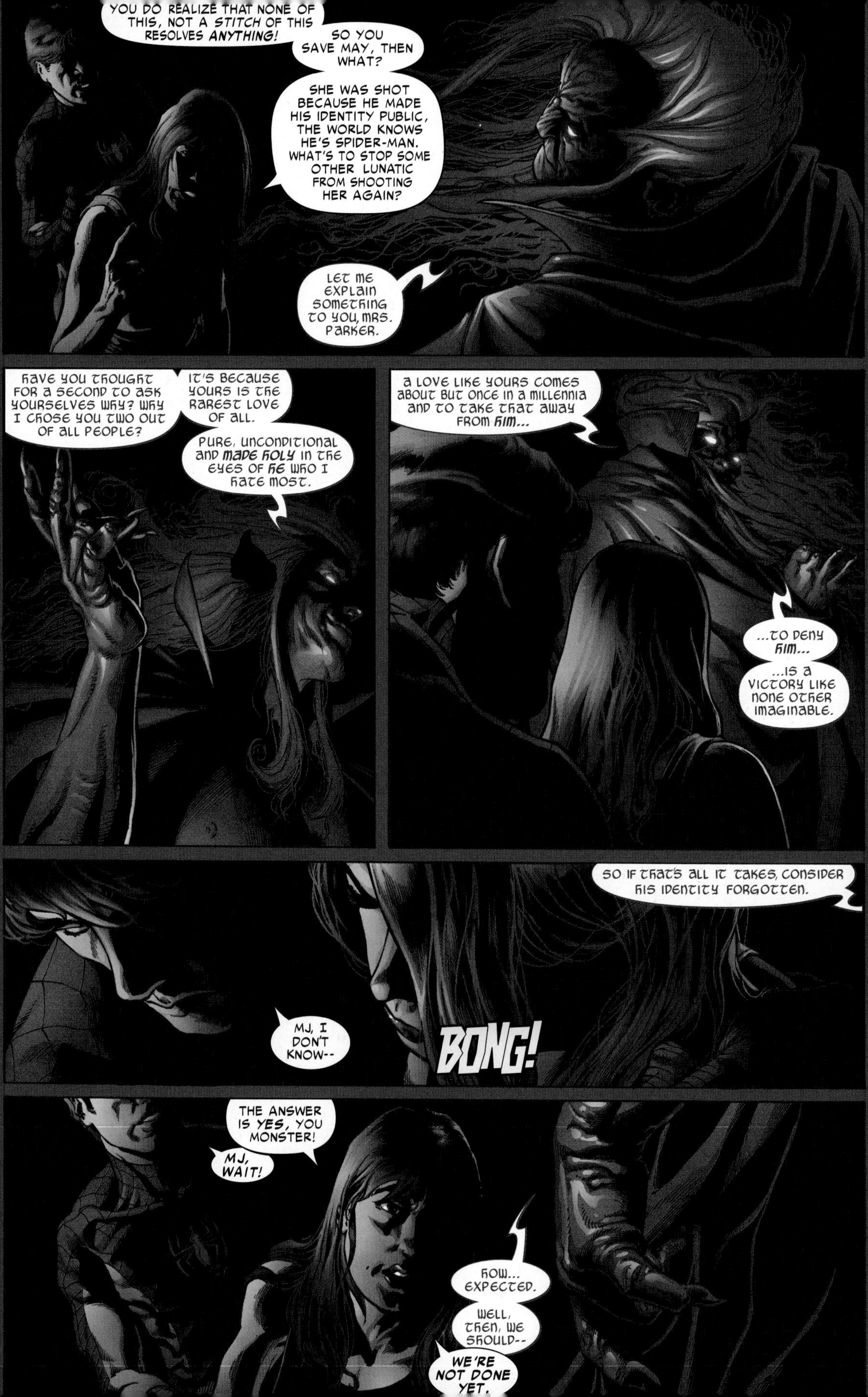
YOU DO REALIZE THAT NONE OF THIS, NOT A STITCH OF THIS RESOLVES ANYTHING!
SO YOU SAVE MAY, THEN WHAT?
SHE WAS SHOT BECAUSE HE MADE HIS IDENTITY PUBLIC, THE WORLD KNOWS HE'S SPIDER-MAN. WHAT'S TO STOP SOME OTHER LUNATIC FROM SHOOTING HER AGAIN?
LET ME EXPLAIN SOMETHING TO YOU, MRS. PARKER.
HAVE YOU THOUGHT FOR A SECOND TO ASK YOURSELVES WHY? WHY I CHOSE YOU TWO OUT OF ALL PEOPLE?
IT'S BECAUSE YOURS IS THE RAREST LOVE OF ALL.
PURE, UNCONDITIONAL AND MADE HOLY IN THE EYES OF HE WHO I HATE MOST.
A LOVE LIKE YOURS COMES ABOUT BUT ONCE IN A MILLENNIA AND TO TAKE THAT AWAY FROM HIM...
...TO DENY HIM...
...IS A VICTORY LIKE NONE OTHER IMAGINABLE.
SO IF THAT'S ALL IT TAKES, CONSIDER HIS IDENTITY FORGOTTEN.
MJ, I DON'T KNOW--
BONG!
THE ANSWER IS YES, YOU MONSTER!
MJ, WAIT!
HOW... EXPECTED.
WELL, THEN, WE SHOULD--
WE'RE NOT DONE YET.

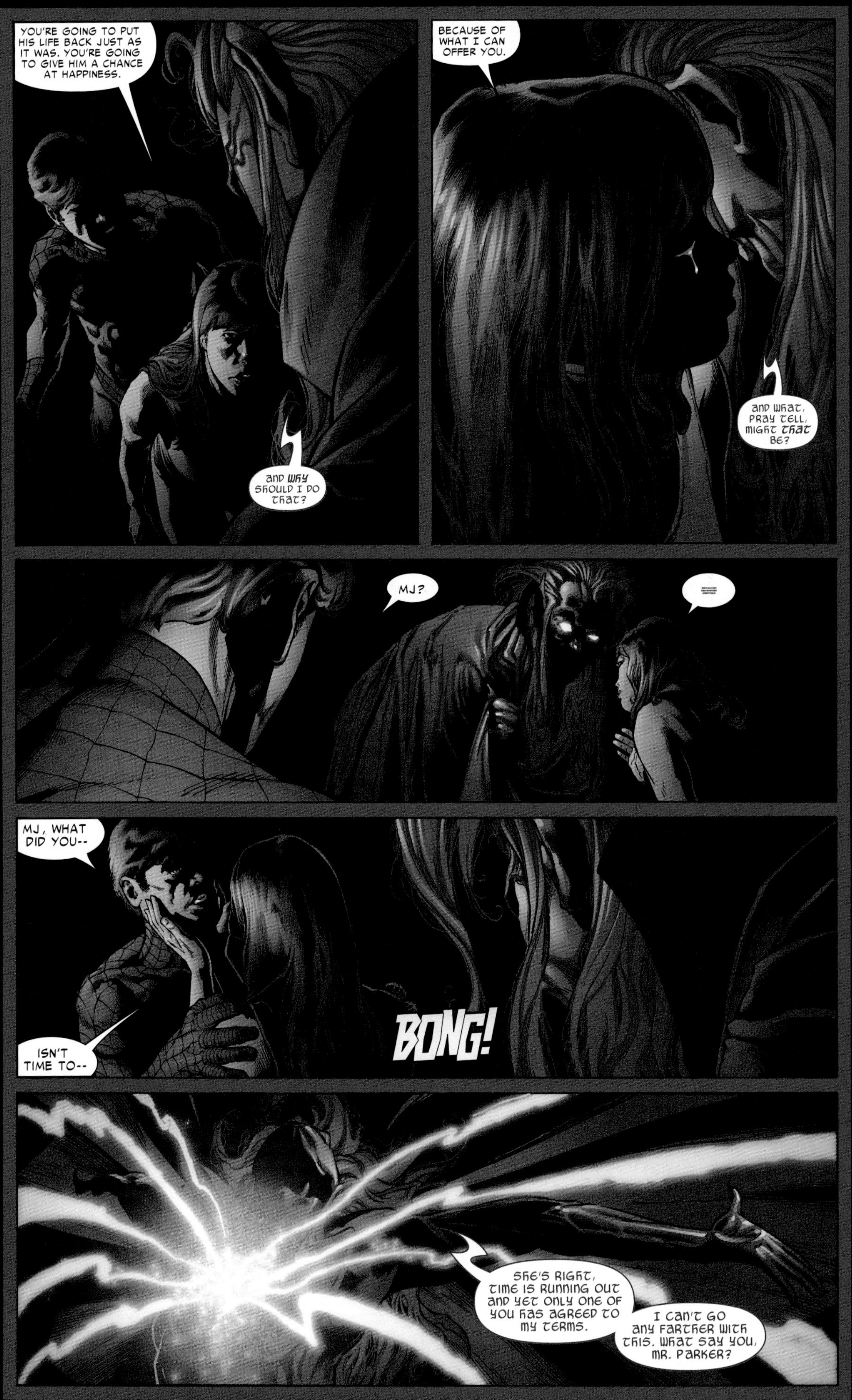

YOU'RE GOING TO PUT HIS LIFE BACK JUST AS IT WAS. YOU'RE GOING TO GIVE HIM A CHANCE AT HAPPINESS.
AND WHY SHOULD I DO THAT?
BECAUSE OF WHAT I CAN OFFER YOU.
AND WHAT, PRAY TELL, MIGHT THAT BE?
MJ?
MJ, WHAT DID YOU--
ISN'T TIME TO--
BONG!
SHE'S RIGHT, TIME IS RUNNING OUT AND YET ONLY ONE OF YOU HAS AGREED TO MY TERMS.
I CAN'T GO ANY FARTHER WITH THIS. WHAT SAY YOU, MR. PARKER?

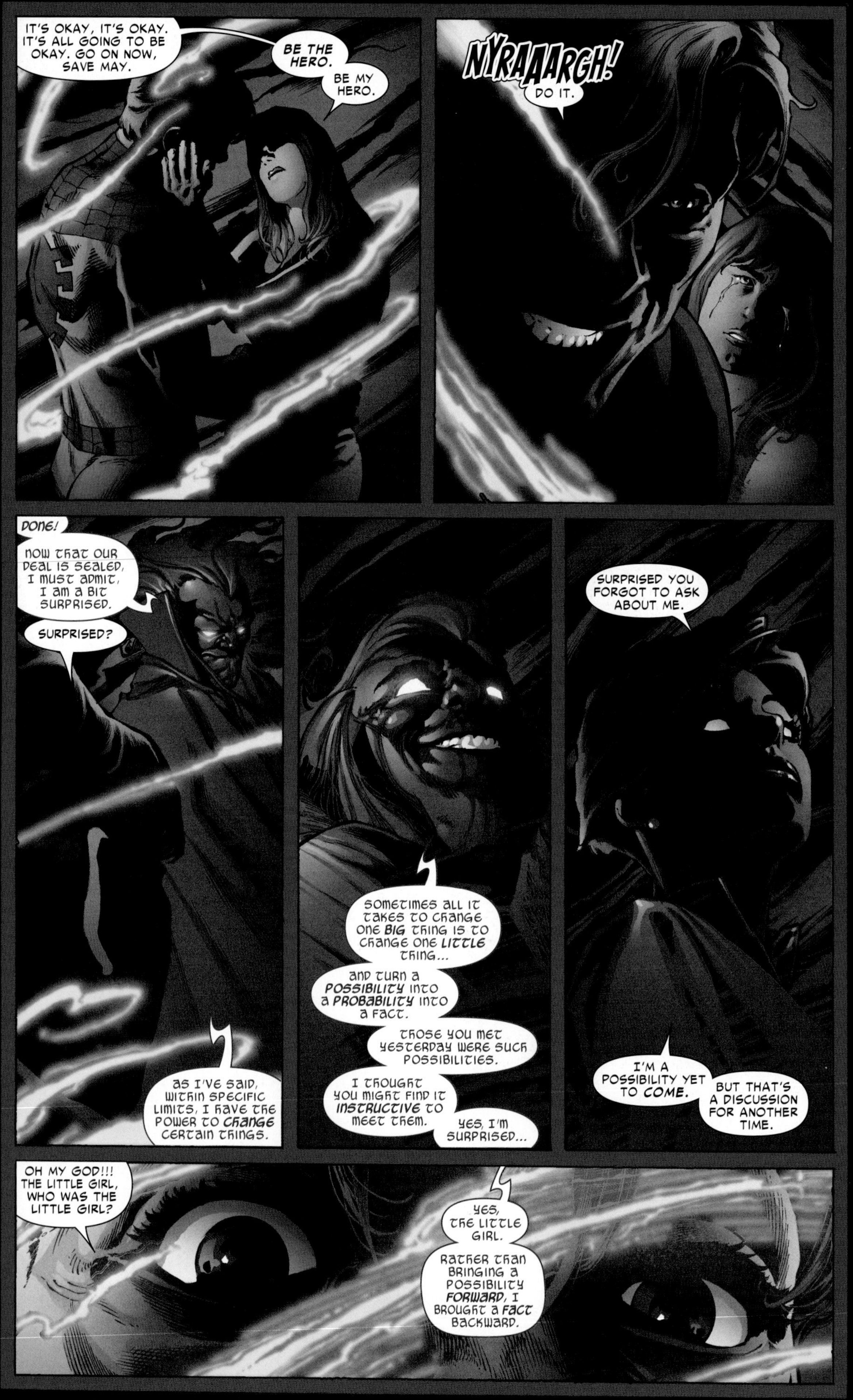
IT'S OKAY, IT'S OKAY. IT'S ALL GOING TO BE OKAY. GO ON NOW, SAVE MAY.
BE THE HERO.
BE MY HERO.
NYRAAARGH!
DO IT.
DONE!
NOW THAT OUR DEAL IS SEALED, I MUST ADMIT, I AM A BIT SURPRISED.
SURPRISED?
AS I'VE SAID, WITHIN SPECIFIC LIMITS, I HAVE THE POWER TO CHANGE CERTAIN THINGS.
SOMETIMES ALL IT TAKES TO CHANGE ONE BIG THING IS TO CHANGE ONE LITTLE THING...
AND TURN A POSSIBILITY INTO A PROBABILITY INTO A FACT.
THOSE YOU MET YESTERDAY WERE SUCH POSSIBILITIES.
I THOUGHT YOU MIGHT FIND IT INSTRUCTIVE TO MEET THEM.
YES, I'M SURPRISED...
SURPRISED YOU FORGOT TO ASK ABOUT ME.
I'M A POSSIBILITY YET TO COME.
BUT THAT'S A DISCUSSION FOR ANOTHER TIME.
OH MY GOD!!! THE LITTLE GIRL, WHO WAS THE LITTLE GIRL?
YES, THE LITTLE GIRL.
RATHER THAN BRINGING A POSSIBILITY FORWARD, I BROUGHT A FACT BACKWARD.

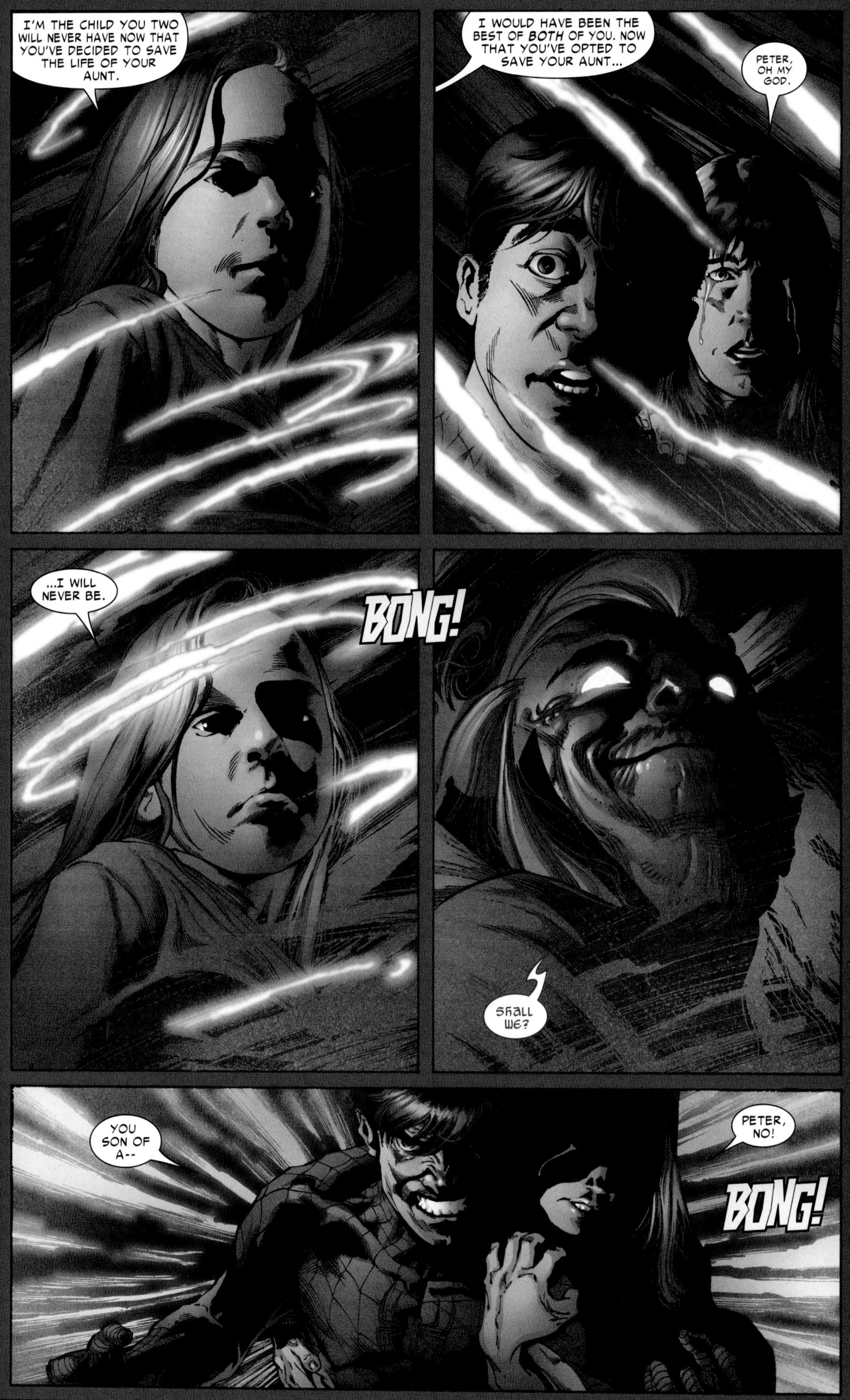
I'M THE CHILD YOU TWO WILL NEVER HAVE NOW THAT YOU'VE DECIDED TO SAVE THE LIFE OF YOUR AUNT.
I WOULD HAVE BEEN THE BEST OF *BOTH* OF YOU. NOW THAT YOU'VE OPTED TO SAVE YOUR AUNT...
PETER, OH MY GOD.
...I WILL NEVER BE.
BONG!
SHALL WE?
YOU SON OF A--
PETER, NO!
BONG!

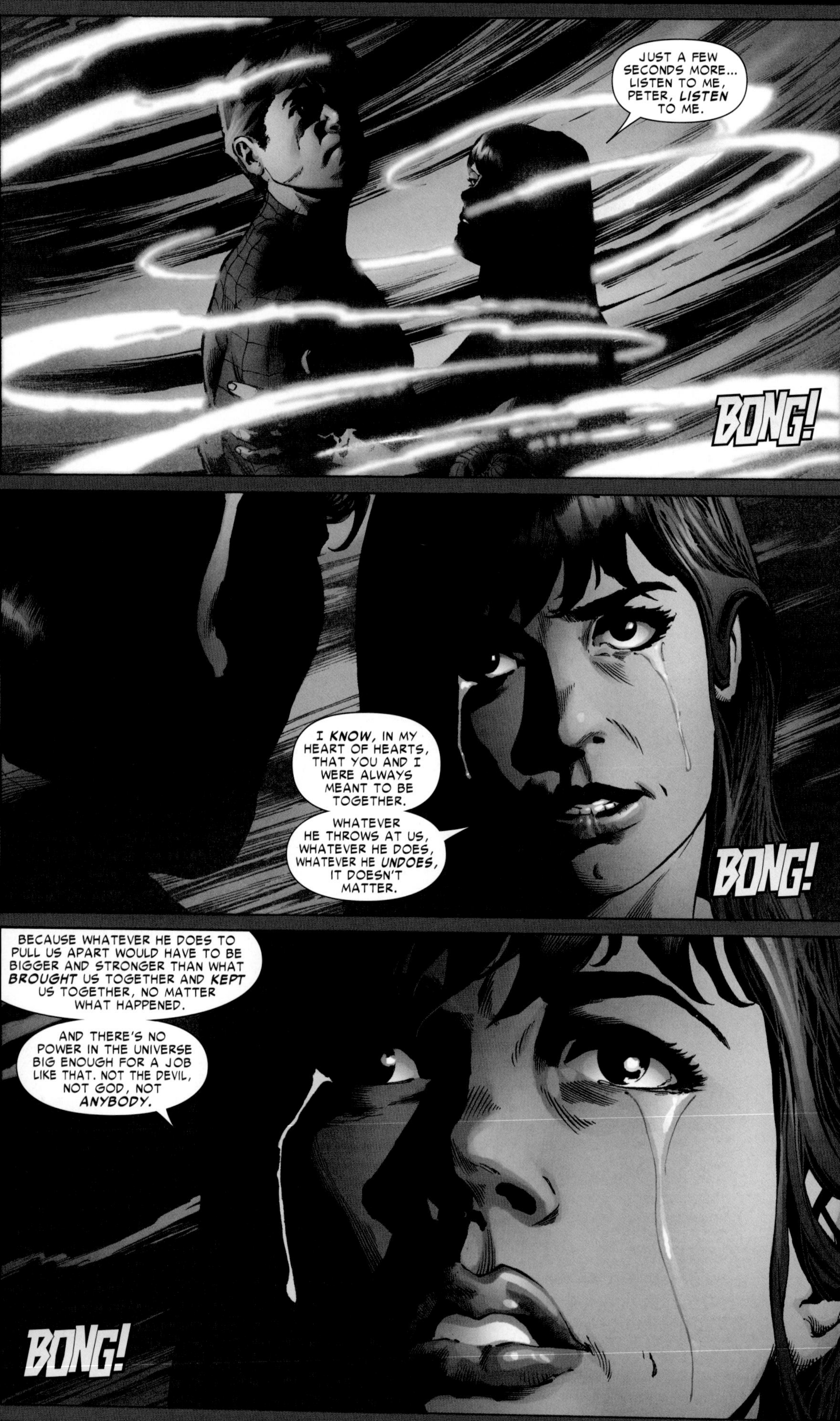
JUST A FEW SECONDS MORE... LISTEN TO ME, PETER, LISTEN TO ME.
BONG!
I KNOW, IN MY HEART OF HEARTS, THAT YOU AND I WERE ALWAYS MEANT TO BE TOGETHER.
WHATEVER HE THROWS AT US, WHATEVER HE DOES, WHATEVER HE UNDOES, IT DOESN'T MATTER.
BONG!
BECAUSE WHATEVER HE DOES TO PULL US APART WOULD HAVE TO BE BIGGER AND STRONGER THAN WHAT BROUGHT US TOGETHER AND KEPT US TOGETHER, NO MATTER WHAT HAPPENED.
AND THERE'S NO POWER IN THE UNIVERSE BIG ENOUGH FOR A JOB LIKE THAT. NOT THE DEVIL, NOT GOD, NOT ANYBODY.
BONG!

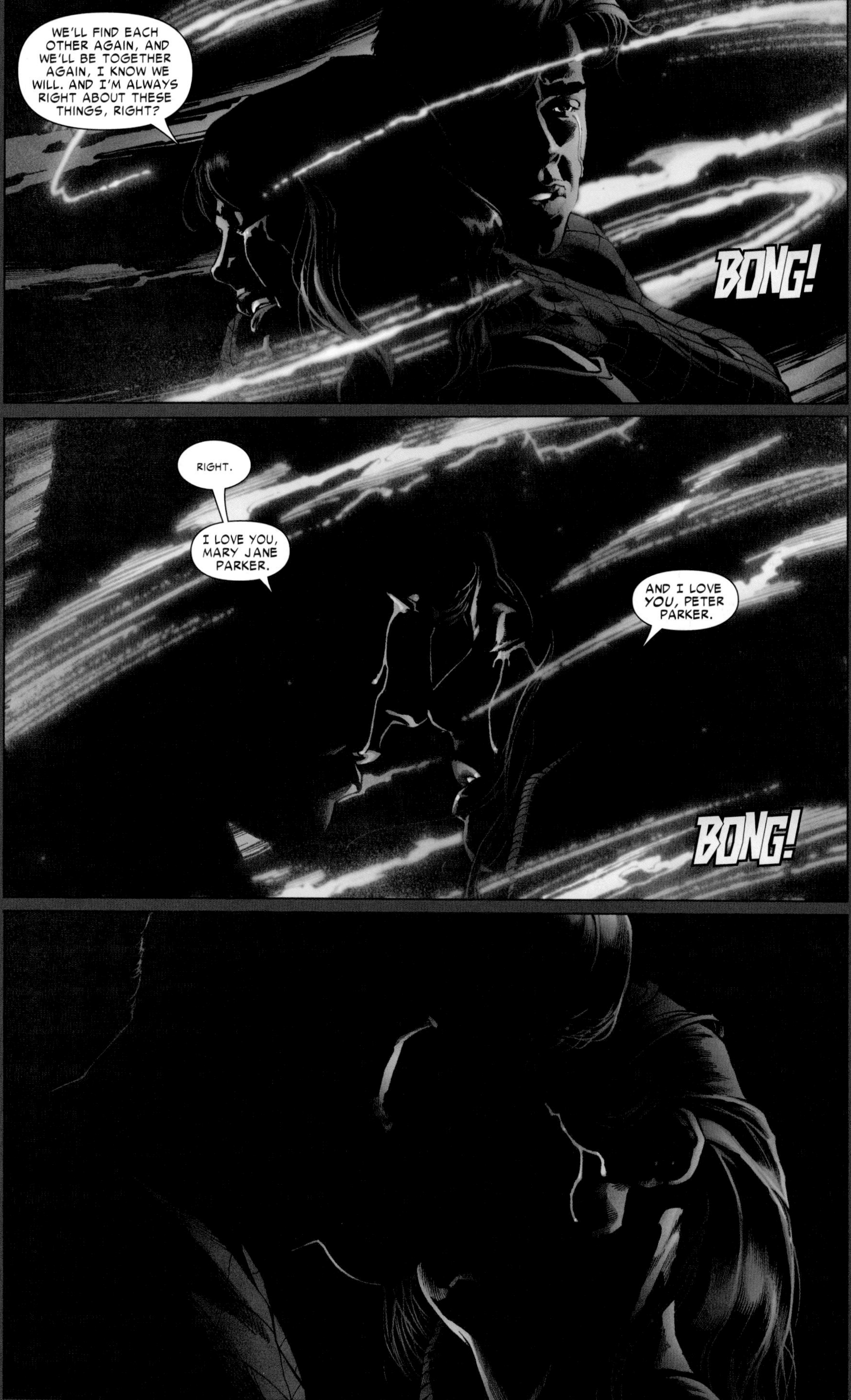
WE'LL FIND EACH OTHER AGAIN, AND WE'LL BE TOGETHER AGAIN, I KNOW WE WILL. AND I'M ALWAYS RIGHT ABOUT THESE THINGS, RIGHT?
BONG!
RIGHT.
I LOVE YOU, MARY JANE PARKER.
AND I LOVE YOU, PETER PARKER.
BONG!

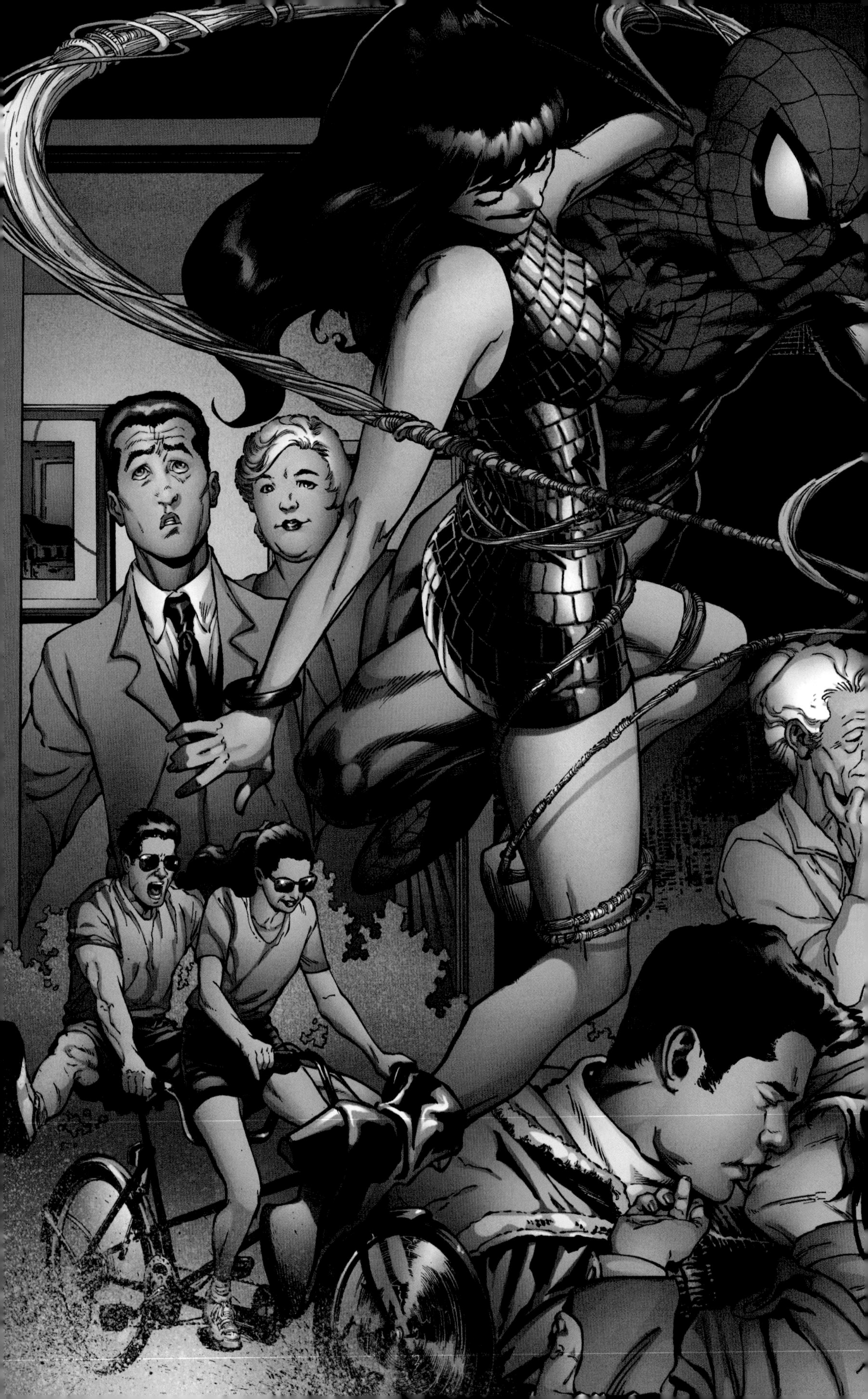

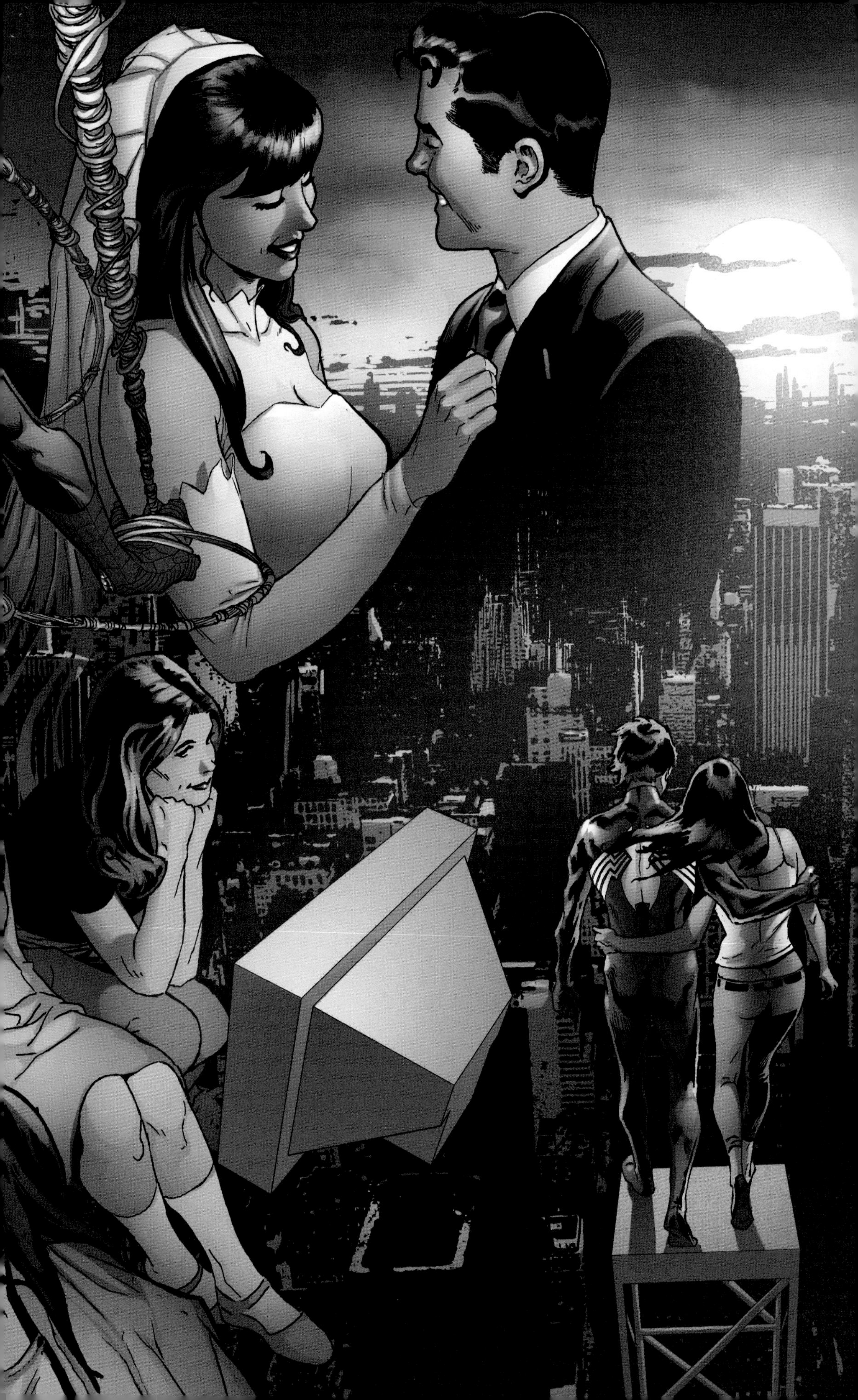

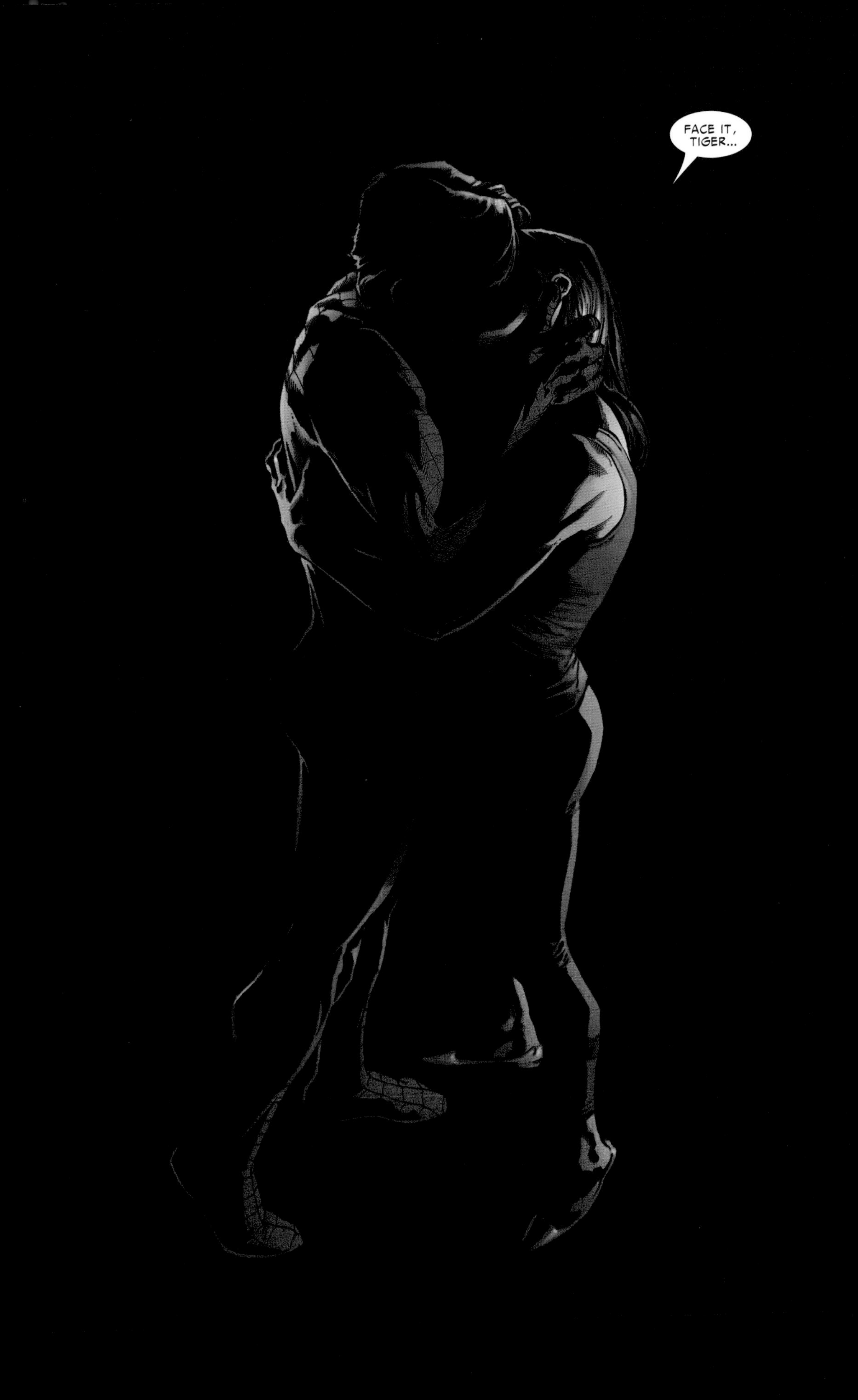
FACE IT, TIGER...

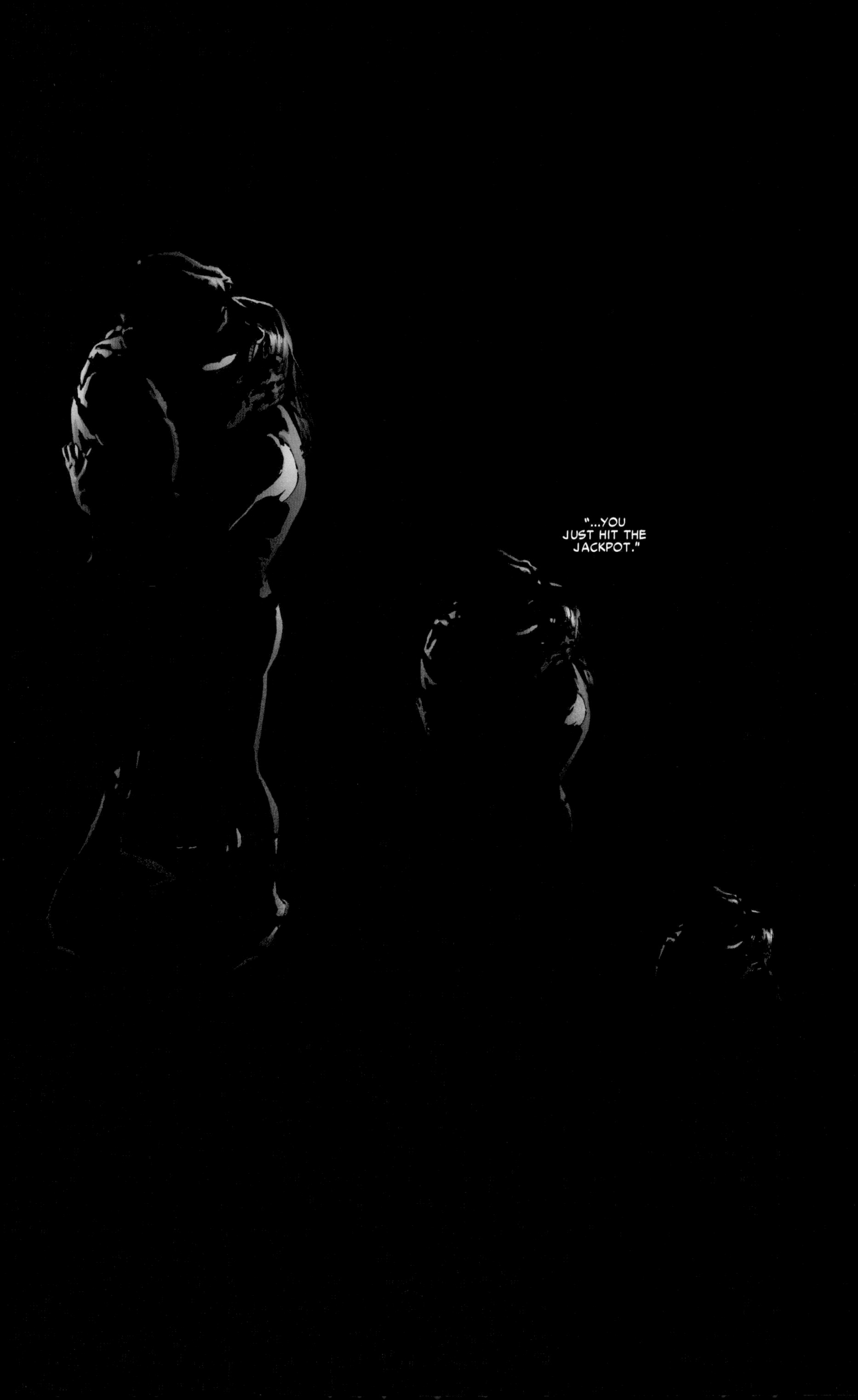
"...YOU JUST HIT THE JACKPOT."

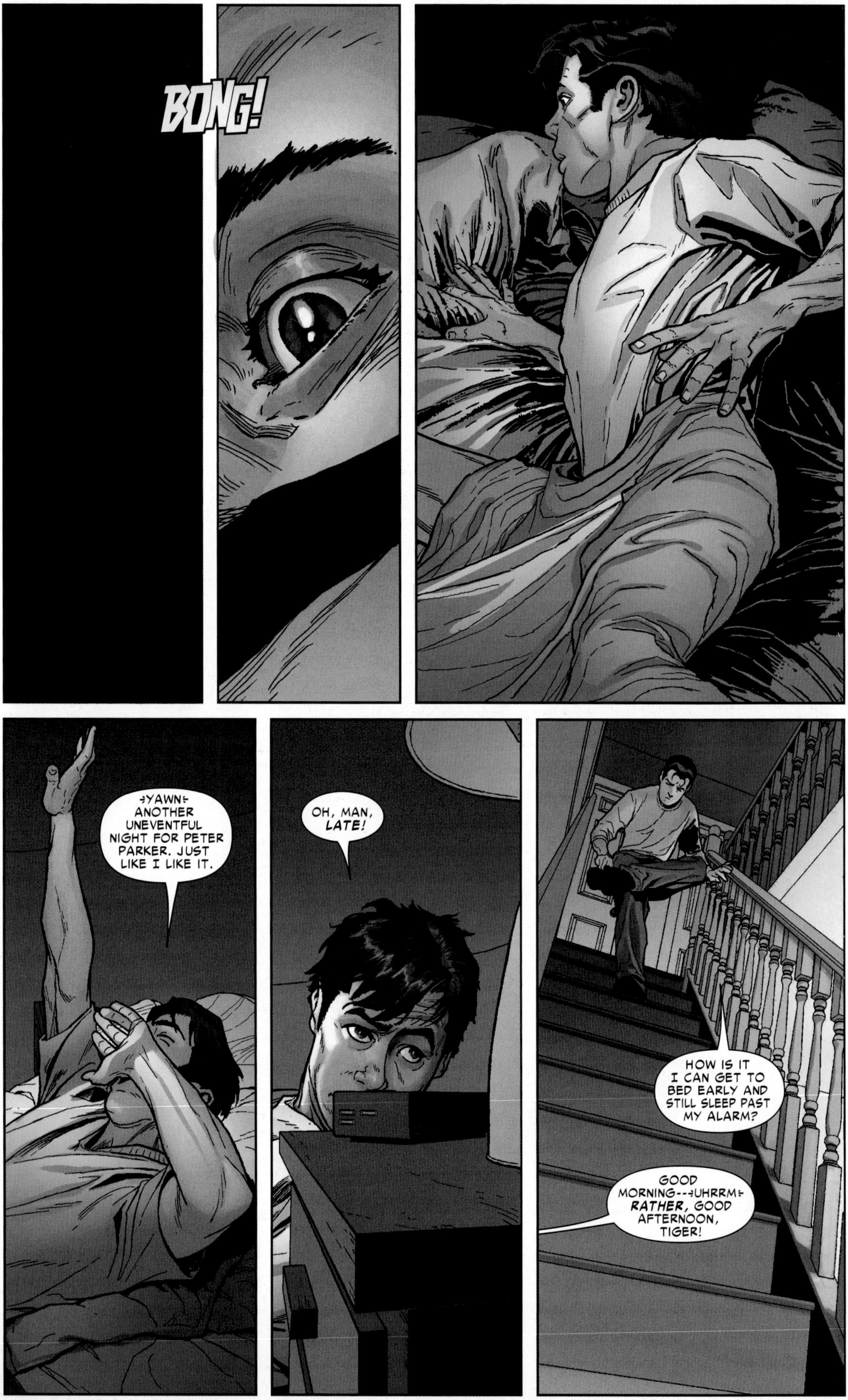
BONG!
=YAWN= ANOTHER UNEVENTFUL NIGHT FOR PETER PARKER. JUST LIKE I LIKE IT.
OH, MAN, LATE!
HOW IS IT I CAN GET TO BED EARLY AND STILL SLEEP PAST MY ALARM?
GOOD MORNING-- =UHRRM= RATHER, GOOD AFTERNOON, TIGER!

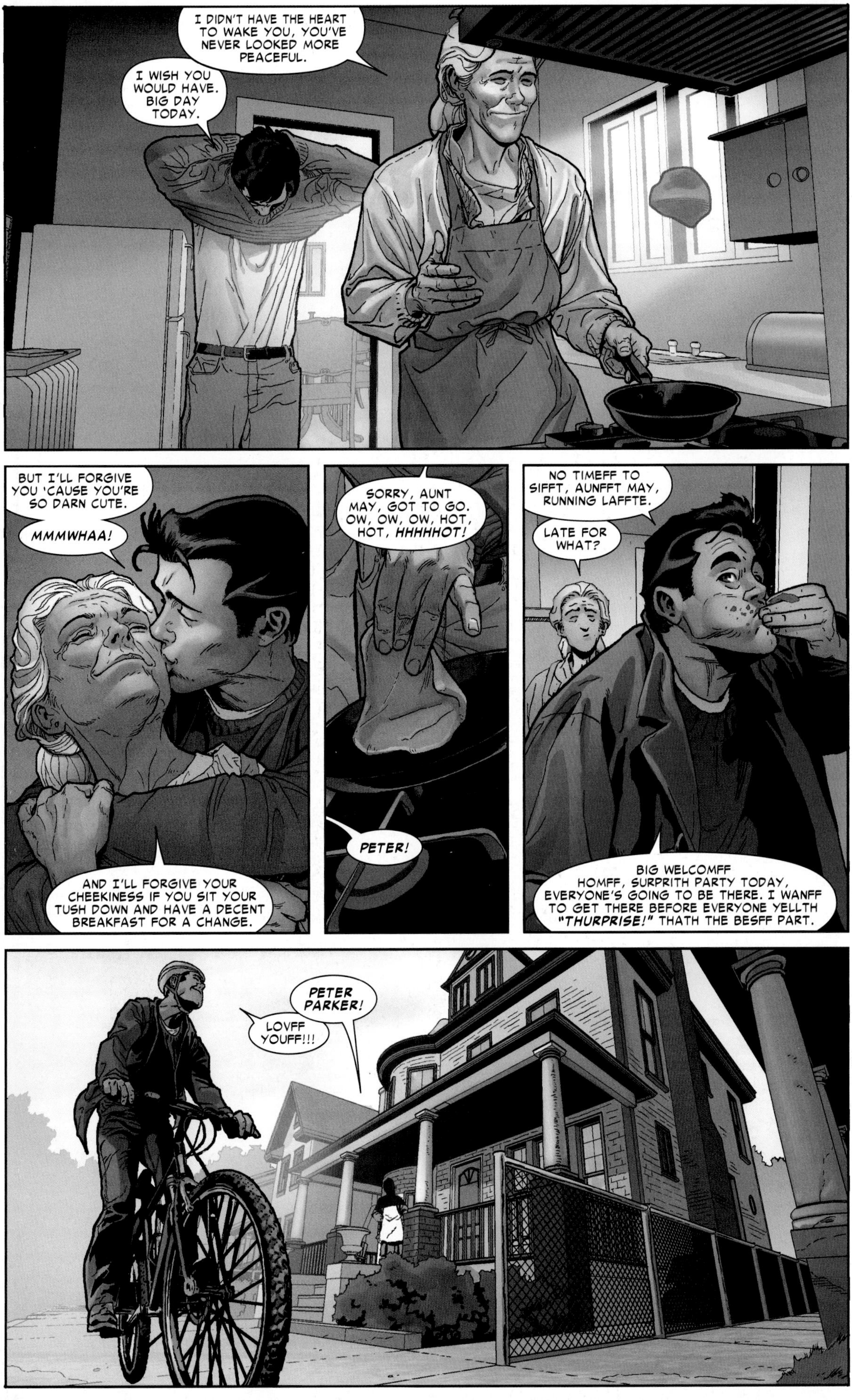
I DIDN'T HAVE THE HEART TO WAKE YOU, YOU'VE NEVER LOOKED MORE PEACEFUL.
I WISH YOU WOULD HAVE. BIG DAY TODAY.
BUT I'LL FORGIVE YOU 'CAUSE YOU'RE SO DARN CUTE.
MMMWHAA!
AND I'LL FORGIVE YOUR CHEEKINESS IF YOU SIT YOUR TUSH DOWN AND HAVE A DECENT BREAKFAST FOR A CHANGE.
SORRY, AUNT MAY, GOT TO GO. OW, OW, OW, HOT, HOT, HHHHHOT!
PETER!
NO TIMEFF TO SIFFT, AUNFFT MAY, RUNNING LAFFTE.
LATE FOR WHAT?
BIG WELCOMFF HOMFF, SURPRITH PARTY TODAY, EVERYONE'S GOING TO BE THERE. I WANFF TO GET THERE BEFORE EVERYONE YELLTH "THURPRISE!" THATH THE BESFF PART.
PETER PARKER!
LOVFF YOUFF!!!

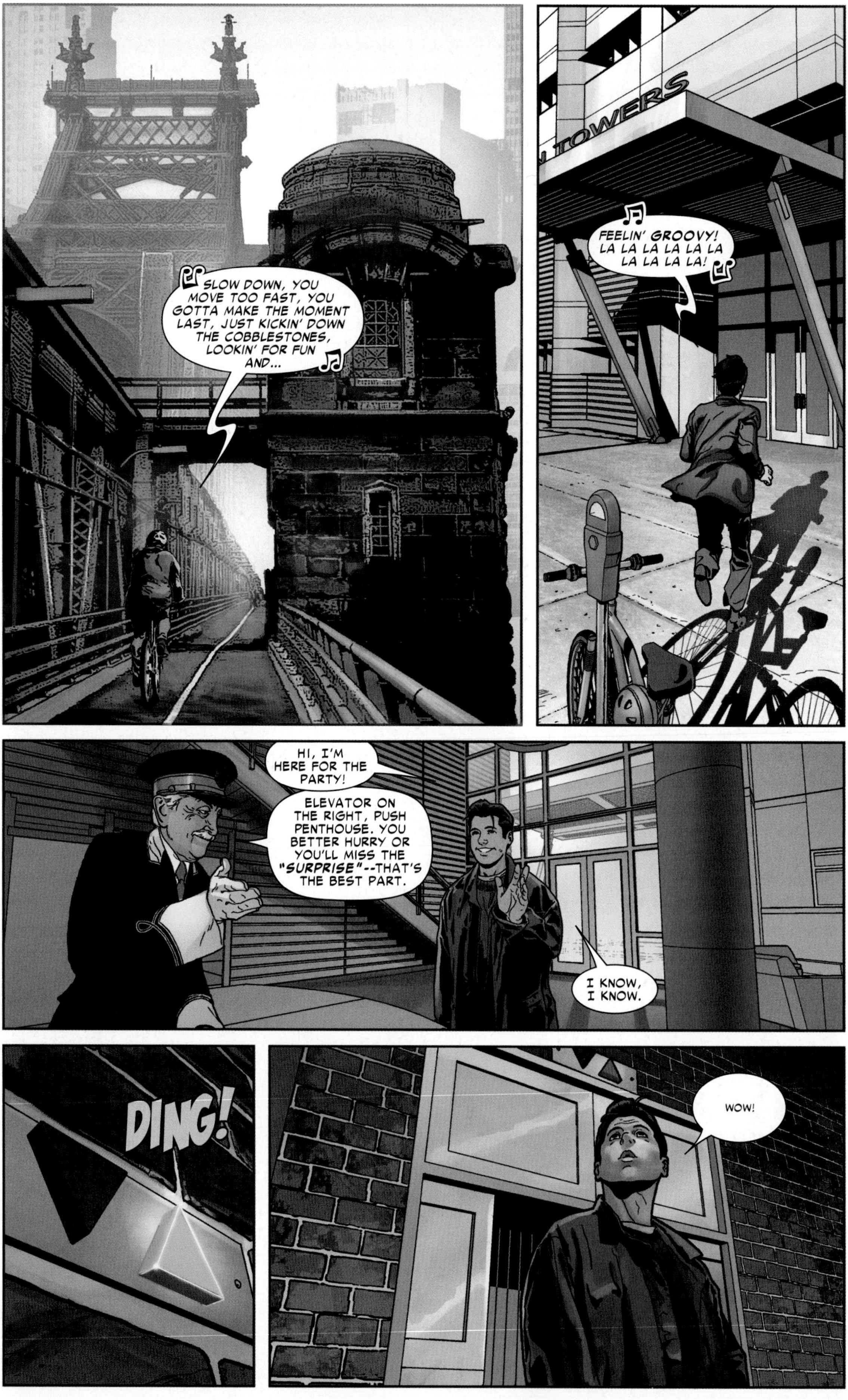
SLOW DOWN, YOU MOVE TOO FAST, YOU GOTTA MAKE THE MOMENT LAST, JUST KICKIN' DOWN THE COBBLESTONES, LOOKIN' FOR FUN AND...
TOWERS
FEELIN' GROOVY! LA LA LA LA LA LA LA LA LA!
HI, I'M HERE FOR THE PARTY!
ELEVATOR ON THE RIGHT, PUSH PENTHOUSE. YOU BETTER HURRY OR YOU'LL MISS THE "SURPRISE"--THAT'S THE BEST PART.
I KNOW, I KNOW.
DING!
WOW!

SWANKY DIGS.

PARKER!

'SUP, FLASH!

WHERE THE HECK HAVE YOU BEEN?!

FRANK SINATRA
DEAN MARTIN
SAMMY DAVIS JR.
PETER LAWFORD
JOEY BISHOP

IN THE LOUNGE

JONAH JONES

YOU ALMOST MISSED THE "SURPRISE," AND THAT'S THE BEST PART.

I KNOW, I KN--

YIKES, AWKWARD! THINGS STILL FROSTY WITH MJ, HUH?

YEAH, I GUESS YOU CAN SAY THAT. I DON'T KNOW IF SHE'LL EVER FORGIVE ME FOR--

SHHHHHH, EVERYBODY!

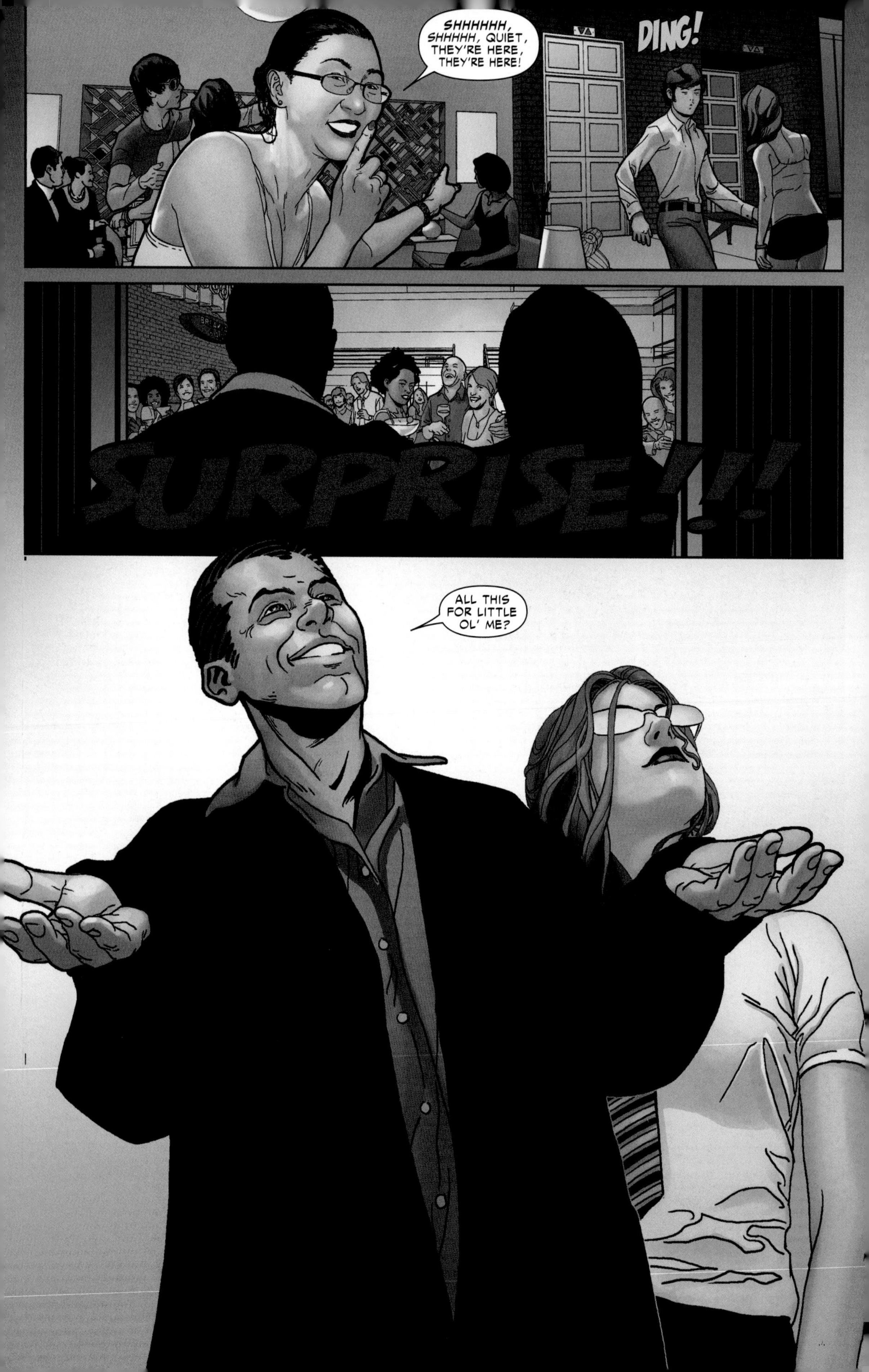
SHHHHHH, SHHHHH, QUIET, THEY'RE HERE, THEY'RE HERE!
DING!
SURPRISE!!!
ALL THIS FOR LITTLE OL' ME?

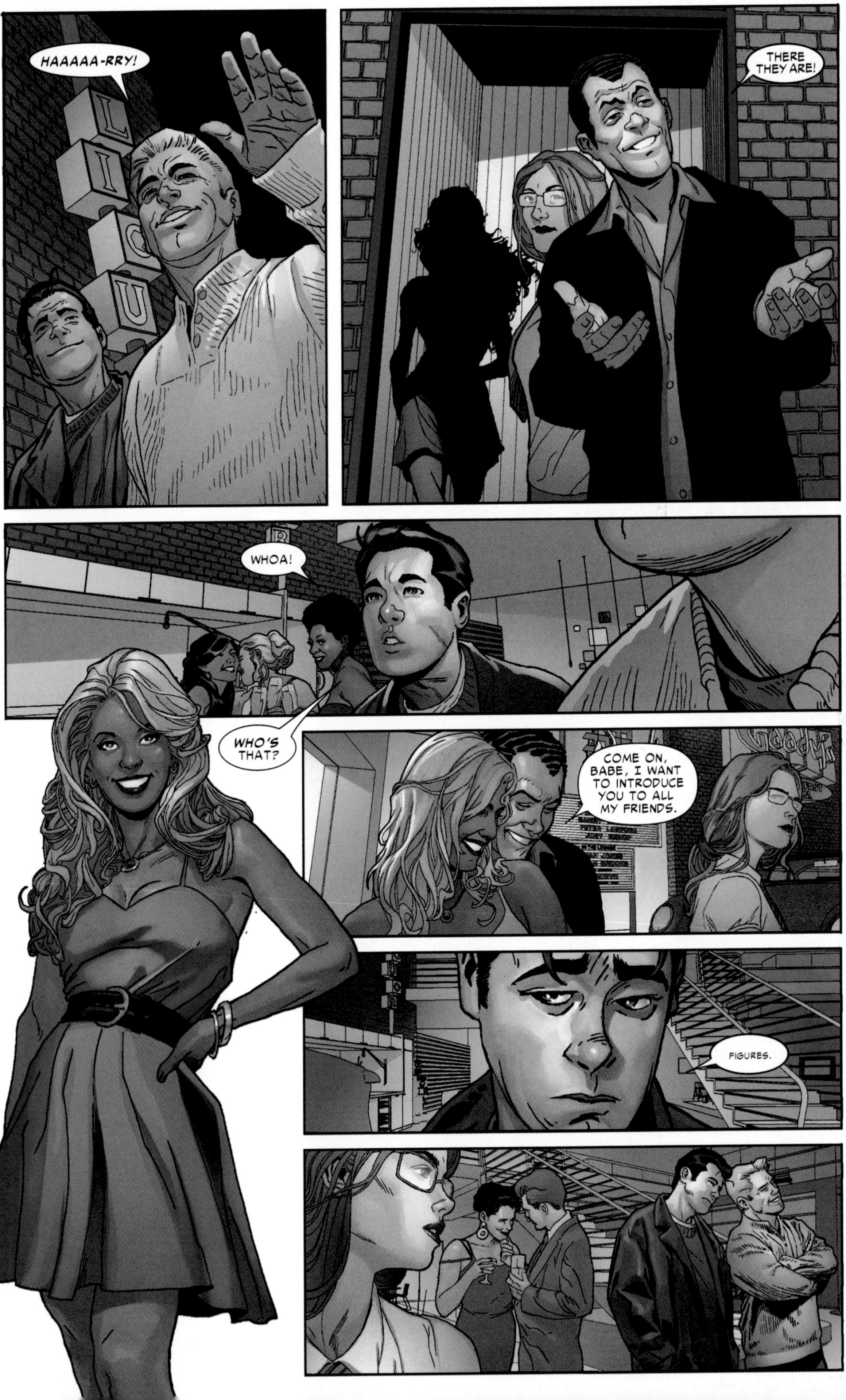
HAAAAA-RRY!
THERE THEY ARE!
WHOA!
WHO'S THAT?
COME ON, BABE, I WANT TO INTRODUCE YOU TO ALL MY FRIENDS.
FIGURES.

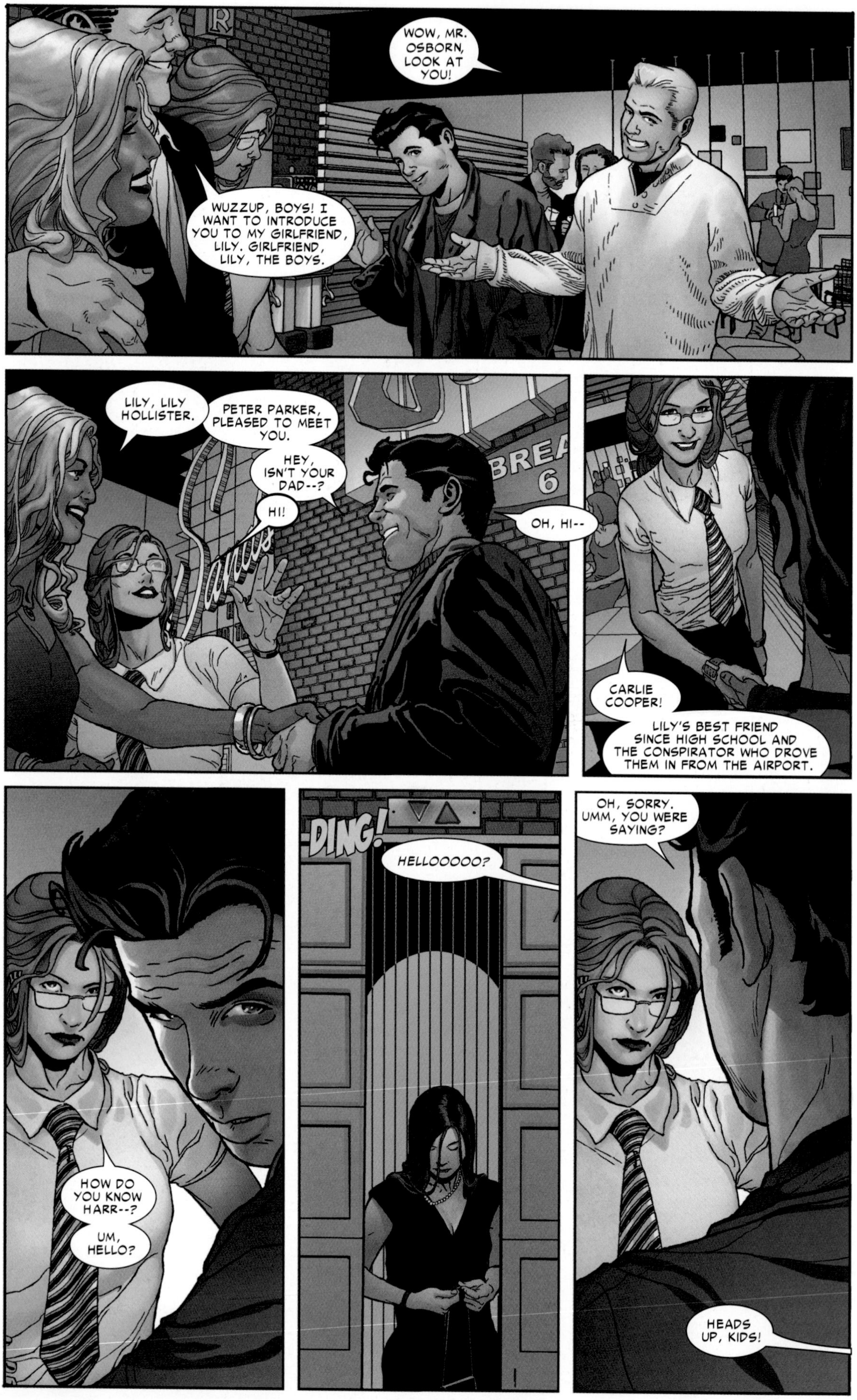
WOW, MR. OSBORN, LOOK AT YOU!
WUZZUP, BOYS! I WANT TO INTRODUCE YOU TO MY GIRLFRIEND, LILY. GIRLFRIEND, LILY, THE BOYS.
LILY, LILY HOLLISTER.
PETER PARKER, PLEASED TO MEET YOU.
HEY, ISN'T YOUR DAD--?
HI!
BREA
6
OH, HI--
CARLIE COOPER!
LILY'S BEST FRIEND SINCE HIGH SCHOOL AND THE CONSPIRATOR WHO DROVE THEM IN FROM THE AIRPORT.
HOW DO YOU KNOW HARR--?
UM, HELLO?
DING!
HELLOOOOO?
OH, SORRY. UMM, YOU WERE SAYING?
HEADS UP, KIDS!

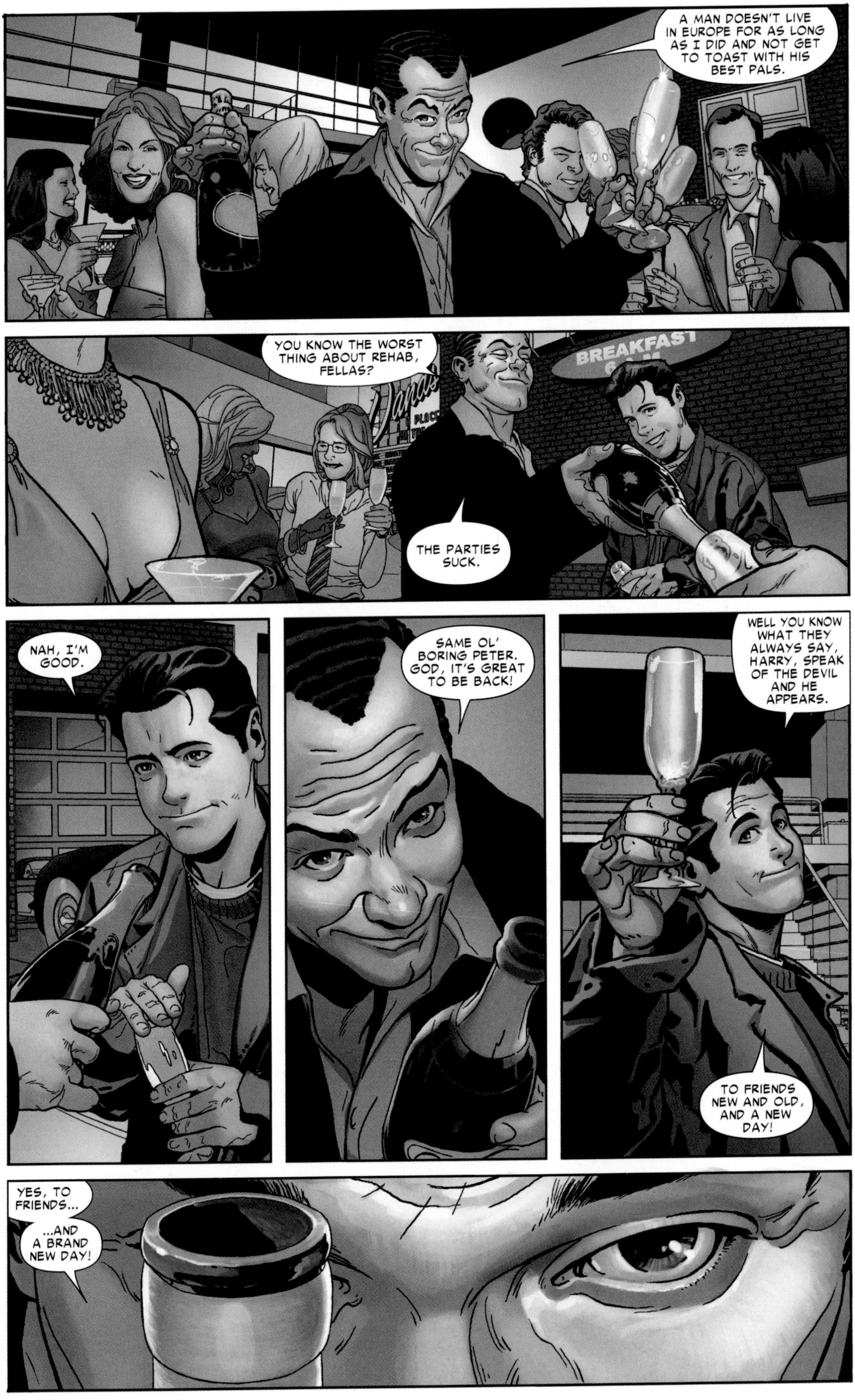
A MAN DOESN'T LIVE IN EUROPE FOR AS LONG AS I DID AND NOT GET TO TOAST WITH HIS BEST PALS.
YOU KNOW THE WORST THING ABOUT REHAB, FELLAS?
BREAKFAST
THE PARTIES SUCK.
NAH, I'M GOOD.
SAME OL' BORING PETER. GOD, IT'S GREAT TO BE BACK!
WELL YOU KNOW WHAT THEY ALWAYS SAY, HARRY, SPEAK OF THE DEVIL AND HE APPEARS.
TO FRIENDS NEW AND OLD, AND A NEW DAY!
YES, TO FRIENDS...
...AND A BRAND NEW DAY!

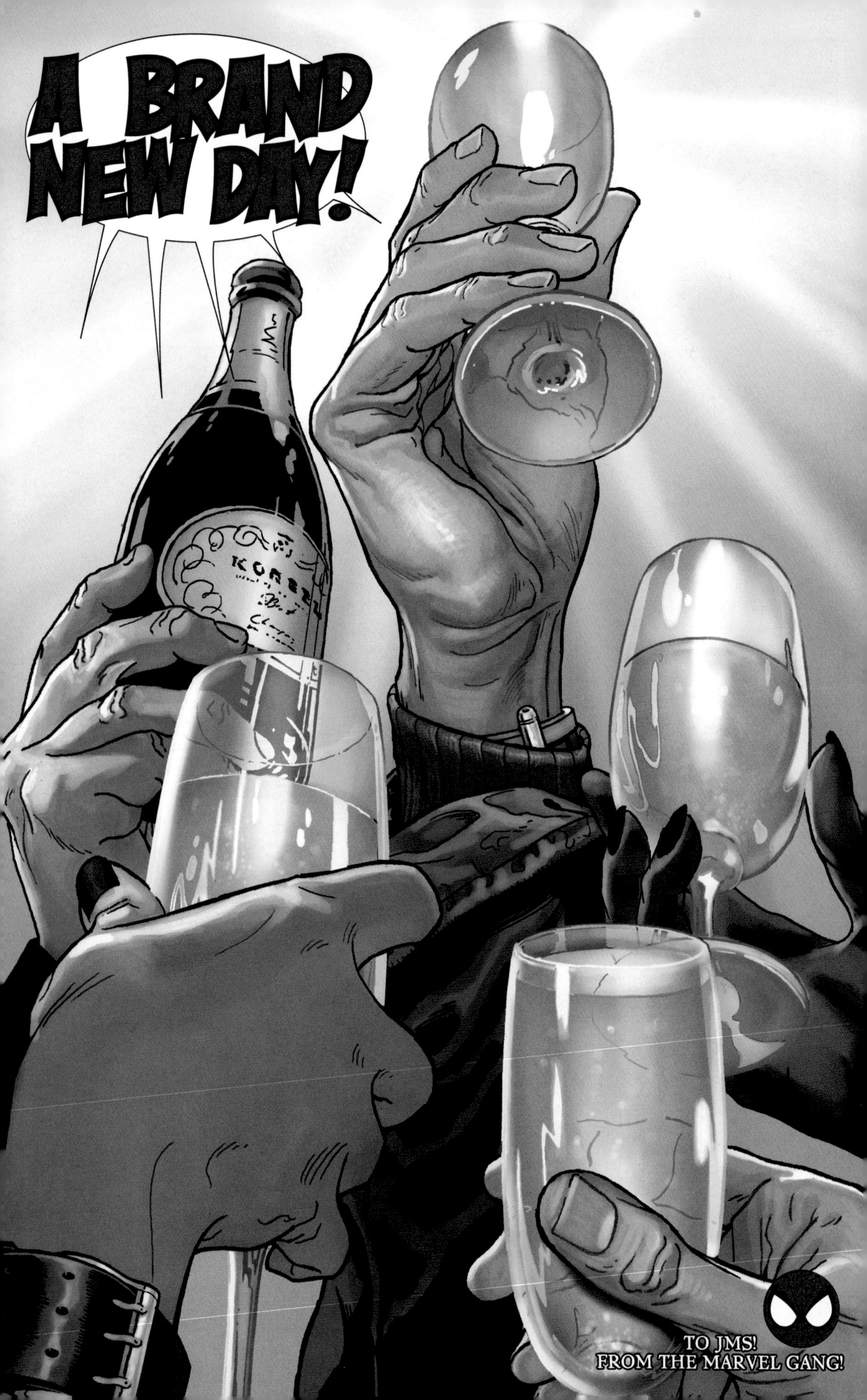
A BRAND NEW DAY!
TO JMS!
FROM THE MARVEL GANG!

AFTERWORD
By STAN LEE

Wow! Talk about courage! Just imagine what cojónes it must have taken for Joey the Q and his Marvel madmen to separate Spidey and MJ after years of married bliss.

I know this new, startling development will anger some readers — might even make 'em think that Marvel has lost its collective mind. But me — I think the Bullpen deserves a medal. In fact, I hereby award them a rare, digital No-Prize.

You see, I haven't forgotten that day, many years ago, when I decided to have Peter and MJ get hitched. You should'a heard the uproar from True Believers around the globe! "You're killing the strip, Lee!" "If they get married, I'll never read another Spider-Man!" "How can you do this to your own characters? Have you lost what little was left of your mind?!" And those were the kinder messages.

Sometimes readers forget that a series can't continue going down the same road forever. Think about it. In real life, people may make friends, lose friends, stay single, get married, get divorced, get sick, die, whatever. All the Bullpen is brilliantly doing is giving you characters whose lives are as full of surprises as your own. I applaud them for that.

As for the future, who knows what it holds? Will our star-crossed lovers stay apart? Will they be reunited one day? Or, will something even more unexpected occur? Look, neither you nor I can ever know what tomorrow holds for us, right? That's the mystery and wonder of life.

And that's what makes Spider-Man and the rest of the magnificent Marvel characters the most exciting and compelling heroes of all.

So be proud, O Keeper of the Flame; you're part of the Mighty Marvel Literary Renaissance!

And congratulations, Joey. You and the Bullpen are the greatest!

EXCELSIOR!

Stan Lee

STAN

COVER GALLERY

AMAZING SPIDER-MAN #544 VARIANT

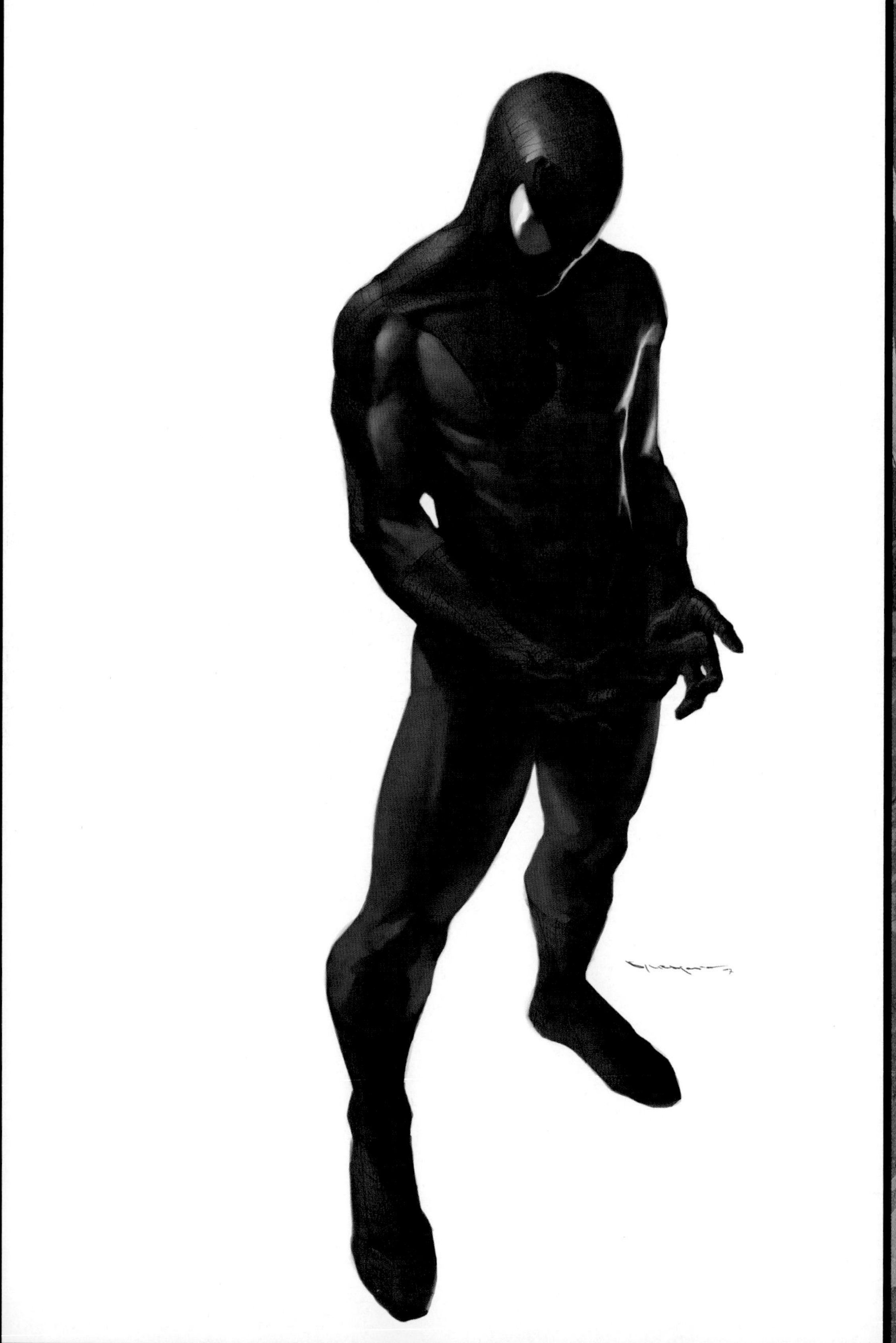

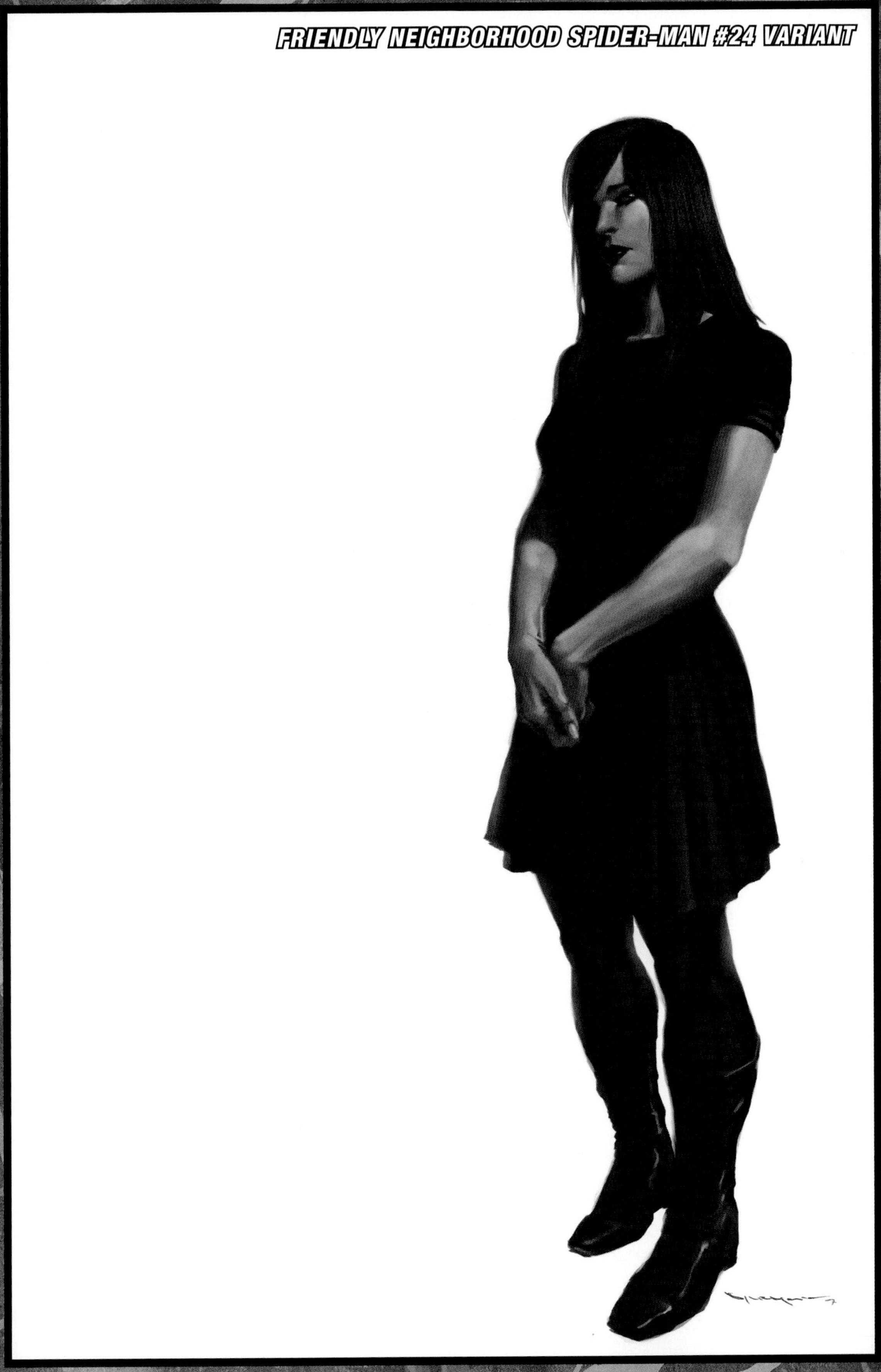

FRIENDLY NEIGHBORHOOD SPIDER-MAN #24 VARIANT

SENSATIONAL SPIDER-MAN #41 VARIANT

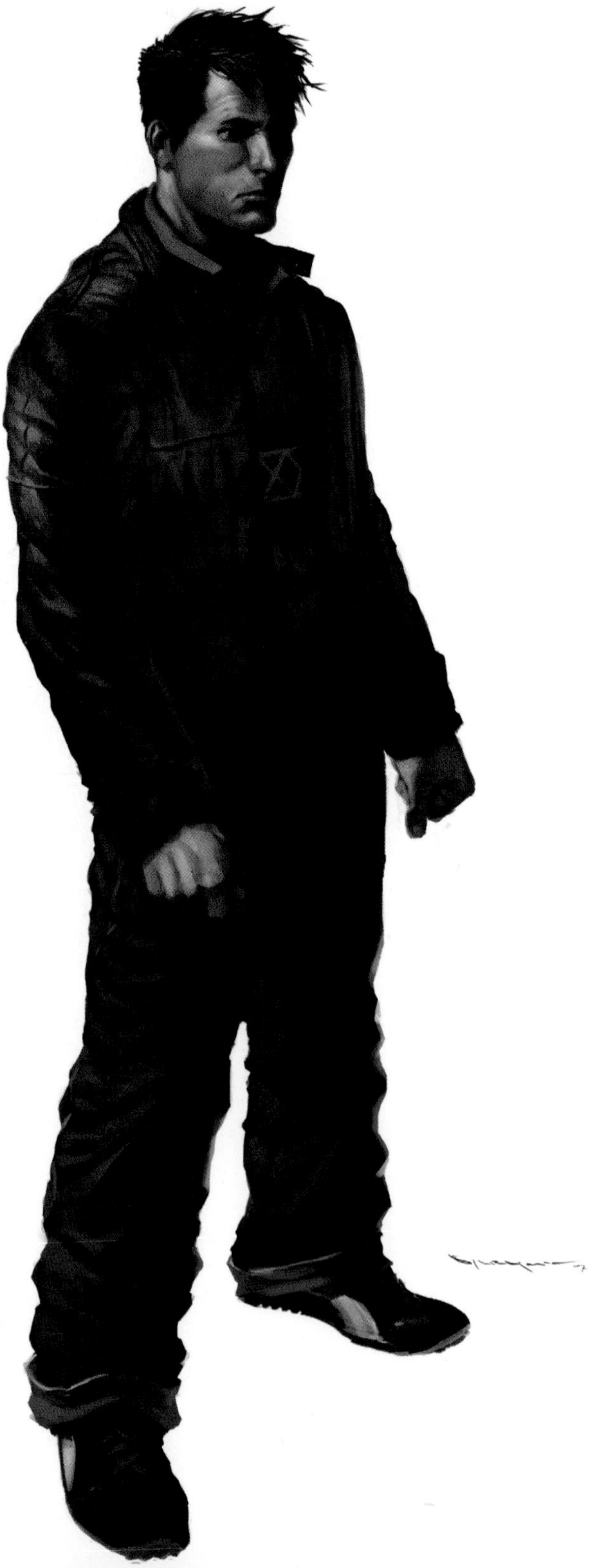

AMAZING SPIDER-MAN #545 VARIANT

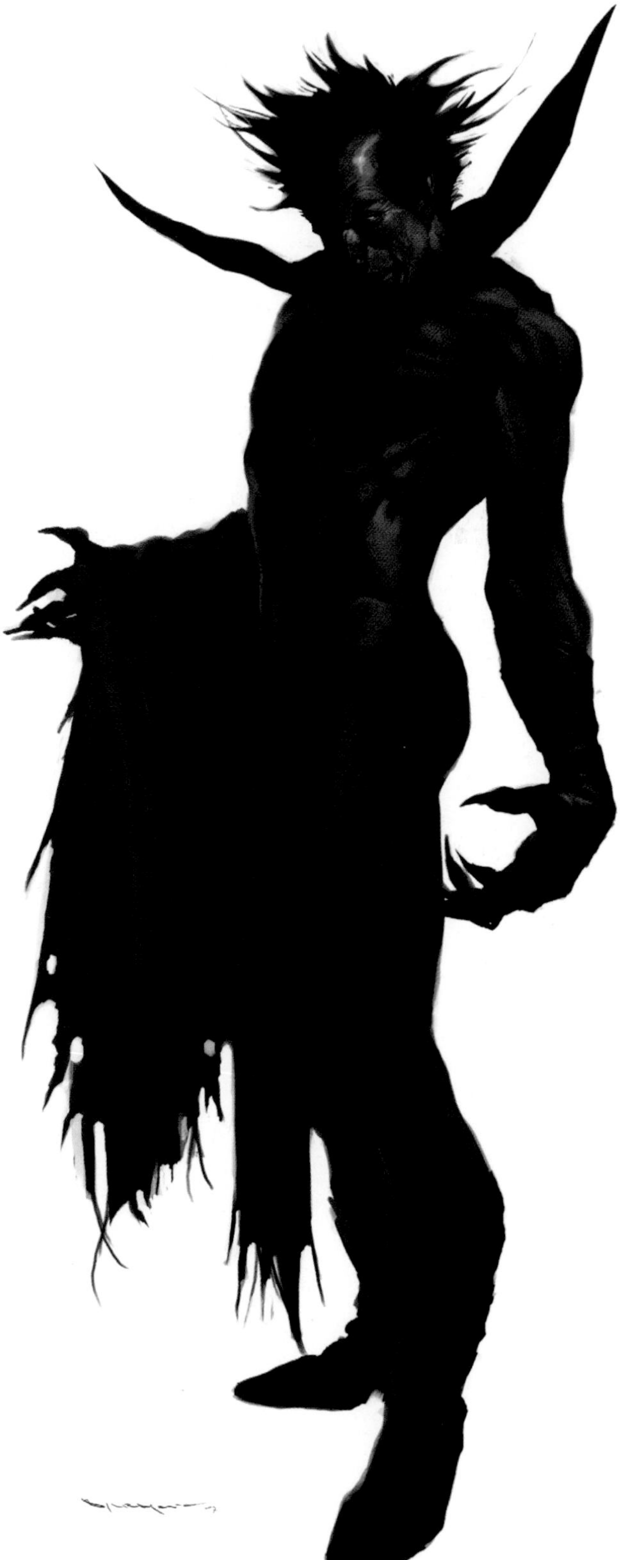

AMAZING SPIDER-MAN #544

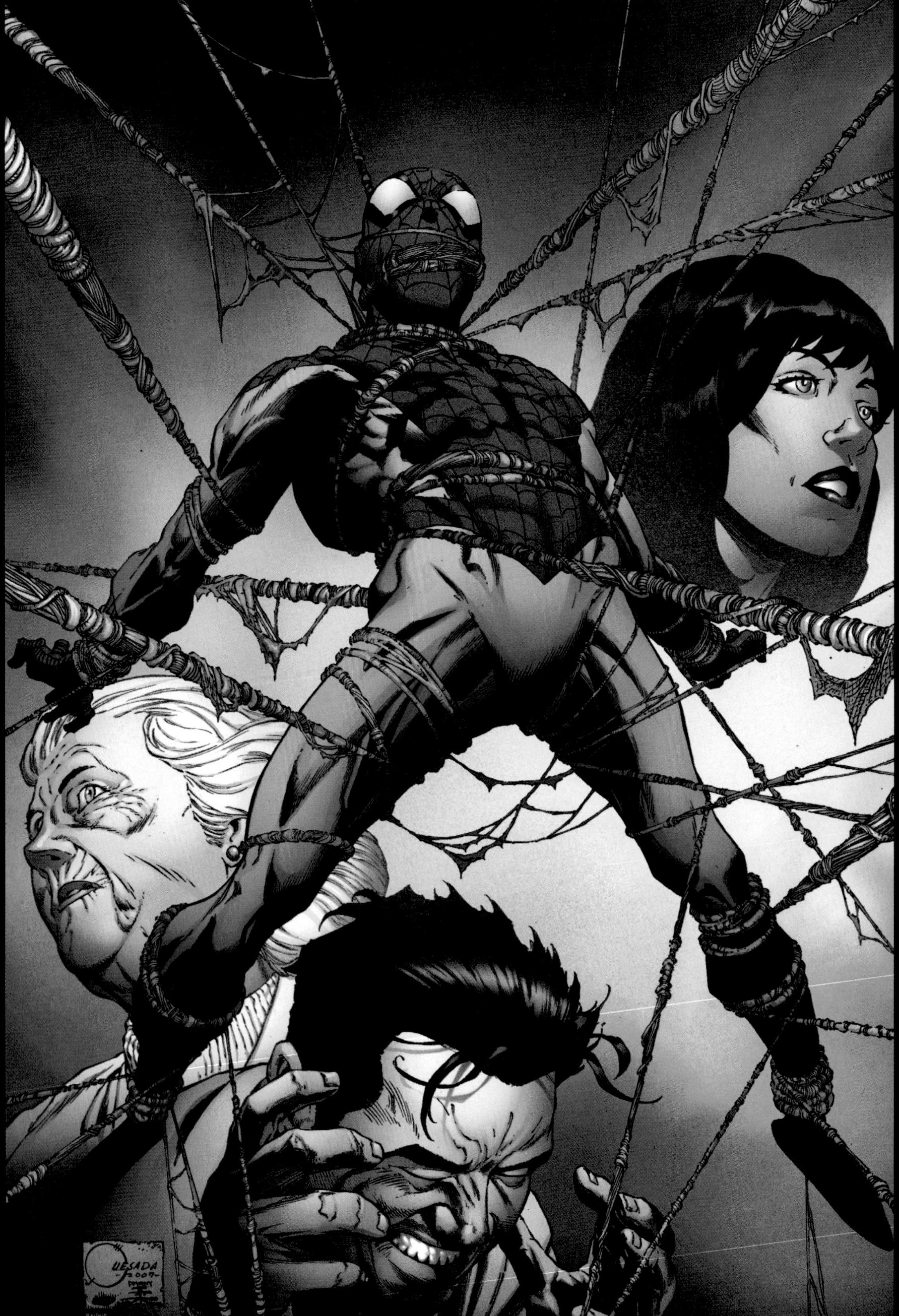

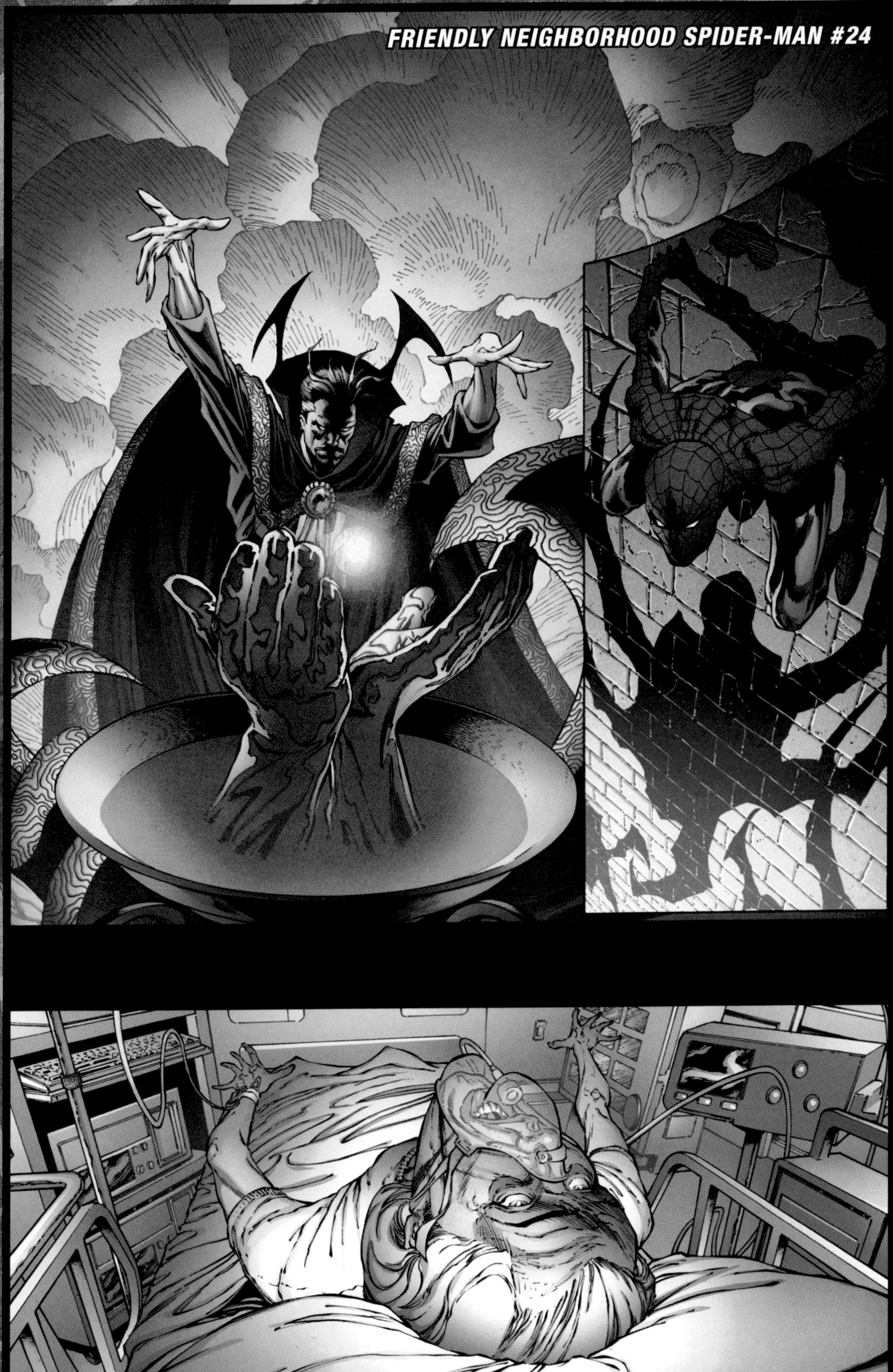
FRIENDLY NEIGHBORHOOD SPIDER-MAN #24

SENSATIONAL SPIDER-MAN #41

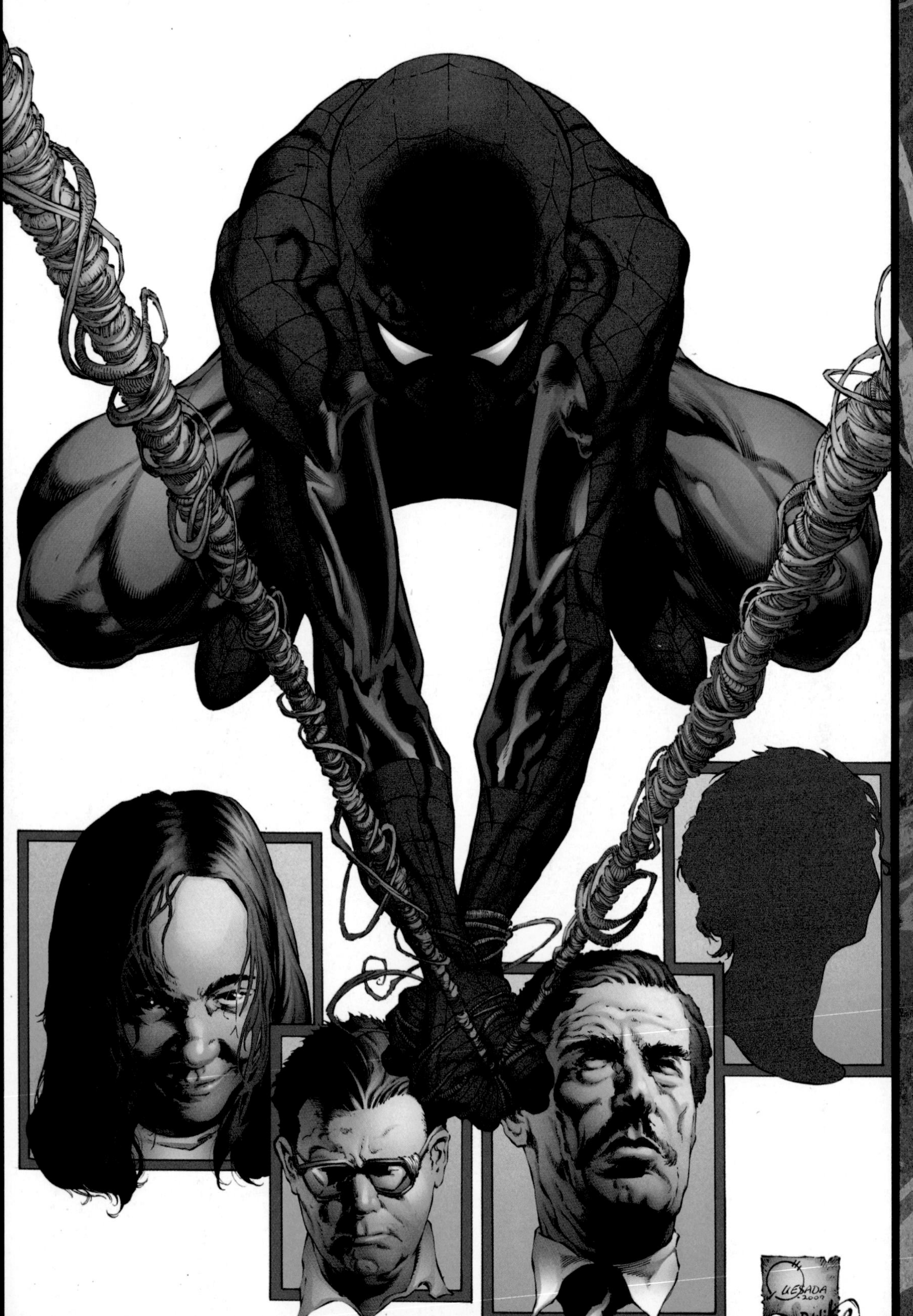

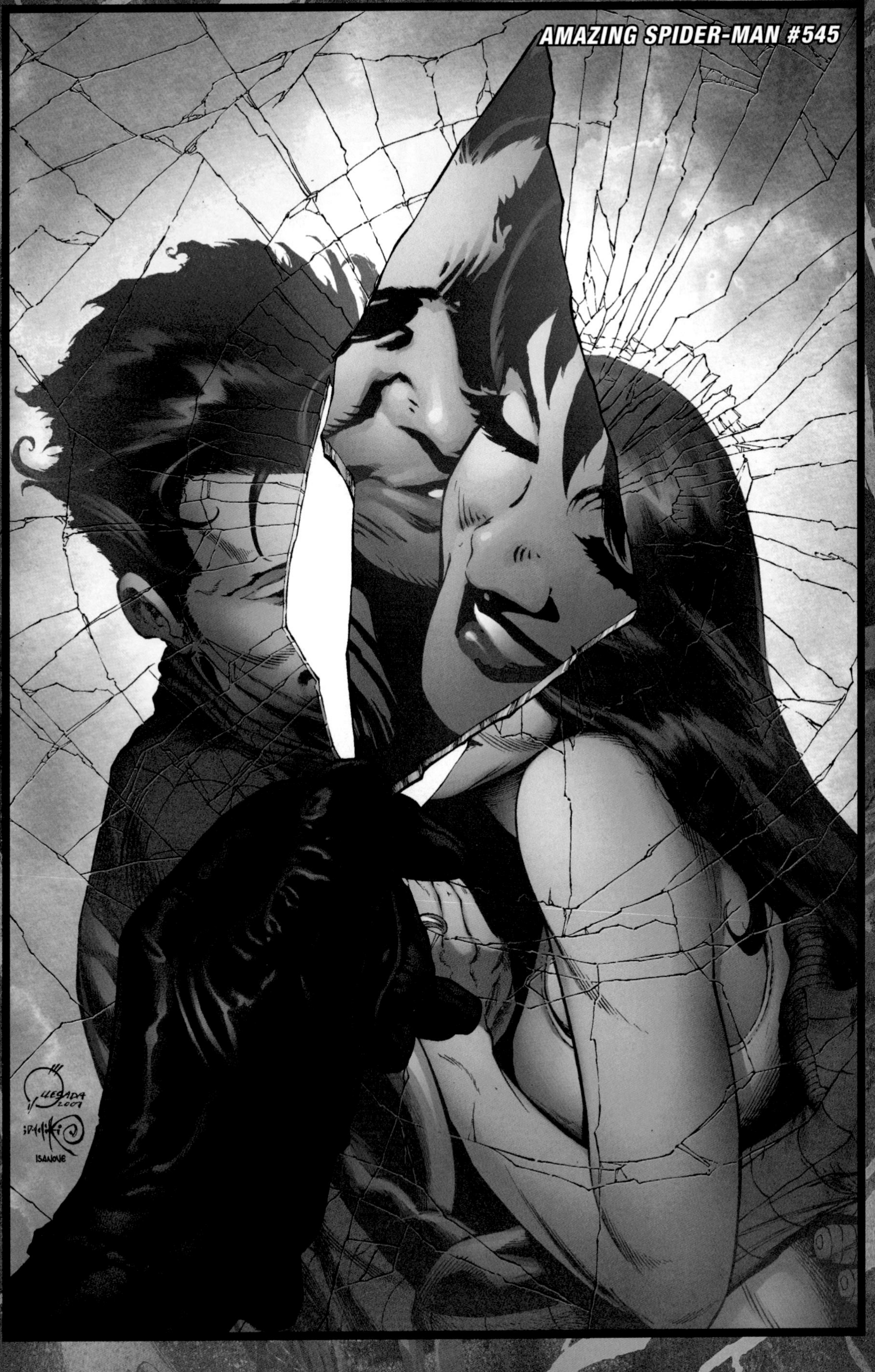
AMAZING SPIDER-MAN #545

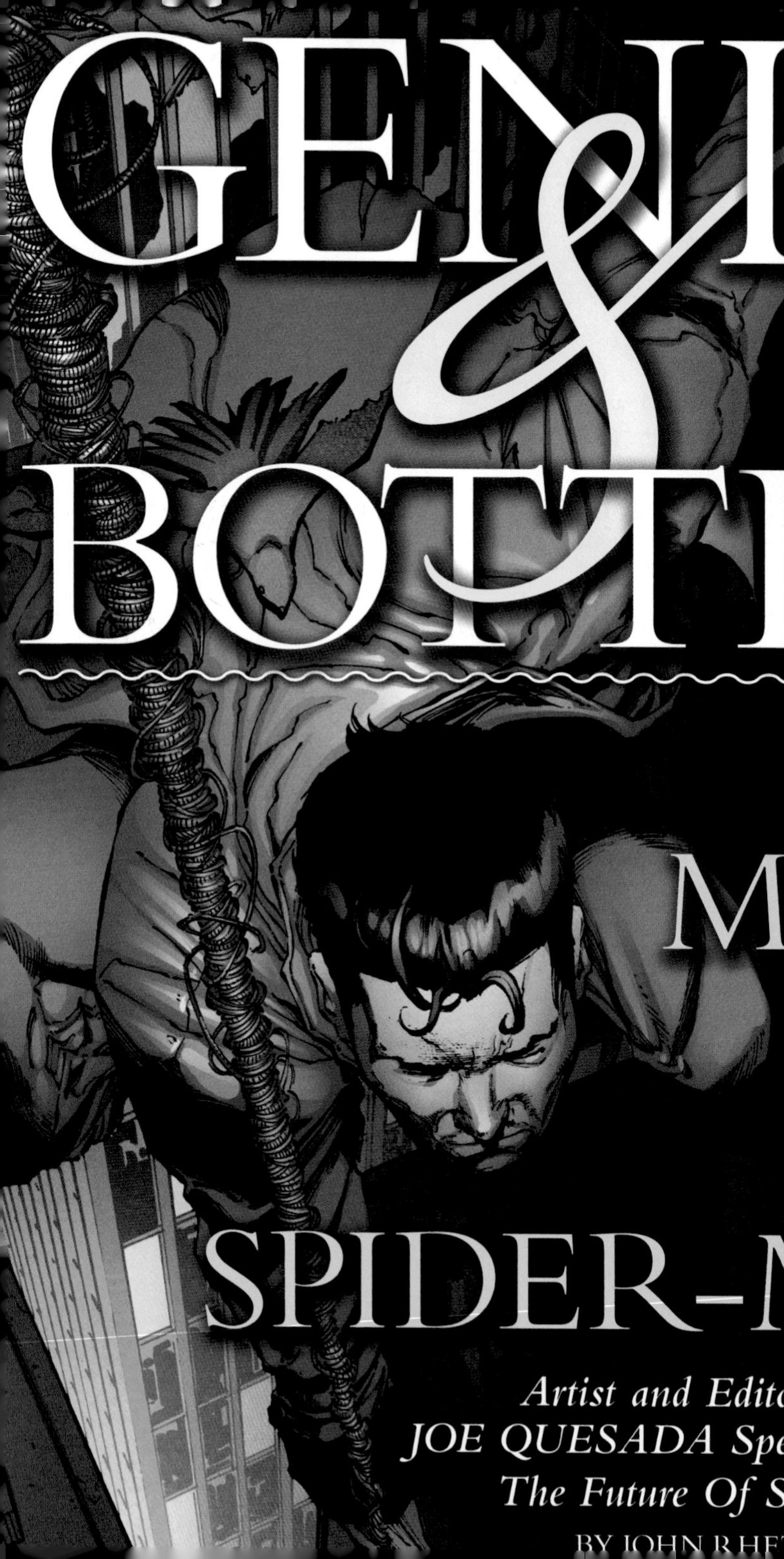

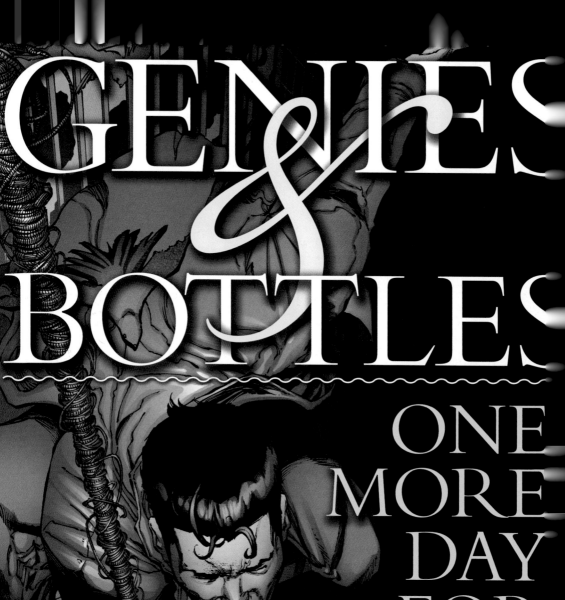

GENIES & BOTTLES

ONE MORE DAY FOR SPIDER-MAN

Artist and Editor in Chief JOE QUESADA Speaks About The Future Of Spider-Man

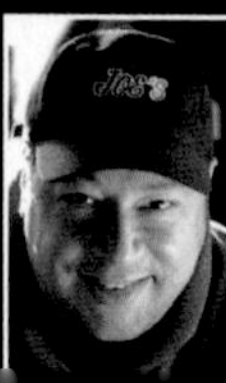

BY JOHN RHETT THOMAS

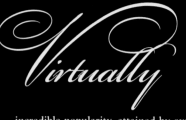

Virtually all fans of the Marvel Universe feel some sort of ownership over their favorite characters and have followed their every move since that first momer they developed a bond with them. Any slight change in the fortunes o these favorites risks the wrath of any number of these fans, and this true whether we're talking about characters that have less of the limeligh like Hellcat or Ant-Man, or the iconic characters that drive the Marv Universe—like Wolverine, Thor or Captain America. By virtue of h incredible popularity, attained by exposure through TV shows, movies, a daily comic strip and decades of som of the finest storytelling in comics history, Spider-Man is probably at the top of the list of characters that carr the most risk in managing through the years of changing tastes and degrees of popularity. ♦ So when it cam time to talk with Joe Quesada, who is not only the artist of the "One More Day" event, which seeks to reorier Spider-Man's direction for the future, but the Editor in Chief of the company that made the decisions on this nev direction, I was sure I'd uncover some trepidation, some fear about taking the bold moves highlighted in "On More Day" and "Brand New Day". I was wrong. I found out that any trepidation or fear I sensed from the man is probably best interpreted as outward manifestations of the awe and respect for the characters of Peter Parker and Spider-Man, and the steadfast intent on making sure that this new phase in Spider-Man history is approached with the utmost care. In the lead interview of our *Spotlight* coverage of "One More Day/Brand New Day," Joe Quesada takes us inside his thoughts on the gravity of altering Spider-Man's destiny and shines a spotlight on the "Brand New Day" that is coming.

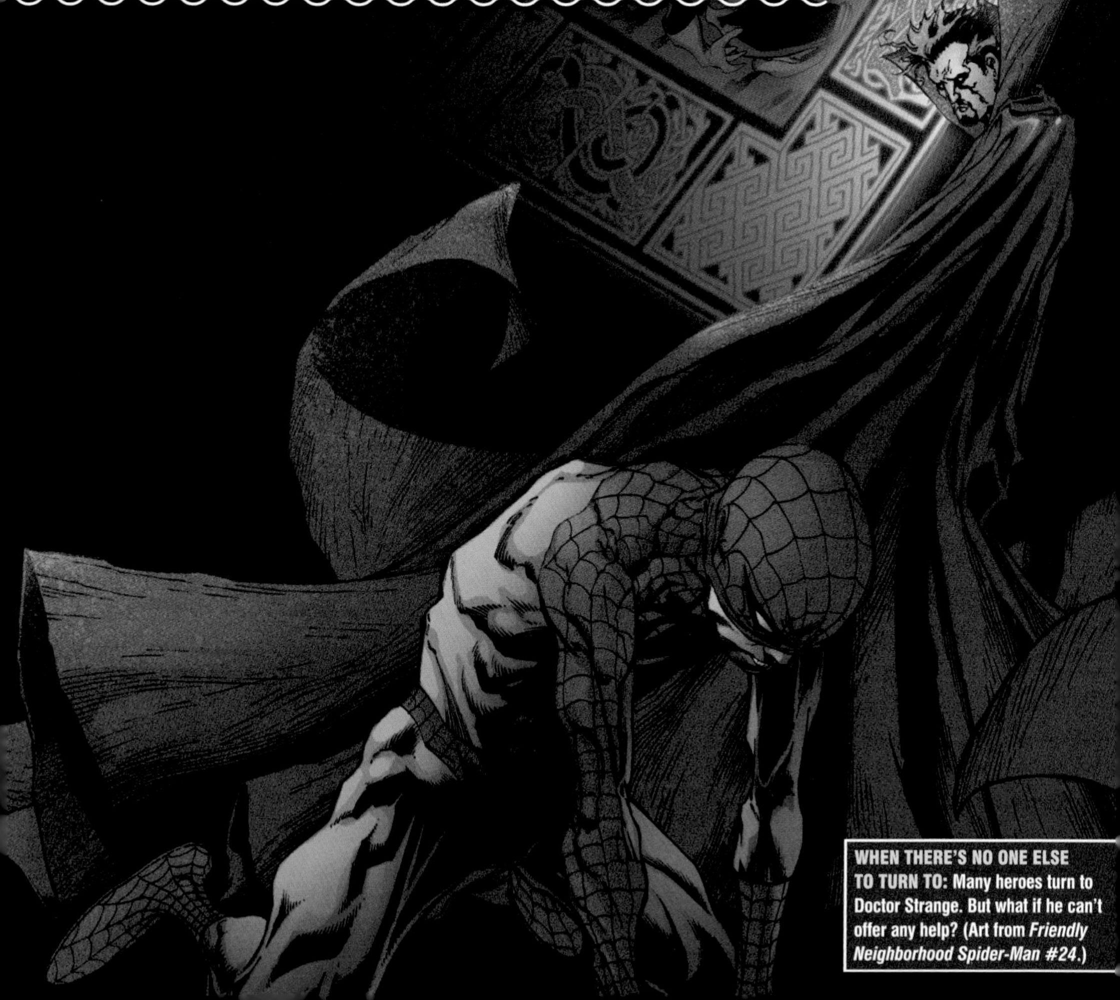

WHEN THERE'S NO ONE ELSE TO TURN TO: Many heroes turn to Doctor Strange. But what if he can't offer any help? (Art from *Friendly Neighborhood Spider-Man #24*.)

SPOTLIGHT: Your available time outside of being Marvel's editor in chief is very limited, which means you can only choose a few projects to do as an artist. So why choose this one over other worthy projects?

JOE: I just felt very close to this story. This was a project I really wanted to do, I really *could* do, I really *needed* to do, and something I hoped I could really knock out of the park. Another reason why I wanted to do this was that I've been talking about this for some time now, so I needed to put my money where my mouth is! It's my decision, though obviously we work as a company and we agree as a company, but I believe if anyone should come under fire it should be me.

SPOTLIGHT: Spider-Man is the cornerstone character in the Marvel corporate structure: so much begins and ends with Spider-Man, so there must be a really tremendous weight on his caretakers to make sure this goes well. The ramifications of "One More Day" are obviously something you believe in, you've talked about it for so long and now it's really come to fruition. Can you share with us the weight upon you to do this and get it right?

JOE: Well, I don't know if "weight" is the right word for it, but I do feel a sense of responsibility for it. The reason Marvel has hired me to be editor in chief is to be a caretaker to these characters and do what's best for these characters. This has nothing to do with my personal taste of things. Although I suspect it is in part my personal vision (those who hired me) want as well, especially if that vision adds up to better comics, better sales, etc., etc.

'I WOULD ARGUE THAT PETER PARKER IS MIX OF SPIDER-MAN. IT'S ALL REALLY AI HAPPENS WHEN HE PUTS ON THE SUIT IS

But I've always felt, along with many other people in the comics industry—editors, editors in chief, past and present—that this is something that needed to be done; we just needed to find the right way to do it. To find a methodology that really worked, and once we came upon that methodology I felt that we needed to get on it and fix these elements of Spider-Man that could really be improved on.

SPOTLIGHT: It sounds to me that you are confident that what you are doing is definitely going to be received well, at least well enough to merit doing it in the first place. And that sort of ameliorates any trepidation you might have.

JOE: Well, yeah, let's be honest: We don't go into any decision here thinking it's going to fail, or else why are we doing it? This is not about ego or anything. What it's about is the longevity of the character, and it makes sense in my world that this is something that is needed for better Spider-Man stories. How will it be received? I don't know. I speculate that anything with a radical change will be received with shock and trepidation and that's okay - that's what fans do, and I've grown accustomed to it

SHOWDOWN WITH STARK: The steep breakdown of friendship between Peter and Tony Stark has its culmination in *Amazing Spider-Man* #544.

There has never been a single, significant moment here at Marvel —or a single, significant moment in comic books overall - that the status quo has ever stayed the same, or people weren't doing something for the betterment of the books or the characters. So with all that in mind, I can't tell you if the fans are immediately going to embrace this. But I do think, like a lot of things that we've done in these past few years, that given a year, a month, or however long, once we actually settle into the type of stories we really want to tell, I think it's going to gel with the readers.

SPOTLIGHT: Now let's talk about the character. So much has been made about who Spider-Man is now, and over the years you've been indicating that maybe he's not really where he needs to be to tell the most effective stories. So who is Peter Parker right now?

JOE: Peter Parker to me is the everyday shlub of the Marvel Universe. He is our everyman, he's you, he's me. I think the beauty of Spider-Man is that everyone—*everyone*—can relate to his character, everyone sees a little bit of themselves in Spider-Man. And that's part of the character's allure, and I think when we step away from that it shouldn't be surprising to us that the character doesn't resonate as much with fans. So we have had an incredible J. Michael Straczynski run, and we're going to continue to have great runs after Joe leaves, but I think getting back to the status quo, to Peter's roots, is a very important thing for the characters for the next twenty to thirty years.

SPOTLIGHT: It's funny, Spider-Man is the most important character in the Marvel stable, but his condition as a character is vitally dependent on two different identities. He really

THE MOST IMPORTANT PERSON IN THE
OUT PETER PARKER, AND REALLY WHAT
JUST GRAVY." – ARTIST/EDITOR IN CHIEF JOE QUESADA

defines what it means to be a super hero with an alter ego, with all the frailties and the faults that humans have. We talk about Peter Parker, but how substantially will Spider-Man —the hero, the costumed identity—be affected as "One More Day" evolves into "Brand New Day"?

JOE: I would argue that Peter Parker is the most important person in the mix of Spider-Man. It's all really about Peter Parker, and really what happens when he puts on the suit is just gravy, so I think when you see the changes that will occur in Peter in "Brand New Day", you will know how it affects Spider-Man, as there is additional and added soap opera to his life. There will be new and interesting problems, new and interesting people, a brand new cast, a whole new mix of characters and villains for us to play with. It's really going to open the floodgates of creativity for Spider-Man. I think the fans are truly going to get a kick out of what we're going to do.

SPOTLIGHT: One of the elements of the book that I enjoyed while reading over the last few years has been the relationship Peter has developed with Tony Stark. I thought it was

really novel and interesting relationship to build up. Was the interaction between Iron Man and Spider-Man in the first chapter of "One More Day" (*ASM #544*) pretty much the resolution of that arc between the two characters?**

JOE: Well, probably for now it will be. There is more stuff happening with respect to Iron Man in his world, and where that character is going, that I think it will cause him to have continual run-ins with other members of his super-hero fraternity, but I think for the time being that's going to be it for Peter and Iron Man.

SPOTLIGHT: You mention JMS' run earlier: what are your impressions of him as lead Spidey-writer over the past few years, and now dealing with him directly in this arc? What do you think he feels right now as he is getting ready to leave a title that has obviously meant a lot to him?

JOE: I don't know how he actually feels, but I can certainly tell you: I don't think Joe realizes the impact he's had on this character after so many years. His run has been historic in length and quality. That many wonderful Spider-Man stories after so long, that kind of consistency for so long is pretty remarkable, and that's something for which I will always be appreciative to Joe. He always gave us his "A" game. Not every story is going to be met with critical success, but on a day-to-day basis what he did for the character is truly remarkable. So I can't speak for what he's feeling but I sure hope he's proud of it, because man, we sure are.

SPOTLIGHT: When you spoke about looking for the methodology in which to tell new Spider-Man stories, you mentioned you were looking for the right opportunity to take the plunge. At what point did you sense that the events of *Civil War* were serving up the kind of pitch that you could hit over the fence?

JOE: It's very easy to un-marry a character, or fix something like that: you just do a huge universal retcon, and say a few events in history didn't happen. But that's really not the way we do it here at Marvel. That's the reason why over the years, while other editors in chief have tried to find a way to get to this point, the idea just wasn't there. Then one day we came upon the idea, and it was this moment that allowed us to do the unmasking of Peter Parker, because we knew that one idea would run into the other and make the other idea possible, so it was just finding a way to make the other idea possible. Once we found the way to do it, we asked ourselves, "Okay, now where do we put it on the time line?" And away we went.

SPOTLIGHT: How did you feel when you stumbled upon that moment and you realized that the stuff you've been talking about for so long now many seemed feasible, like something that could actually happen?

JOE: Yeah, I have to tell you, a lot of our writers helped come up with that and it was like striking gold. It was one of those moments when we were like, "Oh, my God, we've got it!" And it was also so funny because it was so simple. It's just the same feeling we had about the *Civil War*, when we were trying to bring back the edginess that we had lost over the last forty years. So again, one thing fit into the other, which fit into the other. We were just very fortunate that these things came along at the time that they did.

"IT'S VERY EASY TO UN-MARRY A CHA[RACTER, OR FIX SOME]THING...YOU JUST DO A HUGE UNIV[ERSAL RETCON, AND] SAY A FEW EVENTS IN HISTORY DIDN'[T HAPPEN. BUT THAT'S] REALLY NOT THE WAY WE DO IT HERE[...]

SPOTLIGHT: How important was getting Steve Wacker on board as editor to the success of "Brand New Day"? From a structural standpoint, it would seem like he couldn't be overvalued because of his experience with *52* and getting that rolling. What can you say about him, and what he brings to the "Brand New Day" experience?

JOE: Steve is made for this job; he has had his baptism of fire. We had planned out "Brand New Day" before Steve was hired on here, but we didn't ask to bring to him Marvel based upon this idea. It just sort of fit in and we were all like, "Hey, wait a minute...." It was just the stars aligning for lack of a better word.

SPOTLIGHT: Who stood with you when you were conceptualizing what "Brand New Day" would mean to Spider-Man?

JOE: For "One More Day" it was basically the guys who had been on big creative retreats with us. You end up with a list of guys and a huge e-mail chain, which started one day talking about Spider-Man and then evolved into a two week long email chain of ideas being thrown around about "One More Day," with ideas about how it would work. With respect to "Brand New Day," that's really the writers group, the guys who were writing the book plus a few others, we all sat in a room and started batting about what to do with Spider-Man and what to do to make it fun again, and away we went.

SPOTLIGHT: You had the Spider-Man book that came out on Free Comic Book Day back in the spring, well before anything about "One More Day" or "Brand New Day" had hit the grapevine. You must have felt very mischievous when that book came out: by all appearances it was a stand-alone, "What If?" type of Spider-Man story, but there was something going on underneath the surface, wasn't there? A sort of "Brand New Day" preview?

...CTER, OR FIX SOME-...SAL RETCON, AND ...APPEN. BUT THAT'S MARVEL." —QUESADA

ONE MORE DAY COMES TO A CLOSE: Joe Quesada and his team have designed "One More Day" as the endpoint from which a new beginning starts, sending Spidey webswinging toward a "Brand New Day".

JOE: Absolutely, that's just what we were doing. That was the fun part. Phil Jimenez was giggling all the way to the bank with that one. He knew what we were doing as well.

SPOTLIGHT: What was the feedback you got from people who may not have known what was at stake with that story? Did you get any positive feedback, any negative feedback?

JOE: No negative feedback; it was all positive. I mean, most people didn't know what they had, but a few fans were guessing and they'd say, "Hey, wait a minute, what's going on here?"

SPOTLIGHT: What's great is it really drives home the fact that you guys aren't giving up on Mary Jane. I think a lot of people assume that just because the status quo in Spider-Man's life is changing and they think the marriage will be a part of that change, she is apparently still involved in a certain way of his life.

JOE: Absolutely. There was no reason to get rid of Mary Jane. She is a wonderful character. Part of "Brand New Day" and "One More Day" is our answer to the fact that we acknowledge that over the course of many, many years, and many, many Spider-Man stories, and many, many Spider-Man writers, a lot of damage has been done to the cast in the sense that we've had many great characters who eventually were lost to character death, or whatever other pitfalls, but those things happen in the course of the years of storytelling. So we wanted to make sure we didn't make those mistakes again in a rushed, hasty fashion. We knew that Mary Jane was a great character regardless of how involved she is in Peter's life or

not - there was no reason to kill her off, and that would really just defeat the purpose of what we were trying to do.

SPOTLIGHT: On the eve of its introduction, can you sum up your feelings about how "Brand New Day" is shaping up? Looking at the way the Spider-Man office has set this up, they've pieced together some very interesting creative teams to deliver these thrice monthly story lines. So wearing your editor in chief hat, but also as a fan of good Spider-Man stories, what kind of a job do you think they're doing?

JOE: I think they're doing an incredible job. I think that my favorite moment came when we were in the writers room and we were playing around with the stories and there was someone there who was not a writer. They turned to me after the first day of coming up with story concepts and said, "You know what? I have to be honest with you. I wasn't a believer in un-marrying Peter and Mary Jane. I didn't grow up in that golden age of Spider-Man, but now sitting here and listening to all those stories you all are coming up with, now I understand what you're talking about. I completely get it." And that was really kind of cool, to get that kind of feedback from someone who was not a believer, and I really suspect that the fans will have the same feeling we get when we're sitting here coming up with ideas in the writers room.

By now, "One More Day" is complete and in the record books, and now we turn things over to the "Brand New Day" crew for more great Spidey stories! Thanks to Joe for taking the time to take us inside his thinking about "One More Day"!

ONE MORE DAY, SIX AMAZING YEARS:

A SPIDER-MAN STORYTELLER

WRITER J. MICHAEL STRACZYNSKI LOWERS THE CURTAIN ON HIS CAREER AS SPIDER-MAN'S CHIEF SCRIBE. By Chris Arrant

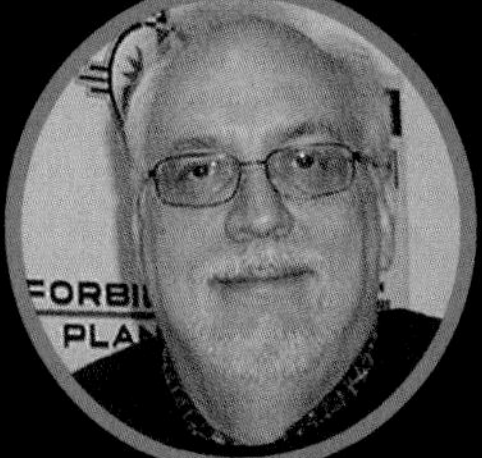

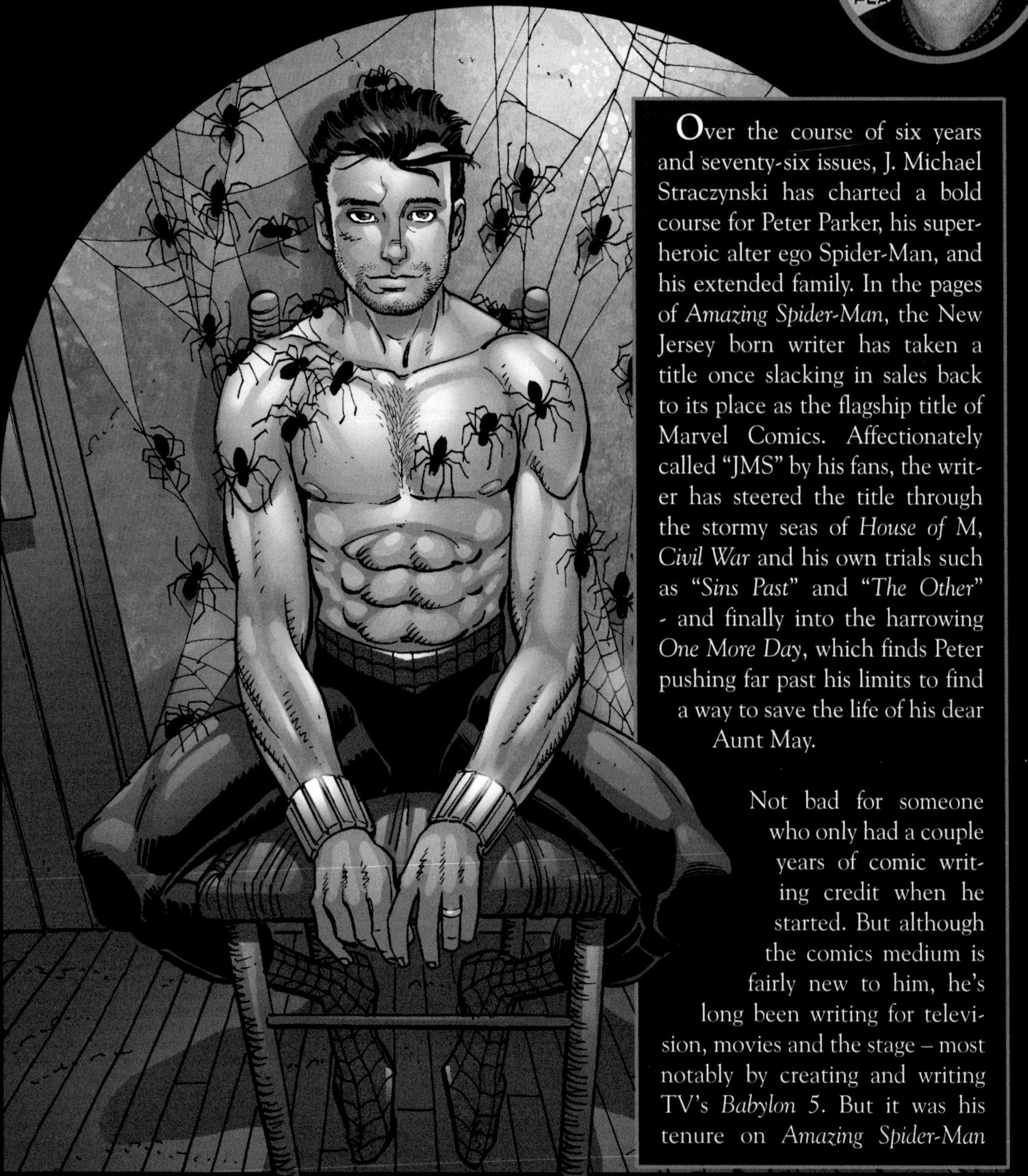

Over the course of six years and seventy-six issues, J. Michael Straczynski has charted a bold course for Peter Parker, his super-heroic alter ego Spider-Man, and his extended family. In the pages of *Amazing Spider-Man*, the New Jersey born writer has taken a title once slacking in sales back to its place as the flagship title of Marvel Comics. Affectionately called "JMS" by his fans, the writer has steered the title through the stormy seas of *House of M*, *Civil War* and his own trials such as "*Sins Past*" and "*The Other*" - and finally into the harrowing *One More Day*, which finds Peter pushing far past his limits to find a way to save the life of his dear Aunt May.

Not bad for someone who only had a couple years of comic writing credit when he started. But although the comics medium is fairly new to him, he's long been writing for television, movies and the stage – most notably by creating and writing TV's *Babylon 5*. But it was his tenure on *Amazing Spider-Man* that made his name in the comics arena, and a great name it has made for him.

As his swan song is released in stores, it's high time to sit down with JMS to talk about *One More Day*: the ending, the beginning…and everything in between.

SPOTLIGHT: Let's jump right into it: We're knee-deep in the middle of Spider-Man's "*One More Day*" event, with you and Joe Quesada

adrenaline, he's on the wrong side of the law…he's screwed and he knows it.

SPOTLIGHT: Once Peter is faced with the reality that modern medicine can do nothing to help Aunt May, he begins to reach out to his super hero friends… first to Tony Stark. Spider-Man had developed quite a friendship with Tony prior to *Civil War*, only to become bitterly opposed to him with more than one altercation. Why was Tony first on Peter's list?

"He's certainly desperate, and determined, and more liable to make a reckless mistake that he might not make under other circumstances. He's running on adrenaline, he's on the wrong side of the law…he's screwed and he knows it."
— JMS on the state of Spider-Man in *One More Day*.

making your swan song an epic ordeal. How did this final story come together?

JMS: I'm trying to remember the exact time, but I can only dimly recall…it was at either a retreat or Philly Con that Joe first broached the idea of it. He knew that I was going to stop on Spidey at some point, and wanted this to be the end of the road for my run. He and Marvel editorial had specific ideas they wanted to address with the character, and wanted to be able to use this series to accomplish them.

SPOTLIGHT: In *Amazing Spider-Man* #544 we fully see the fragility of Aunt May's condition. With Aunt May being so central to Peter Parker's life, in some ways more vital than even Mary Jane, how does that affect his mental state?

JMS: He's certainly desperate, and determined, and more liable to make a reckless mistake that he might not make under other circumstances. He's running on

JMS: Tony was up first because Peter needed money for May, and Tony had it. He also knew that Tony was fond of May and might be able to get past the registration issue to be of aid, especially since to some extent May was injured because Peter listened to him and unmasked. I also wanted Tony to be the one to help out because though I've written him that way to editorial specs, I've

FRIENDS NOW FOES: One of the best assets of JMS' tenure on *Amazing Spider-Man* was the emotional connection made between Peter and Tony Stark, a connection now tragically sundered by *Civil War*. (Art from *ASM #544*.)

never really bought into Tony as a bad guy. I liked Tony as the mentor figure, and writing that period where he and Peter were working together at Stark Tower was the part of him I enjoyed most.

SPOTLIGHT: At the end of *Amazing Spider-Man* #544, Spider-Man hints at going to Dr. Strange for help. With all Spider-Man's acquaintances, why is Stephen Strange on his list second only to Tony Stark?

JMS: Tony represents whatever science and money can do. Having exhausted science and money, the non-scientific remains. Hence Stephen.

SPOTLIGHT: In some ways, your entire run on *Amazing Spider-Man* has been building up to this arc. You've effectively put Peter at the end of his rope, placing him at the point where any normal person wouldn't have any options.

JMS: When we developed the story, there was nothing else one could really do other than put him in a corner emotionally, so yes on that score.

SPOTLIGHT: Let's step back from '*One More Day*' and look at the big picture – your run on *Amazing Spider-Man*. You started back in June 2001 with issue #471 – your first work with Marvel Comics. You were familiar with comic readers through your work on *Rising Stars* but still best known by your hit TV show *Babylon 5*. What was going through your mind?

JMS: I really saw it as what it became: a chance to work on a flagship character with whom I greatly identified as a kid who was also a big fan of the character growing up. Marvel was in desperate straits then, and needed something to boost the character from where he'd been at the time, selling something like 30,000 copies per month. Since I've been on the book, it's rarely dropped below triple that number, and that was my hope: to bring it up to the top tier again, where it belongs.

SPOTLIGHT: How did you and Marvel originally get on the same page and get you on *Amazing Spider-Man*?

JMS: On the one hand, it's their character, and I made it clear that I viewed it that way. I'm a hired gun. At the end of the day, I or any other writer moves on and you have to be sure not to damage

JMS' TOP FIVE SPIDEY CHARACTERS TO WRITE

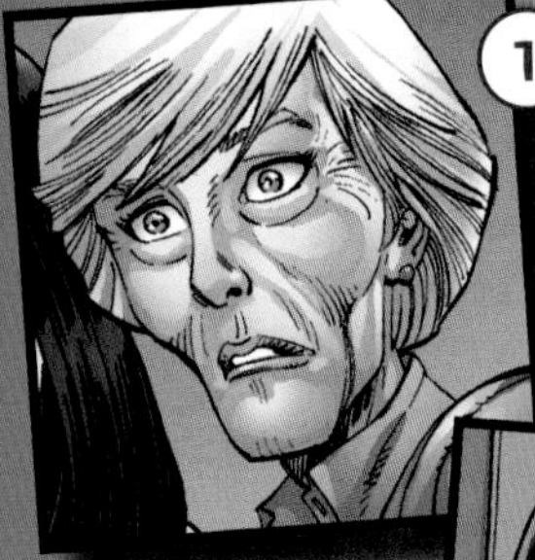

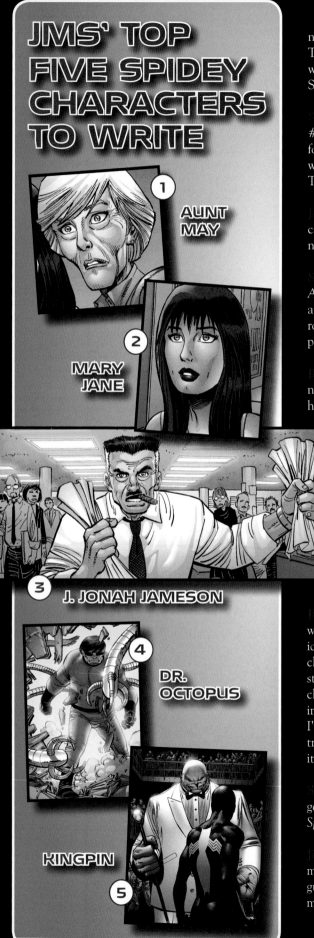

1 AUNT MAY

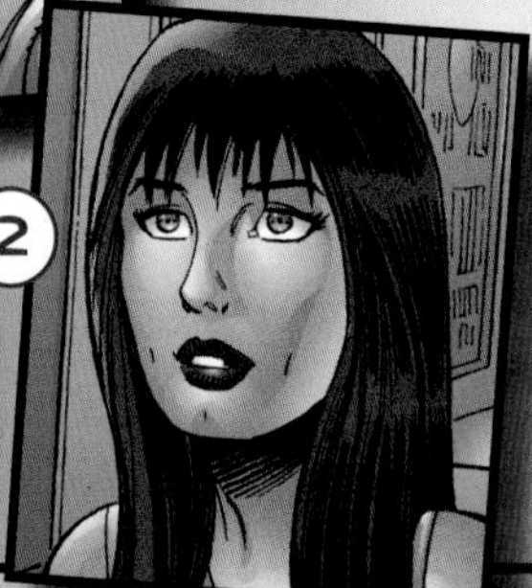

2 MARY JANE

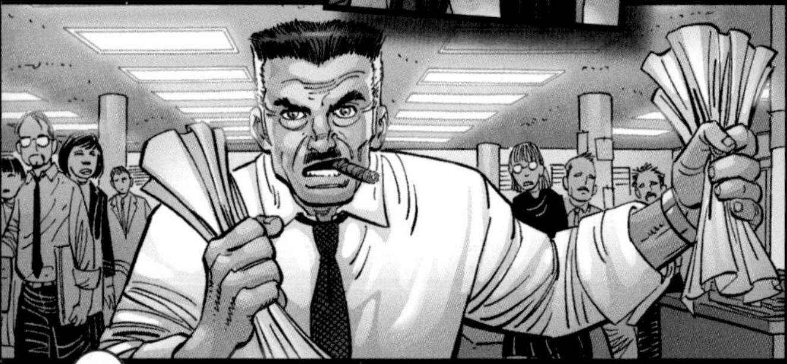

3 J. JONAH JAMESON

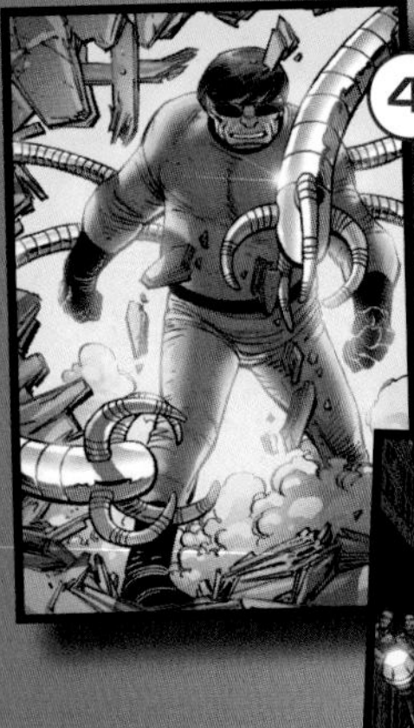

4 DR. OCTOPUS

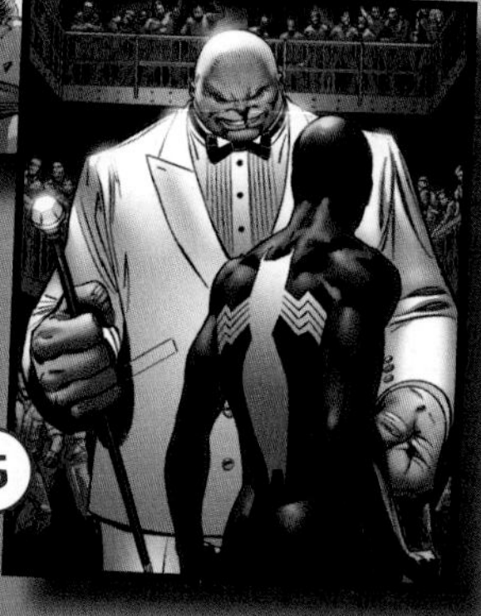

5 KINGPIN

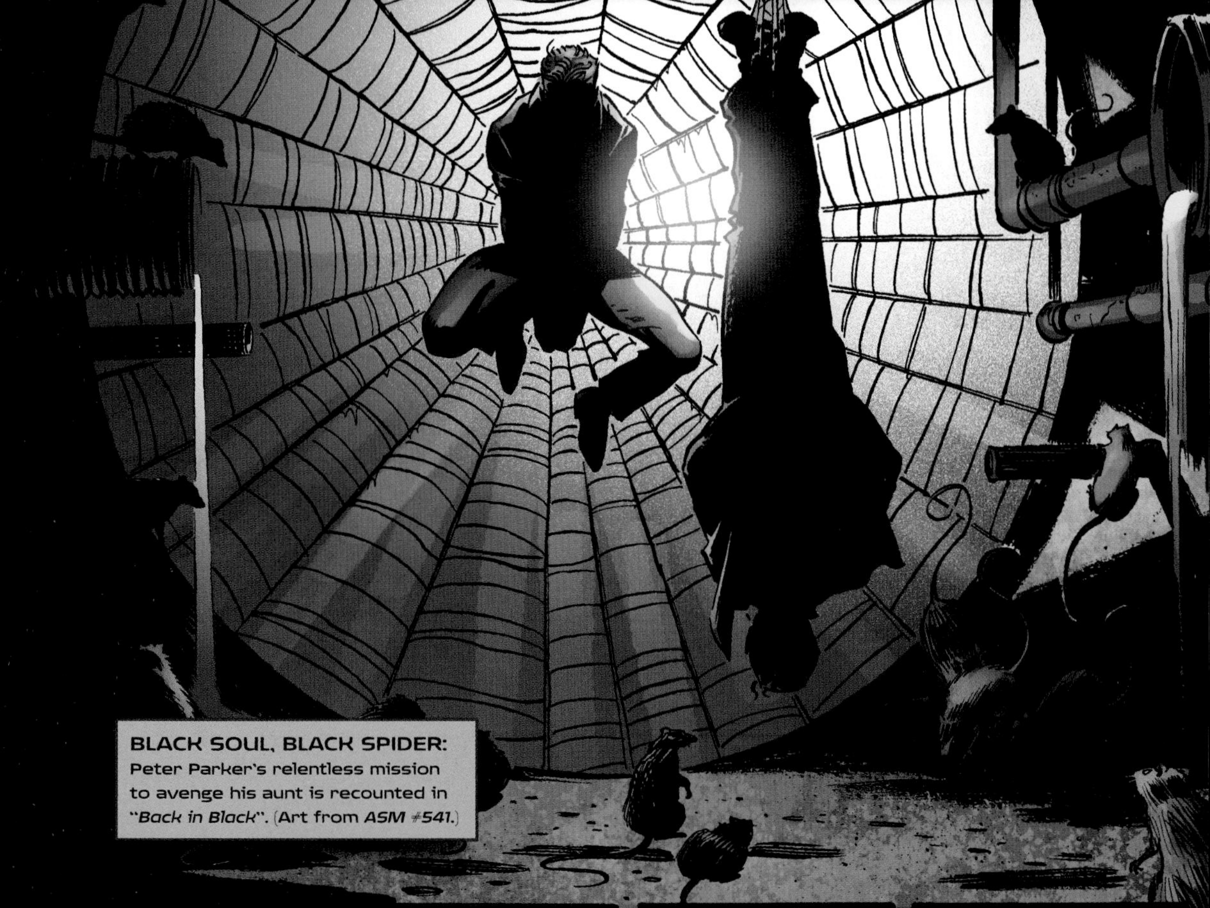

BLACK SOUL, BLACK SPIDER: Peter Parker's relentless mission to avenge his aunt is recounted in "*Back in Black*". (Art from *ASM #541.*)

the character beyond recall. On the other hand, I told them that I was going to try a lot of different things in order to bring up the character's profile, some of it probably controversial, and from time to time I'd probably fail. If they were cool with that, we'd proceed, and we did.

SPOTLIGHT: The first page of your first issue really sets the status quo of the time, with Peter living solo in NYC and without Mary Jane. They were separated during that time – how did you wrap your head around that, and did you have firm ideas for how you would proceed with their relationship?

JMS: I really wanted to get them together ASAP because I liked that dynamic, so that was one of the first things I told Marvel I wanted to do. I wanted to show a loving couple, not two people who just bicker and bite at each other over petty stuff, which is how a lot of writers view conflict.

SPOTLIGHT: Aunt May has always been an integral character to the Spider-Man family, but over the course of your run you've elevated her to being perhaps the most genuine character in comics. How did you approach writing Aunt May, and did you have any guidelines ingrained from the get-go?

JMS: I just tried to always visualize her as a real person of great inner strength, not a liability, not someone who was there just for the purpose of fainting and being cross and weak all the time. She raised Peter by herself; that requires inner strength. I wanted to validate and reinforce that.

SPOTLIGHT: You sent the fans reeling early on when Aunt May discovered that Peter was Spider-Man. Teased for ages, what made then the right time to do it? And how do you think it evolved Peter's relationship with May?

JMS: It's something I wanted to do and it just felt like the right time to do it. I wanted to send a message that those we love can bear our secrets without being killed by them, a message that I think a lot of people needed to hear, given the response and emails that followed. I think it matured his relationship with May and made them closer.

SPOTLIGHT: In the first issue, you move Peter into a new vocation – no longer a photographer, but a schoolteacher. What brought this on?

JMS: It just felt like the right thing to do, and I wanted to explore it more, but the overall shape it became difficult to continue to play that thread out as planned. I just thought it could be a cool story element to have Peter giving back to kids like he used to be.

SPOTLIGHT: A bevy of new characters entered the Spider-Man mythos during your run: Ezekiel, Morlun, Shathra, Shade, a new Dr. Octopus, The Digger, Killshot, and Gabriel and Sarah Stacy. I think I've forgotten a few in there somewhere. Anyway…. Why'd you go this route instead of going straight to Spidey's all-too-familiar rogue's gallery?

JMS: Your last clause has the answer to that: we'd seen the rogue's gallery used so much that it just felt like it needed freshening. I don't think any of the characters I introduced are really worth keeping over the years; they were introduced for specific story purposes in terms of Peter's character. How many times can you have Spidey fight Electro (as much as I enjoy Electro) before it begins to parody itself? I figured, let's have some guest characters to cleanse the palate for a while before bringing back the original group.

SPOTLIGHT: Early on in your run, you introduced a new aspect to Spider-Man's origin – that

"I wanted to send a message that those we love can bear our secrets without being killed by them, a message that I think a lot of people needed to hear…"

— JMS on Aunt May discovering the secret of Peter's dual life as Spider-Man.

of totems. The mysterious Ezekiel was the one that slowly unraveled the mystery to Peter, and it took Peter on a wild ride culminating with 'The Other' crossover. Given that Spider-Man's origin is so ingrained in comic consciousness, did you have any apprehension at introducing this new element?

JMS: I always have apprehension when introducing something new. But as I told Marvel at the

SPIDER-MAN VS. DIGGER: One of JMS's cool additions to Spidey's rogues gallery was featured in *ASM #53*.

beginning, I wanted to try some new things, some of which would work, while others wouldn't. The totem aspect came to me when I looked over his rogue's gallery and saw that something like 90% of them were other animal figures: Rhino, Doc Ock, the Vulture, Croc, the list goes on and on. There was an animal totem thing going on before I ever touched it, I was just the first guy to say "maybe there's a connection and a reason." But I always kept Peter skeptical about the whole thing.

SPOTLIGHT One of the most poignant and popular issues of your run was the famous 'Black Issue', commemorating 9-11. Back during the time you said you wrote it in a blur of a couple hours, and John Romita, Jr. said he illustrated it in a similar haze. Looking back at it now, what are your thoughts on it?

JMS: I'm still very happy about it. (And for those who complained about it, Doctor Doom wasn't in the script I gave to Marvel, I just noted that there were a number of villains who were moved by the event, and Doom was one of those drawn, so I won't cop to that one.) It was a very different style of writing for me, and to this day I continue to get people coming up to me and thanking me for that issue, so I did something right for a change.

SPOTLIGHT Peter got his share of good with the bad though, and one of Peter's highest moments was reuniting with his wife, Mary Jane. How did you approach this make-up for the Parkers?

JMS: I just tried to imagine how it'd go if I were in that position, then had Peter act smarter than me since I always screw these things up when I'm in that position.

SPOTLIGHT One of the most controversial parts of your run on *Amazing Spider-Man* was the reveal that Gwen Stacy had a one-night stand with Norman Osborn – aka The Green Goblin – while she was dating Peter, and had twins that Peter didn't know about until recently. When the ideas that became this story starting coming to you, did you realize the fan upheaval it would cause – and how do you think it serves to color and broaden Spider-Man, and Gwen Stacy's effectiveness as characters?

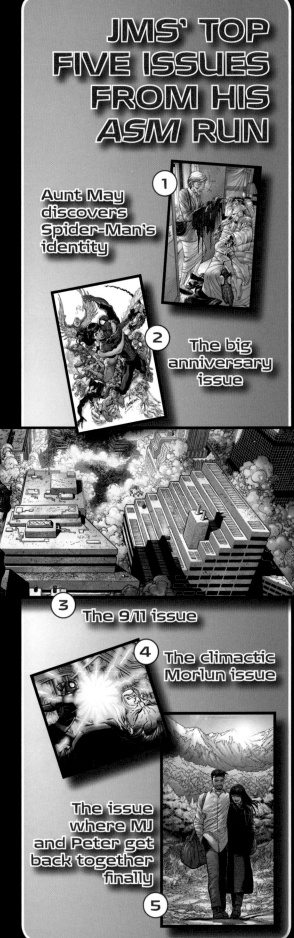

JMS' TOP FIVE ISSUES FROM HIS *ASM* RUN

1 Aunt May discovers Spider-Man's identity

2 The big anniversary issue

3 The 9/11 issue

4 The climactic Morlun issue

5 The issue where MJ and Peter get back together finally

TOP FIVE THINGS JSM DIDN'T GET A CHANCE TO DO

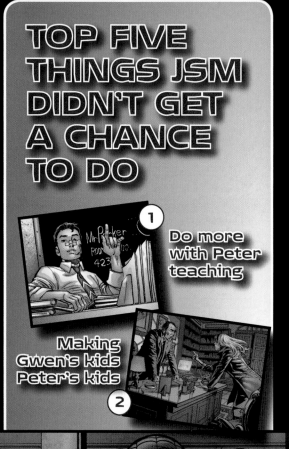

1 Do more with Peter teaching

2 Making Gwen's kids Peter's kids

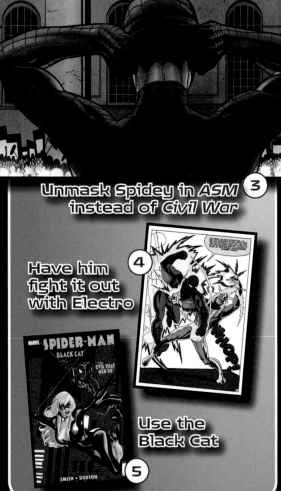

3 Unmask Spidey in *ASM* instead of *Civil War*

4 Have him fight it out with Electro

MARVEL
SPIDER-MAN
BLACK CAT
THE EVIL THAT MEN DO
SMITH • DODSON

5 Use the Black Cat

JMS: I didn't anticipate the whole madonna/whore complex that came out in a lot of people. I thought it showed strength for her to make a mistake, own up to it, have the kids, and come back to confront Norman and marry Peter. (And for those who kept saying "how could she do this with Spidey's enemy?", she didn't know he was Spidey's enemy.) But it didn't quite go down that way. The irony is that I had at first proposed making this a story about Gwen having Peter's kids, but Marvel vetoed the idea because it would make Peter feel too old, and at the last moment they suggested Norman as a way to shake things up, but "the fans'll love it." I kind of wanted to back away from the story at that point, but the solicitations were already going out with the first issue of the arc, and it was too late to do much about it but buy the ticket and take the ride.

SPOTLIGHT: Spider-Man became more of a central figure in the tight-knit Marvel Universe as the war drums began beating for *Civil War*, joining the Avengers, having a camaraderie with Tony Stark (aka Iron Man), and moving his family into Avengers Headquarters. As the chief Spider-Man writer, how did this change Peter?

JMS: Peter was always a lone wolf, and joining the Avengers gave him a context, and people he could rely on and confide in and share techniques with, and I think that meant a lot to him.

SPOTLIGHT: Peter's friendship with Tony Stark grew rapidly, and despite its ultimate demise mid-way through *Civil War*, it was an interesting friendship. What do you think Tony and Peter's relationship was about, and how do you think Peter viewed Tony?

JMS: I think in many ways Tony was a father figure for Peter, in that they had a lot in common and there was a real friendship there. Which is why I liked writing that mentor-ish relationship and didn't much like turning it around later.

SPOTLIGHT: The Spider-Man unmasking during *Civil War* – we have to talk about it. Introduced in *Civil War*, it was in your title that the repercussions were felt. As a writer, how did this change for Peter color your outlook on writing the title?

LAYING DOWN THE LAW: Peter Parker gets the final word in the climax of one of JMS' most rawly emotional scripts. (Art from *ASM #553*)

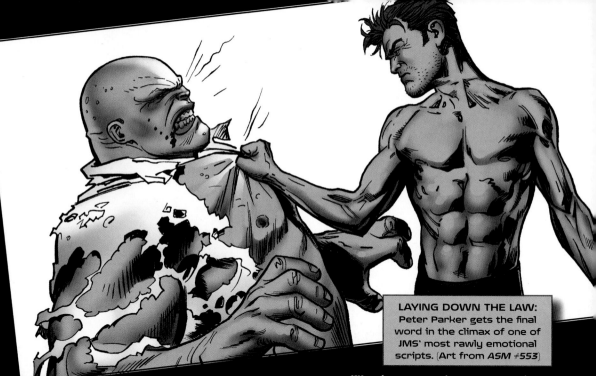

JMS: It was an editorial decision made at one of the retreats, and I had to work with it as best I could. It opened up a lot of story possibilities; I went to the mattress on a number of things in *Civil War*, but again, it's Marvel's character and they have the right and the purview to make decisions about the fate of their characters, that's not really my call.

SPOTLIGHT: Changing gears to "*The Other*" storyline, it saw you working in tandem with the other Spider-Man creative teams and titles to culminate the "*Totem*" story first introduced in your inaugural June 2001 issue. Peter died, and sort-of evolved in a cocoon to a next stage of life. This new Peter Parker, how is he different from the one from before?

JMS: I was never really very happy with how "*The Other*" was handled, and Marvel has fessed up to some problems in coordinating the thing. I felt it was kind of disconnected and lost its focus through diverse writers and elements being put in by one writer that writer B didn't know about. I wanted to use the moment to reset Peter physically and to give him a new lease on life.

SPOTLIGHT: Shortly after "*The Other*", you barreled into "*Back In Black*" which saw an attempt on Peter's life tragically hit Aunt May instead, leaving her on death's door and Peter on the brink. This led to the return of the darker "Black" costume. Was this a natural progression of your arc, or was some of it informed by others?

JMS: I'd wanted, and had always planned, to go right from the issue where Aunt May is shot into "*One More Day*", which if you look carefully at those two issues, they fold right into one another.

SPOTLIGHT: Although your final issue isn't out yet, you've surely turned in your script months ago. How does it feel to be over?

JMS: It feels good on one level, having done the book for this long, and having achieved some good things with it. It's odd not to be writing it, but that's to be expected...like when your tongue keeps going over a tooth that's just been pulled and it's not there anymore.

SPOTLIGHT: Was it a tough decision to leave *Amazing Spider-Man*?

JMS: Not really. If I stayed much longer, I think I would've begun to suck. ("Too late," some might say.)

Thanks, JMS, for taking the time to recount your tenure on AMAZING SPIDER-MAN. The entire run of JMS's Spidey is available in collected edition hardcovers and TPBs. JMS newest title is the sensational revival of a certain Norse God of Thunder in the pages of THOR. And in 2008, he will premiere the new series THE TWELVE, featuring a cast of Golden Age Timely heroes.

"J.M.S. had the brave heart to take an icon in new uncharted waters from the moment he took the book. All-new characters, villains, scenarios and controversy on an almost monthly basis. From the on-his-sleeve emotions of 9/11, to Aunt May and Peter finally having it out, I do believe this will be remembered as one of the great runs, not only of *Spider-Man*, but of all of comics."

— BRIAN MICHAEL BENDIS

"I remember when he was just "J.S." Then he got the spider book, and all of a sudden he's "J.S.M." — Joe Spider-Man. Which is clever, but they would not cash his checks. So he settled on J.M.S. That's a true story. What's also true is that J.M.S. is the hallmark of a true professional. Dedicated. Loyal. And talented. Buckets of talent as his great run on Spidey will attest, and his current run on *Thor* is furthering the legend. My favorite thing about him? He's a friend of mine. And it doesn't get any cooler than that. Congrats, J.S.M.!

— JEPH LOEB

"There are many more eloquent quotes before mine, and I won't attempt to compete with the authors of them. I can come up with two semi-intelligent words that can be construed as a compliment of Joe's run on the *Amazing Spider-Man*: Sales tripled! Thanks, Joe."

— JOHN ROMITA, JR.

"Joe has always been capable of The Big Surprise, but his run on *Amazing Spider-Man* shows that unique flair to mature, full-blown uniqueocity. You go, Joe!."

— HARLAN ELLISON

"I read (almost) every Marvel comic that is published each and every week. For me, it's homework, research, and, of course, fun. I usually organize my pile of 'to read' based on what films we are currently developing and what character is undergoing a renaissance in the comics. For the past six years, Joe's run on Spidey has been the one on top. I would sit and read it the moment it landed in my inbox. Joe's creative daring is an inspiration and his imaginative storytelling transcends all forms of media. My favorite J.M.S. Spidey moment also happens to be my favorite Spidey moment period: Aunt May discovers Peter's secret. It has become my mission to put that moment up on screen. Someday we will. I promise."

— KEVIN FEIGE
Producer/President of Marvel Studios

"In case you need reminding, Joe picking up the writing duties on *Amazing Spider-Man* was a seismic moment in modern comics. He, together with *Daredevil* writer Kevin Smith, showed Hollywood that far from slumming it in comic books, these guys were having the time of their lives. Joe not only doubled the sales of Marvel's flagship book, but has been responsible for the most radical and inventive Spider-Man stories in a generation. It's true he has a silly, virtually unpronounceable name that sensible people like to reduce to three letters, but as far as Spider-Man goes I think he's up there with Stan."

— MARK MILLAR

"I may have difficulty spelling his name, but there's nothing difficult about praising the terrific job that Joe Straczynski has done in his truly unforgettable eight-year run of *Spider-Man* scripting. Of course, from where I sit, an eight-year run is like — what'samatter, you didn't have the patience to stay with it for a while?

"But, despite his dawdling, for Joe to have been so inventive and creative and just plain exciting during so many issues of Spidey is beyond remarkable. His stories made the web-spinner's mag sell better than ever and his far-out themes and unexpected concepts kept the readers totally hooked for all those years. Of course, my biggest regret is that I never really got to work with the guy so it's hard for me to take any credit for what he's done.

"Hey, I'd like to add a lot more compliments and laudatory remarks, which Joe certainly deserves but, as I'm sure he'll understand, it's too difficult when you're consumed by envy!"

EXCELSIOR!

(that's "Straczynski" spelled backwards)

— STAN LEE